ARMSTRONG'S HANDBOOK

OF PERFORMANCE MANAGEMENT

An evidence-based guide to
delivering high performance

4TH EDITION

Michael Armstrong

KoganPage

LONDON PHILADELPHIA NEW DELHI

Publisher's note

Every possible effort has been made to ensure that the information contained in this book is accurate at the time of going to press, and the publishers and author cannot accept responsibility for any errors or omissions, however caused. No responsibility for loss or damage occasioned to any person acting, or refraining from action, as a result of the material in this publication can be accepted by the editor, the publisher or the author.

First published in Great Britain and the United States in 1994 by Kogan Page Limited as *Performance Management*
Second edition 2000
Third edition 2006
Fourth edition 2009 published as *Armstrong's Handbook of Performance Management*
Reprinted 2012 (three times)

120 Pentonville Road
London N1 9JN
United Kingdom
www.koganpage.com

1518 Walnut Street, Suite 1100
Philadelphia PA 19102
USA

4737/23 Ansari Road
Daryaganj
New Delhi 110002
India

© Michael Armstrong, 1994, 2000, 2006, 2009

ISBN 978 0 7494 5392 3

British Library Cataloguing-in-Publication Data

A CIP record for this book is available from the British Library.

Library of Congress Cataloging-in-Publication Data

Armstrong, Michael, 1928–
    Armstrong's handbook of performance management : an evidence-based quide to delivering high performance / Michael Armstrong. — 4th ed.
        p. cm.
    Rev. ed. of: Performance management. 3rd ed. 2006.
    ISBN 978-0-7494-5392-3
    1. Employees—Rating of. 2. Performance standards. 3. Performance.
I. Armstrong, Michael, 1928– Performance management. II. Title. III.
Title: Handbook of performance management.
    HF5549.5.R3A758 2009
    658.3'125--dc22

                                        2009016886

Typeset by Saxon Graphics Ltd, Derby
Print production managed by Jellyfish
Printed and bound by CPI Group (UK) Ltd, Croydon, CR0 4YY

Contents

This book is accompanied by additional online material. To access these resources go to www.koganpage.com/resources and under 'Academic Resources' click on either 'Student Resources' or 'Lecturer Resources' as appropriate.

Introduction

This book is concerned with the management of performance. It deals with performance management as a system consisting of interlocking elements deliberately designed to achieve a purpose, that of achieving high performance. Within that system performance management is carried out through the processes of planning, goal setting, monitoring, providing feedback, analysing and assessing performance, reviewing, dealing with under-performers and coaching.

A vast amount has been written about performance management since the first article by Warren in 1972 – an EBSCO search in January 2009 produced 6,607 references. Much of this has been based on research and one of the aims of this book is to distil the results of that research in order to produce evidence-based material to inform understanding of the position performance management has reached after 37 years and to provide practical guidance on how this evidence can be interpreted and applied by those concerned with developing and introducing performance management.

The process of performance management

The process of performance management was defined by Latham, Sulsky and Macdonald, 2007 as follows:

The process of performance management

The process of performance management consists of the following four steps:

1. Desired job performance is defined.

2. Specific challenging goals are set as to what the person or team should start doing, stop doing or do differently.

3. The individual's performance on the job is observed.

4. Feedback is provided and a decision is made about, training, transferring, promoting, demoting or terminating the contract of an individual.

The Work Foundation research into performance management conducted by Kathy Armstrong and Adrian Ward (2005) reached the following conclusion about the impact of performance management:

> Performance management has the potential to improve the performance of organizations and act as a lever to achieve cultural change. A focus on performance can bring real rewards for organizations. Performance management can be the key space or mechanism for dialogue in an organization. An organization's choice of where to focus its attention in relation to performance management may in part determine its future and can certainly guide its culture.

Performance management is easy to describe but hard to operate. And there is no such thing as 'one best way' to carry it out. As Pulakos, Mueller-Hanson and O'Leary (2008) comment:

> ### The problem of performance management
>
> Performance management is often referred to as the 'Achilles heel' of HRM. All modern organizations face the challenge of how best to manage performance. That is, they must determine the best ways to set goals, evaluate work and distribute rewards in such a way that performance can be improved over time. While all firms face similar challenges, the way a firm responds to these challenges will depend on where the firm is located and the context within which it is operating. Differences in culture, technology or simply tradition make it difficult to directly apply techniques that have worked in one setting to a different setting.

Themes

This book is permeated by a number of themes as set out below that have emerged from the study of the literature and from research into current practice.

Focus on organizational capability

Performance management has to focus on organizational as well as individual capability. Processes for improving individual performance will not necessarily result in improvements in organizational performance. A strategic approach is required that involves fitting the performance management strategy to the firm's business strategy and context, and supporting the business and HR strategies through activities designed to improve organizational effectiveness.

The significance of the organizational context

Performance management functions within a context to influence behaviour in directions that will meet the needs of the stakeholders in the organization. It is as much if not more about managing the context, including the system of work, as about managing individual performance.

The significance of the work system

Individual performance is influenced by systems factors as well as person factors. These will include the support they get from the organization and other factors outside their control. It was stated by Deming (1986) that differences in performance are largely due to systems variations. Gladwell (2008) also argues that success isn't primarily down to the individual, but to his or her context. Coens and Jenkins 2002) believe that: 'Individual performance is mostly determined by the system in which the work is done rather than by the individual's initiative, abilities and efforts.'

Performance management values

Performance management values are based on the ethical principles of respect for the individual, mutual respect, procedural fairness and transparency-based performance management.

Performance management should be evidence based. It is an analytical process in which the factors influencing performance are identified. And this is not just about performance measures. They are important but it is always easy for people to hide behind the figures. It is necessary to drill down and uncover the real reasons for good or not-so-good performance.

Running the business

Performance management is about running the business. It is a natural and continuous process of management. It is not an annual appraisal meeting.

The aims of performance management

Performance management is a forward-looking process primarily concerned with developing people and the systems in which they work to deliver sustained high performance. It is not just about looking backwards and improving indifferent or poor performance in the short term. The aims of performance management as stated by CEMEX and Hitachi are set out in Appendix B.

The nature of performance management

Performance management involves a continuing dialogue between managers and the people they manage. The dialogue is based on goal achievement, performance analysis and constructive feedback, and leads to performance and personal development plans.

Successful performance management

Gillian Henchley, Head of HR at the Victoria & Albert Museum quoted by Armstrong and Baron (1998), believes that the keys to successful performance management are:

- being clear about what is meant by 'performance';

- understanding where the organization is and needs to be in its 'performance culture';

- being very focused on how individual employees will benefit and play their part in the process.

Plan of the book

Part 1 of the book begins with a short history of performance management. Much current practice is based on past experience in such areas as management by objectives and performance appraisal. But the first chapter also provides a background to the emerging themes referred to earlier. Performance management has a strong conceptual base consisting of various aspects of motivational theory, organizational behaviour concepts, systems theory and contingency theory, and these are covered in Chapter 2. The practice of performance management has attracted a great deal of criticism over the years. Some of it focuses on performance appraisal and some seems to be based on labour process theory (ie quasi-Marxist) notions. A lot of it is rightly concerned with the practical problems of implementing an effective performance management system, which are formidable. Chapter 3 sums up the views of the leading critics. You may not agree with all of them but they have much to teach us.

Part 2 of the book describes the nuts and bolts of how performance systems work, how they can be managed and what can be done about under-performers.

Part 3 deals with each of the main processes of performance management in turn, starting with goal or objective setting in Chapter 7. The two terms are virtually synonymous but 'goal' is generally favoured in this book to recognize the significance of the goal theory created by Latham and Locke in 1979, which has had a lot of influence on the practice of performance management. The succeeding chapters in this part cover feedback, performance reviews, analysing and assessing performance and coaching. These chapters describe the considerable skills required to practise performance management.

Part 4 describes performance management in action. It refers to the research conducted recently through a number of surveys and how performance management can be modelled (a valuable way of conveying to those concerned how it works). Research is summarized on how people react to performance management (more favourably than any commentators think) and the evidence of research on the impact of performance management (often equivocal) is reviewed in Chapter 16.

Part 5 is concerned with how performance management is applied in organizations and for teams, and how it relates to learning and development and reward. The management of organizational performance is covered in Chapter 17, which, because of its emphasis on the significance of performance management at a strategic level as a means of developing organizational capability, is one of the most important ones in the book. The strangely neglected subject of performance management for teams is dealt with in Chapter 18.

Part 6 deals with how performance management should be developed and the role of line managers, upon whom the effectiveness of performance management largely depends. It also covers performance management training and, importantly, the evaluation of performance management, another strangely neglected subject. In these hard times it is more essential than ever to ensure that added value is provided by what can often be a complex and expensive management system.

Appendix A contains a comprehensive toolkit that provides practical guidance on analysing current performance arrangements and developing, implementing, operating and evaluating performance management systems.

Appendix B contains case studies specially commissioned from e-reward.

Further reading

The bibliography contains 292 references obtained from the literature search. The most original, penetrating and illuminating of these were:

Armstrong, K and Ward, A (2005) *What Makes for Effective Performance Management?* The Work Foundation, London

Bevan, S and Thompson, M (1991) Performance management at the crossroads, *Personnel Management*, November, pp 36–39

Coens, T and Jenkins, M (2002) *Abolishing Performance Appraisals: Why they backfire and what to do instead*, Berrett-Koehler, San Francisco

Egan, G (1995) A clear path to peak performance, *People Management*, 18 May, pp 34–37

Latham, G P and Locke, E A (1979) Goal setting: a motivational technique that works, *Organizational Dynamics*, Autumn, pp 442–47

Lee, C D (2005) Rethinking the goals of your performance management system, *Employment Relations Today*, **32** (3), pp 53–60

McGregor, D (1957) An uneasy look at performance appraisal, *Harvard Business Review*, May–June, pp 89–94

Strebler, M T, Bevan, S and Robertson D (2001) *Performance Review: Balancing objectives and content*, Institute of Employment Studies, Brighton

Part I

The Background to Performance Management

The Foundations of
Performance Management

The aim of this chapter is to provide a lead in to the rest of this book by tracing the evolution of performance management in the shape of the various approaches to assessing performance that have contributed to the concept as we know it today. In the first section of the chapter a broad definition of performance management is given that will be expanded in Chapter 4. This provides the background to the remaining sections of the chapter, which cover:

1. A short history of performance management.

2. The main developments leading to performance management, ie:

    –   merit rating;

    –   management by objectives;

    –   assessment techniques;

    –   performance appraisal.

3. The development of performance management.

4. The differences between management by objectives, performance appraisal and performance management.

Performance management defined

Performance management is a systematic process for improving organizational performance by developing the performance of individuals and teams. It is a means of getting better results by understanding and managing performance within an agreed framework of planned goals, standards and competency requirements. Processes exist for establishing shared understanding about what is to be achieved, and for managing and developing people in a way that increases the probability that it will be achieved in the short and longer term. It is owned and driven by line management.

As an operational process, performance management can be defined as follows:

> ### Performance management (Briscoe and Claus, 2008)
>
> Performance management is the system through which organizations set work goals, determine performance standards, assign and evaluate work, provide performance feedback, determine training and development needs and distribute rewards.

Performance management as practised today incorporates processes such as management by objectives and performance appraisal that were first developed some time ago. But its overall approach is significantly different. As Mohrman and Mohrman (1995) emphasize: 'Performance management is managing the business.' It is what line managers do continuously, not an HR-directed annual procedure. It is a natural process of management.

Performance management is much more than appraising individuals. It contributes to the achievement of culture change and it is integrated with other key HR activities, especially human capital management, talent management, learning and development and reward management. Thus performance management helps to achieve horizontal integration and the 'bundling' of HR practices so that they are interrelated and therefore complement and reinforce each other. As an important part of a high-performance work system, it contributes to the development of more effective work systems that largely determine levels of performance.

As this book will explain, performance management is a natural process that can be enhanced if it is conducted systematically and those concerned have and use the demanding skills required.

A short history of performance management

According to Koontz (1971), the first known example of performance appraisal took place during the Wei dynasty (AD 221–65) when the emperor employed an 'imperial rater' whose task it was to evaluate the performance of the official family. In the 16th century Ignatius Loyola established a system for formal rating of the members of the Jesuit Society.

The first formal monitoring systems, however, evolved out of the work of Frederick Taylor and his followers before the First World War. Rating for officers in the US armed services was introduced in the 1920s and this spread to the UK, as did some of the factory-based American systems. Merit rating came to the fore in the United States and the UK in the 1950s and 1960s, when it was sometimes re-christened performance appraisal. Management by objectives then came and largely went in the 1960s and 1970s, and simultaneously, experiments were made with assessment techniques such as behaviourally anchored rating scales. A revised form of results-orientated performance appraisal emerged in the 1970s and still exists today. The term performance management was first used in the 1970s but it did not become a recognized process until the latter half of the 1980s.

Merit rating

Merit rating was the process of assessing how well someone was regarded in terms of personality traits such as judgement or integrity and qualities such as leadership or cooperativeness. The term 'merit' recalled classroom judgements made by teachers. Merit rating often involved the quantification of judgements against each factor, presumably in the belief that the quantification of subjective judgements made them more objective.

W D Scott was the American pioneer who introduced rating of the abilities of workers in industry prior to the First World War. He was very much influenced by F W Taylor (1911) and invented the 'Man to Man Comparison' scale, which was Taylorism in action. Many of the developments that have followed, even to this day, are a form of Taylorism, which is F W Taylor's concept of scientific management, meaning the use of systematic observation and measurement, task specialization and, in effect, the reduction of workers to the level of efficiently functioning machines.

The W D Scott scale was modified and used to rate the efficiency of US army officers. It is said to have supplanted the seniority system of promotion in the army and initiated an era of promotion on the basis of merit. The perceived success of this system led to its adoption by the British army.

The pioneering efforts of Scott were developed in the 1920s and 1930s into what was termed the Graphic Rating Scale, used for reports on workers and for rating managers and supervisors. A typical manager's or supervisor's scale included 'tick box' assessments of various qualities, for example:

Consider his success in winning confidence and respect through his personality:

(a) inspiring ☐   (b) favourable ☐   (c) indifferent ☐
(d) unfavourable ☐   (e) repellent ☐

Times have changed.

The justification made for the use of this sort of scale was that ratings were 'educational'. They ensured, it was said, that those making the reports analysed subordinates in terms of the traits essential for success in their work. The educational impact on employees was described as imparting knowledge that they were being judged periodically on vital and important traits.

The original scale was said to have been based on thorough research by W D Scott and colleagues into what were the key criteria for rating people at work. But the principle of the scale and the factors used were seized on with enthusiasm by organizations on both sides of the Atlantic as merit rating or, later, performance appraisal flourished. This was without any research and analysis of the extent to which the factors were relevant (or whether dubbing someone 'repellent' was a good idea). Surveys conducted by the CIPD (Armstrong and Baron, 1998 and 2004) and e-reward (2005) revealed that there are organizations still using lists of competencies that include items that look suspiciously like some of the traits identified 70 years or more ago. They seemed to have been lifted down from some shelf (or extracted from a 'dictionary of competencies') without any research into the extent to which they were appropriate in the context of the organization. Merit rating still exists in some quarters even if it is now called performance management.

Some companies use the total merit score as the basis for ranking employees, and this is translated into a forced distribution for performance pay purposes; for example, the top 10 per cent in the ranking get a 5 per cent increase, the next 20 per cent a 4 per cent increase and so on. To iron out rating inconsistencies one manufacturing company used a diabolical device that they called 'factorising'. This meant producing an average score for the whole company and amending the allocation of points in each department to ensure that their scores corresponded with the company average. It can be imagined that line managers did not take kindly to the implication that there were no differences between departmental performances.

Attacks on merit rating and performance appraisal

Although merit rating in different guises still persists, a strong attack on the practice was mounted by McGregor in his highly influential *Harvard Business Review* article, 'An uneasy look at performance appraisal' (1957). He made the following suggestion:

> ### Douglas McGregor on performance appraisal
>
> The emphasis should be shifted from appraisal to analysis. This implies a more positive approach. No longer is the subordinate being examined by his superior so that his [sic] weaknesses may be determined; rather he is examining himself, in order to define not only his weaknesses but also his strengths and potentials... He becomes an active agent, not a passive 'object'. He is no longer a pawn in a chess game called management development.

McGregor went on to propose that the focus should be on the future rather than the past in order to establish realistic targets and to seek the most effective ways of reaching them. The accent of the review is therefore on performance, on actions relative to goals.

He went on to write:

> *There is less a tendency for the personality of the subordinate to become an issue. The superior, instead of adopting the position of a psychologist or a therapist, can become a coach helping subordinates to reach their own decisions on the specific steps that will enable them to reach their targets. In short, the main factor in the management of individual performance should be the analysis of the behaviour required to achieve agreed results, not the assessment of personality. This is partly management by objectives, which is concerned with planning and measuring results in relation to agreed targets and standards, but retains the concept that individual performance is about behaviour as well as results (a notion that management by objectives ignored).*

A research project conducted by Rowe (1964) in the UK came to broadly the same conclusion as McGregor – that managers do not like 'playing at being God' in rating the personalities of their subordinates:

> *Managers admitted they were hesitant [to appraise] because what they wrote might be misunderstood, because they might unduly affect a subordinate's future career, because they could only write what they were prepared to say and so on.*

One comment made to Rowe was that: 'You feel rather like a schoolmaster writing an end-of-term report'. Rowe's conclusions were that:

- Appraisers were reluctant to appraise.

- The follow-up was inadequate.

- No attempt should be made to clarify or categorize performance in terms of grades. The difficulty of achieving common standards and the reluctance of appraisers to use the whole scale made them of little use.

These comments, especially the last one, are as relevant today as they were when they were made some time ago. Yet commentators are still producing these precepts as original truths. It is remarkable how much re-inventing the wheel goes on in the field of performance management. Another example is the replacement of the somewhat discredited management by objectives by performance management, at least in its earlier versions.

The attack on merit rating or the earlier versions of performance appraisal, as it came to be known in the 1960s, was often made on the grounds that it was mainly concerned with the assessment of traits. These could refer to the extent to which individuals were conscientious, imaginative, self-sufficient and cooperative, or possessed qualities of judgement, initiative, vigour or original thinking. Traits represent 'pre-dispositions to behave in certain ways in a variety of different situations' (Chell, 1992) Trait theorists typically advance the following definition of personality: 'More or less stable internal factors that makes one person's behaviour consistent from one time to another and different from the behaviour other people would manifest in comparable situations' (Hampson, 1982). But the belief that trait behaviour is independent of situations (the work system) and the people with whom an individual is interacting is questionable. Trait measures cannot predict how a person will respond in a particular situation (Epstein and O'Brien, 1985). And there is the problem of how anyone can be certain that someone has such and such a trait. Assessments of traits are only too likely to be prompted by subjective judgements and prejudices.

Management by objectives

The management by objectives movement claimed that it overcame the problems of trait rating. It was based on the writings of Peter Drucker and Douglas McGregor.

Peter Drucker

The term 'management by objectives' was first coined by Peter Drucker (1955) as follows:

Peter Drucker on management by objectives

What the business enterprise needs is a principle of management that will give full scope to individual strength and responsibility and at the same time give common direction of vision and effort, establish teamwork and harmonize the goals of the individual with the common weal. The only principle that can do this is management by objectives and self-control.

Drucker emphasized that 'an effective management must direct the vision and efforts of all managers towards a common goal'. This would ensure that individual and corporate objectives are integrated and would also make it possible for managers to control their own performance: 'Self-control means stronger motivation: a desire to do the best rather than just enough to get by. It means higher performance goals and broader vision.'

Douglas McGregor

McGregor's (1960) contribution arose from his Theory Y concept. He wrote: 'The central principle that derives from Theory Y is that of integration: the creation of conditions such that the members of the organization can achieve their own goals best by directing their efforts towards the success of the organization'. This is McGregor's principle of 'management by integration and self-control', which he insisted should be regarded as a strategy – a way of managing people:

> ### *Douglas McGregor on the principle of integration and self-control*
>
> The tactics are worked out in the light of the circumstances. Forms and procedures are of little value… 'selling' management a programme of target setting and providing standardized forms and procedures is the surest way to prevent the development of management by integration and self-control.

This principle may not have entered the vocabulary of performance management but is fully absorbed into current thinking about it. Many writers and management consultants recycle McGregor's philosophy without ever acknowledging its source.

The management by objectives system

Management by objectives was defined by John Humble (1972), a leading British enthusiast, as: 'A dynamic system that seeks to integrate the company's need to clarify and achieve its profit and growth goals with the manager's need to contribute and develop himself [sic]. It is a demanding and rewarding style of managing a business.'

> ### *Management by objectives as described by John Humble*
>
> Management by objectives is a continuous process of:
>
> - reviewing critically and restating the company's strategic and tactical plans;
> - clarifying with each manager the key results and performance standards he [sic] must achieve, and gaining his contribution and commitment to these, individually and as a team member;
> - agreeing with each manager a job improvement plan that makes a measurable and realistic contribution to the unit and company plans for better performance;
> - providing conditions (an organization structure and management information) in which it is possible to achieve the key results and improvement plan;
> - using systematic performance review to measure and discuss progress towards results;
> - developing management training plans to build on strengths, to help managers to overcome their weaknesses and to get them to accept responsibility for self-development;
> - strengthening the motivation of managers by effective selection, salary and succession plans.

Humble emphasized that these activities are interdependent and he illustrated the dynamic nature of the system as shown in Figure 1.1:

Figure 1.1 The management by objectives cycle

Except for the insistence that this system is exclusively for managers (who, presumably, were always men) much of what Humble wrote would be acceptable today as good performance management practice. The performance management cycle as usually described today (see Chapter 4) certainly derives from his management by objectives cycle. And the focus on objectives or goals is still a fundamental characteristic of performance management.

Management by objectives was adopted enthusiastically by many companies in the 1960s and 1970s. But it became discredited by the 1990s – why?

Criticisms of management by objectives

One of the first and most formidable attacks on management by objectives was made in the *Harvard Business Review* by Levinson (1970). His criticisms were:

● Every organization is a social system, a network of interpersonal relationships. A person doing an excellent job by objective standards of measurement may fail miserably as a partner, superior, subordinate or colleague.

● The greater the emphasis on measurement and quantification, the more likely it is that the subtle, non-measurable elements of the task will be sacrificed. Quality of performance frequently loses out to quantification.

● It (management by objectives) leaves out the individual's personal needs and objectives, bearing in mind that the most powerful driving force for individuals comprises their needs, wishes and personal objectives.

These points are just as relevant to performance management practices today that focus on objectives.

The following criticisms were made by Schaffer (1991) in the *Harvard Business Review*:

R H Schaffer on management by objectives

Ironically, management by objectives programmes often create heavy paper snowstorms in which managers can escape from demand making. In many MBO programmes, as lists of goals get longer and thicker, the focus is diffused, bulk is confused with quality, and energy is spent on the mechanics rather than the results. A manager challenged on the performance of her group can safely point to the packet of papers and assert: 'My managers have spent many hours developing their goals for the year.'

The demise of management by objectives was mainly due to the process becoming over-systematized (often under the influence of package-orientated management consultants) and too much emphasis being placed on the quantification of objectives. The originators of the concept may not have advocated lots of forms and they recognized, as John Humble did, that qualitative performance standards could be included in the system, by which was meant 'a statement of conditions which exist when the result is being satisfactorily achieved'. But these principles were often ignored in practice. In addition, management by objectives often became a top-down affair with little dialogue, and it tended to focus narrowly on the objectives of individual managers without linking them to corporate or team goals (although this link was supposed to happen, and it was certainly a major part of Drucker's original concept). The system also tended to concentrate on managers, leaving the rest of the staff to be dealt with by an old-fashioned merit-rating scheme, presumably because it was thought that they did not deserve anything better.

A later comparison of management by objectives and performance management by Fowler (1990) criticized the former because:

- It was not right for all organizations – it required a highly structured, orderly and logical approach that did not fit the opportunistic world of the entrepreneur.

- Only limited recognition was given to the importance of defining the organization's corporate goals and values – the emphasis was on the role of the individual manager.

- Line managers perceived it as a centrally imposed administrative task.

- It became a formal once-a-year exercise bearing little relationship to managers' day-to-day activities.

- There was an overemphasis on quantifiable objectives to the detriment of important qualitative factors.

- The system was administratively top-heavy – form filling became an end in itself.

Developments in assessment techniques

Concurrently with the emergence of management by objectives, consideration was being given to avoiding the misguided use of traits in performance assessment. The critical incident approach developed by Flanagan (1954) changed the focus to the observation of behaviour. Behavioural anchored rating scales (Smith and Kendall, 1963) and behavioural observation scales (Latham and Wexley, 1977) provided for the quantification of behavioural performance. These approaches are described in Chapter 11.

Much research was carried out later on rating, for example, by Bernardin and Buckley (1981), Sulsky and Balzer (1988) and Murphy and Balzer (1989). Such activity reflected the preoccupation of some American academics with rating techniques. This still persists today, in contrast to the UK approach, which has become more concerned with developing performance than rating it. Further consideration to assessment and rating techniques is given in Chapter 11.

Rating source research led to the emergence in the early 1990s of multi-source or 360-degree feedback that provided for upwards and lateral assessments as well as the traditional top-down rating (Hedge, Borman and Birkeland, 2001).

Performance appraisal (1970s version)

In the 1970s a revised approach to performance assessment was developed under the influence of the management by objectives movement. It was sometimes called 'results-orientated appraisal' because it incorporated the agreement of objectives and an assessment of the results obtained against these objectives. Ratings were usually retained of overall performance and in relation to individual objectives. Trait ratings were also used, but more recently these were replaced in some schemes by competency ratings. This form of performance appraisal received a boost during the later 1980s because of the use of performance-related pay based on performance ratings.

As defined by the Advisory, Conciliation and Arbitration Service (ACAS) in 1988: 'Appraisals regularly record an assessment of an employee's performance, potential and development needs. The appraisal is an opportunity to take an overall view of work content, loads and volume, to look back at what has been achieved during the reporting period and agree objectives for the next.'

Appraisal schemes often included ratings of performance factors such as volume of work, quality of work, knowledge of job, dependability, innovation, staff development and communication and an overall rating. Some schemes simply reviewed the achievement of objectives but still included the overall rating. Scope might be allowed for self-assessment, and the forms frequently included spaces for work improvement plans, training requirements and the assessment of potential. There was usually an arrangement for 'countersigning' managers to make comments; this was usually the appraiser's manager – who was originally called the 'grandfather', which later changed to 'grandparent'.

The appraisal was typically an annual event; a meeting convened by a manager in which a top-down opinion was expressed about the performance of a subordinate, followed by a rating.

In principle, many organizations and personnel specialists believed that formal appraisals were desirable. The ACAS (1988) booklet stated that: 'Appraisals can help to improve employees' job performance by identifying strengths and weaknesses and determining how their strengths may be best utilized within the organization and weaknesses overcome.' But many criticisms were made of the ways in which appraisal schemes operated in practice. Levinson (1976) wrote that: 'It is widely recognized that there are many things wrong with most of the performance appraisal systems in use.' He thought that the most obvious drawbacks were:

- Judgements on performance are usually subjective, impressionistic and arbitrary.

- Ratings by different managers are not comparable.

- Delays in feedback occur that create frustration when good performance is not quickly recognized and anger when judgement is rendered for inadequacies long past.

- Managers generally have a sense of inadequacy about appraising subordinates and paralysis and procrastination result from their feelings of guilt about playing God.

He stated that: 'Performance appraisal needs to be viewed not as a technique but as a process involving both people and data, and as such the whole process is inadequate.' He also pointed out that appraisal was not usually recognized as a normal function of management and that individual objectives were seldom related to the objectives of the business.

Another view was expressed by Long (1986) on the basis of the Institute of Personnel Management's research into performance appraisal:

> There is no such thing as the perfect performance review system. None is infallible, although some are more fallible than others. Some systems, despite flaws, will be managed fairly conscientiously, others, despite elegant design, will receive perfunctory attention and ultimately fail. The relative success or failure of performance review, as with any other organizational system, depends very much on the attitudinal response it arouses.

The requirements for success were indeed demanding. These were described by Lazer and Wikstrom (1977): 'A "good" performance appraisal scheme must be job related, reliable, valid for the purposes for which it is being used, standardized in its procedures, practical in its administration and suited to the organization's culture.'

The problem was that performance appraisal was too often perceived as the property of the personnel department. This was where the forms were kept and where decisions were made about performance-related pay. Line managers frequently criticized the system as being irrelevant. They felt they had better things to do and at worst ignored it and at best paid lip service to completing the forms, knowing that they had to make ratings to generate performance pay. Indeed, managers have been known to rate first in accordance with what pay increase individuals should have and then write their comments to justify their marks. In other words, human beings behaved as human beings. Individuals were said to be wary of appraisals and as likely to be demotivated by an appraisal meeting as to be motivated.

Perhaps the worst feature of performance appraisal schemes was that appraisal was not regarded as a normal and necessary process of management. If ratings were based on a review of the extent to which individual objectives were attained, those objectives were not linked to the objectives of the business or department. Appraisal was isolated and therefore irrelevant. Mangers tended to go through the motions when they reluctantly held their yearly appraisal meeting. As described by Armstrong and Murlis (1994) it too often became 'a dishonest annual ritual'.

The concept of 'Appraisal: an idea whose time has gone?' was advanced by Fletcher (1993a) as follows.

Clive Fletcher on appraisal

What we are seeing is the demise of the traditional, monolithic appraisal system… In its place are evolving a number of separate but linked processes applied in different ways according to the needs of local circumstances and staff levels. The various elements in this may go by different names, and perhaps the term appraisal has in some ways outlived its usefulness.

Enter performance management

The concept of performance management incorporates some of the notions and approaches of management by objectives and performance appraisal but it includes a number of significantly different features as described below.

Early days

The earliest reference to performance management in the literature was made by Warren (1972). On the basis of his research in a manufacturing company he defined the features of performance management as follows.

Features of performance management as defined by Malcolm Warren in 1972

- Expectations – a large group of employees – preferably all – must be told clearly, objectively and in their own language what is specifically expected of them.

- Skill – a large group of employees must have the technical knowledge and skill to carry out the tasks.

- Feedback – workers must be told in clear terms, without threats, how they are doing in terms of expectations.

- Resources – employees must have the time, money and equipment necessary to perform the expected tasks at optimal level.

- Reinforcement – employees must be positively reinforced for desired performance.

These requirements may not be expressed in quite the same language today, but they are just as relevant.

Another early use of the term performance management was made by Beer and Ruh (1976). Their thesis was that: 'performance is best developed through practical challenges and experiences on the job with guidance and feedback from superiors.' They described the performance management system at Corning Glass Works, the aim of which was to help managers give feedback in a helpful and constructive way, and to aid in the creation of a developmental plan. The features of this system that distinguished it from other appraisal schemes were as follows:

- emphasis on both development and evaluation;

- use of a profile defining the individual's strengths and development needs;

- integration of the results achieved with the means by which they have been achieved;

- separation of development review from salary review.

Although this was not necessarily a model performance management process it did contain a number of characteristics that are still regarded as good practice.

The concept of performance management then lay fallow for some years but began to emerge in the United States as a new approach to managing performance in the mid-1980s. However, one of the first books exclusively devoted to performance management was not published until 1988 (Plachy and Plachy). They described what had by then become the accepted approach to performance management as follows.

Performance management as described by Plachy and Plachy in 1988

Performance management is communication: a manager and an employee arrive together at an understanding of what work is to be accomplished, how it will be accomplished, how work is progressing toward desired results, and finally, after effort is expended to accomplish the work, whether the performance has achieved the agreed-upon plan. The process recycles when the manager and employee begin planning what work is to be accomplished for the next performance period. Performance management is an umbrella term that includes performance planning, performance review, and performance appraisal. Major work plans and appraisals are generally made annually. Performance review occurs whenever a manager and an employee confirm, adjust, or correct their understanding of work performance during routine work contacts.

In the UK the first published reference to performance management was made at a meeting of the Compensation Forum in 1987 by Don Beattie, Personnel Director, ICL, who described how it was used as 'an essential contribution to a massive and urgent change programme in the organization' and had become a part of the fabric of the business.

By 1990 performance management had entered the vocabulary of human resource management in the UK as well as in the United States. Fowler (1990) defined what has become the accepted concept of performance management:

> *Management has always been about getting things done, and good managers are concerned to get the right things done well. That, in essence, is performance management – the organization of work to achieve the best possible results. From this simple viewpoint, performance management is not a system or technique, it is the totality of the day-to-day activities of all managers. (Emphasis added)*

Performance management established

Full recognition of the existence of performance management was provided by the research project conducted by the Institute of Personnel Management (1992). The following definition of performance management was produced as a result of this research: 'A strategy that relates to every activity of the organization set in the context of its human resources policies, culture, style and communications systems. The nature of the strategy depends on the organizational context and can vary from organization to organization.'

It was suggested that what was described as a 'performance management system' (PMS) complied with the textbook definition when the following characteristics were met by the organization.

Institute of Personnel Management (1992): definition of a performance management system

- It communicates a vision of its objectives to all its employees.

- It sets departmental and individual performance targets that are related to wider objectives.

- It conducts a formal review of progress towards these targets.

- It uses the review process to identify training, development and reward outcomes.

- It evaluates the whole process in order to improve effectiveness.

- It expresses performance targets in terms of measurable outputs, accountabilities and training/learning targets.

- It uses formal appraisal procedures as ways of communicating performance requirements that are set on a regular basis.

- It links performance requirements to pay, especially for senior managers.

With the exception of the link to pay, which applies to many but not all performance management schemes, these characteristics still hold good today.

In the organizations with performance management systems, 85 per cent had performance pay and 76 per cent rated performance (this proportion is lower in later surveys). The emphasis was on objective setting and review that, as the authors of the report mentioned, 'leaves something of a void when it comes to identifying development needs on a longer-term basis... there is a danger with results-orientated schemes in focusing excessively on what is to be achieved and ignoring the how.' It was noted that some organizations were moving in the direction of competency analysis but not very systematically.

Two of the IPM researchers (Bevan and Thompson, 1991) commented on the emergence of performance management systems as integrating processes that mesh various human resource management activities with the business objectives of the organization. They identified two broad thrusts towards integration:

- Reward-driven integration, which emphasizes the role of performance pay in changing organizational behaviour and tends to undervalue the part played by other human resource development activities. This appeared to be the dominant mode of integration.

- Development-driven integration, which stresses the importance of HRD. Although performance pay may operate in these organizations, it is perceived to be complementary to HRD activities rather than dominating them.

Some of the interesting conclusions emerging from this research are set out below.

Conclusions from the IPM 1992 research

- No evidence was found that improved performance in the private sector is associated with the presence of formal performance management programmes.

- An overwhelming body of psychological research exists which makes clear that, as a way of enhancing individual performance, the setting of performance targets is inevitably a successful strategy.

- The process of forming judgements and evaluations of individual performance is an almost continuous one. Most often it is a subconscious process, relying on subjective judgements, based on incomplete evidence and spiced with an element of bias.

- There was little consistency of viewpoint on the motivating power of money. The majority (of organizations) felt that the real motivators at management levels were professional and personal pride in the standards achieved, or loyalty to the organization and its aims, or peer pressure. One line manager commented that he was self-motivated: 'The money comes as a result of that, not as the cause of it.' While the principle of pay for performance was generally accepted, the reservations were about putting it into practice: 'It was often viewed as a good idea – especially for other people – but not something that, when implemented, seemed to breed either satisfaction or motivation.'

- The focus has been on the splendid-sounding notion of the performance-orientated culture and of improving the bottom line, and/or the delivery of services. Whilst this is well and good, the achievement of such ends has to be in concert with the aims and the development needs of individuals.

These conclusions are still relevant.

Performance management: the next phase

The 1998 IPD research project (Armstrong and Baron, 1998) revealed that in many instances performance management practices had moved on since 1992. In the organizations covered by the survey the following trends were observed:

- Performance management is regarded as a number of interlinked processes.

- Performance management is seen as a continuous process, not as a once-a-year appraisal, thus echoing Fowler's (1990) comment that: 'In today's fast-moving world, any idea that effective performance management can be tied neatly to a single annual date is patently absurd.'

- The focus is on employee development rather than on performance-related pay.

- There has been a shift towards getting line managers to accept and own performance management as a natural process of management.

- Some organizations reject the concept of a bureaucratic, centrally controlled and uniform system of performance management, and instead accept that, within an overall policy framework, different approaches may be appropriate in different parts of the organization and for different people.

Another important trend in the 1990s was the increased use of competencies for recruitment and people development purposes. This led to more focus on the nature of performance, which was recognized as being not only about what was achieved but also about *how* it was achieved. The result was the 'mixed model' of performance management as described by Hartle (1995), which covers competency levels and the extent to which behaviour was in line with the core values of the organization, as well as objective-setting and review. At the same time the notion emerged of what Sparrow (2008) calls value-based performance management: that is, including assessments of the extent to which individuals uphold a defined list of core organizational values in the performance review procedure.

The next development was the recognition that performance management had to focus on organizational as well as individual effectiveness. It was not enough to hope that processes for improving individual performance would necessarily result in improvements in organizational performance. As Coens and Jenkins (2002) put it: 'An organization, because it is a system, cannot be significantly improved by focusing on individuals.' A strategic approach was required that involves fitting the performance management strategy to the firm's business strategy and context, and supporting the business and HR strategies through activities designed to improve organizational capability such as human capital management, talent management and the development of high-performance cultures (see Chapter 17).

Why performance management?

Performance management arrived in the later 1980s partly as a reaction to the negative aspects of merit rating and management by objectives referred to earlier. Its strength is that it is essentially an integrated approach to managing performance on a continuous basis. The appeal of performance management in its fully realized form is that it is holistic – it pervades every aspect of running the business and helps to give purpose and meaning to those involved in achieving organizational success.

Of course, performance management at first incorporated many of the elements of earlier approaches: for example, rating, objective setting and review, performance pay and a tendency towards trait assessment. Conceptually, however, performance management is significantly different from previous approaches in that: 1) it is regarded as a continuous process not a single event – (Latham, Sulsky and Macdonald [2007] commented that 'a distinguishing feature of performance management relative to performance appraisal is that the former is an ongoing process whereas the latter is done at discrete time intervals); 2) it is treated as a normal and necessary function of management rather than an HR procedure; and 3) it is therefore owned and driven by line managers rather than HR. But in practice the term has often simply replaced 'performance appraisal', just as 'human resource management' has frequently been substituted for 'personnel management' without any discernible change in approach – lots of distinctions, not many differences.

Performance management may often be no more than new wine in old bottles or, to mix metaphors, a 'flavour of the month'. But it exists and the research quoted in Chapter 13 has demonstrated that interest is growing – why?

The market economy and entrepreneurial culture of the 1980s focused attention on gaining competitive advantage and getting added value from the better use of resources. Performance orientation became important, especially in the face of global competition and recession. The rise of human resource management (HRM) also contributed to the emergence of performance management. As mentioned by Sparrow (2008), this rise was accompanied by a shift in focus from appraisal to a broader agenda of improving performance, an emphasis on more open and honest communication between managers and individuals on behaviours and outcomes, and the need to engage and motivate employees. He listed three developments in HR that reinforced this shift in focus:

- Talent management – the systematic identification and development of talented people.

- Employee segmentation –identifying those segments of employees whose performance really drives business results and treating them accordingly.

- The concept of total rewards – the recognition that the reward system should embrace non-financial as well as financial rewards and that non-financial rewards such as recognition and growth opportunities could be provided through performance management processes.

Another development in the 1990s and beyond was the creation of high-performance, high-commitment or high-involvement management systems in which performance management and the achievement of enhanced levels of employee engagement played an important part.

Comparison of different approaches

A comparison of management by objectives, performance appraisal and performance management is set out below.

Table 1.1 Comparison of management by objectives, performance appraisal and performance management

Management by objectives	Performance appraisal	Performance management
• Emphasis on individual integrating objectives	• Individual objectives may be included	• Focus on organizational, and individual objectives
• Emphasis on quantified requirements and performance measures	• Some qualitative performance objectives may also be included	• Covers both outputs (results) and inputs (competencies)
• Annual appraisal	• Annual appraisal	• All the year round
• No ratings	• Ratings	• May not have ratings
• Backward looking	• Backward looking	• Forward looking
• Focus on performance achievements	• Focus on levels of performance and merit	• Focus on development as well as performance
• Top-down system	• Top-down system	• Joint process
• Monolithic system	• Monolithic system	• Flexible process
• Packaged system	• Usually tailor made	• Tailor made
• Complex paper work	• Complex paper work	• Paper work minimized
• May not be a direct link to pay	• Often linked to performance pay	• May not be linked to performance pay
• Applied to managers	• Applied to all staff	• Applied to all staff
• Owned by line managers and personnel department	• Owned by HR department	• Owned by line managers

The Conceptual Framework of Performance Management

Performance management concepts explain its theoretical basis and how it ought to work in practice. They provide a framework within which performance processes can be developed, operated and evaluated.

This chapter examines the following concepts:

- underpinning theories;
- performance management values;
- the meaning of performance and what determines it;
- contextual factors;
- performance management and motivation;
- performance management and the psychological contract.

Underpinning theories

The following three theories underpinning performance management have been identified by Buchner (2007).

Goal theory

Goal theory as developed by Latham and Locke (1979) highlights four mechanisms that connect goals to performance outcomes: 1) they direct attention to priorities; 2) they stimulate effort; 3) they challenge people to bring their knowledge and skills to bear to increase their chances of success; and 4) the more challenging the goal, the more people will draw on their full repertoire of skills. This theory underpins the emphasis in performance management on setting and agreeing objectives against which performance can be measured and managed.

> ### Robertson, Smith and Cooper (1992) on goal theory
>
> Goals inform individuals to achieve particular levels of performance, in order for them to direct and evaluate their actions; while performance feedback allows the individual to track how well he or she has been doing in relation to the goal so that, if necessary, adjustments in effort, direction or possibly task strategies can be made.

Goal theory supports the agreement of objectives, feedback and review aspects of performance management.

Control theory

Control theory focuses attention on feedback as a means of shaping behaviour. As people receive feedback on their behaviour they appreciate the discrepancy between what they are doing and what they are expected to do and take corrective action to overcome it. Feedback is recognized as a crucial part of performance management processes.

Social cognitive theory

Social cognitive theory was developed by Bandura (1986). It is based on his central concept of self-efficacy. This suggests that what people believe that they can or cannot do powerfully impacts on their performance. Developing and strengthening positive self-belief in employees is therefore an important performance management objective.

Performance management values

Performance management values are based on the ethical principles of respect for the individual, mutual respect, procedural fairness and transparency as defined by Winstanley and Stuart-Smith (1996). The values refer to beliefs that:

- The management of the organization has the overriding responsibility for creating the conditions in which high performance is achievable.

- Everyone is concerned with the improvement of performance; it is the joint responsibility of managers and their teams and they are mutually dependent on one another to attain this purpose.

- People should be valued for what they are as well as what they achieve.

- The needs of individuals as well as those of the organization must be recognized and respected.

- Individuals should be given the opportunity to express their views about the objectives they are expected to achieve.

- Individuals should understand and agree to the measures used to monitor their performance and should be able to track their own performance against those measures.

- Individuals have the right to obtain feedback on their performance and to comment on that feedback.

- Individuals should know how and why decisions affecting them emerging from performance reviews have been made, and should have the right to appeal against those decisions.

- The focus should be on developing performance rather than merely managing it – priority should therefore be given to the developmental aspects of performance management.

There are, however, two superordinate values. First, the values set out above and any others that are believed to be important should not be imposed by management. They should be debated with managers, employees and employee representatives in order to obtain general agreement and understanding that these are the things that matter. Second there should be a process of what Boyett and Conn (1995) call 'reality checking'. This means finding out if behaviour is consistent with espoused values and if not, what needs to be done – change the behaviour or change the value.

The meaning of performance

If you can't define performance you can't measure or manage it. It has been pointed out by Bates and Holton (1995) that: 'Performance is a multi-dimensional construct, the measurement of which varies depending on a variety of factors.' They also state that it is important to determine whether the measurement objective is to assess performance outcomes or behaviour.

Latham, Sulsky and Macdonald (2007) emphasize that an appropriate definition of performance is a prerequisite for feedback and goal setting processes. They state that a performance theory is needed that stipulates:

- the relevant performance dimensions;

- the performance standards or expectations associated with different performance levels;

- how situational constraints should be weighed (if at all) when evaluating performance;

- the number of performance levels or gradients;

- the extent to which performance should be based on absolute or comparative standards.

There are different views on what performance is. It can be regarded as simply the record of outcomes achieved. On an individual basis, it can be a record of the person's accomplishments. Kane (1996) argues that performance 'is something that the person leaves behind and that exists apart from the purpose'. Bernardin *et al* (1995) are concerned that: 'Performance should be defined as the outcomes of work because they provide the strongest linkage to the strategic goals of the organization, customer satisfaction, and economic contributions.'

Guest (1996) also believes that performance is about outcomes but that the concept should be linked to the idea of a balanced scorecard.

Borman and Motowidlo (1993) put forward the notion of contextual performance that covers non-job-specific behaviours such as cooperation, dedication, enthusiasm and persistence and is differentiated from task performance covering job-specific behaviours. As Fletcher (2001) mentions, contextual performance deals with attributes that go beyond task competence and that foster behaviours that enhance the climate and effectiveness of the organization.

The *Oxford English Dictionary* defines performance as: 'The accomplishment, execution, carrying out, working out of anything ordered or undertaken.' This refers to outputs/outcomes (accomplishment) but also states that performance is about doing the work as well as being about the results achieved. Performance could therefore be regarded as behaviour – the way in which organizations, teams and individuals get work done. Campbell (1990) believes that: 'Performance is behaviour and should be distinguished from the outcomes because they can be contaminated by systems factors.' A more comprehensive view of performance is achieved if it is defined as embracing both behaviour and outcomes. This was well put by Brumbach (1988).

Brumbach on performance

Performance means both behaviours and results. Behaviours emanate from the performer and transform performance from abstraction to action. Not just the instruments for results, behaviours are also outcomes in their own right – the product of mental and physical effort applied to tasks – and can be judged apart from results.

This definition of performance leads to the conclusion that when managing the performance of teams and individuals both inputs (behaviour) and outputs (results) need to be considered. This is the mixed model of performance management that covers competency levels and achievements as well as objective setting and review. And it is this model that research (eg Armstrong and Baron, 2004) has shown to be the one that is now interesting many organizations.

Campbell *et al* (1993) are more concerned with measuring performance. They define it as behaviour or action relevant to the attainment of the organization's goals that can be scaled, that is, measured. Their theory states that performance is multidimensional and that each dimension is characterized by a category of similar behaviour or actions. The components consist of: 1) job-specific task proficiency; 2) non-job-specific proficiency (eg organizational citizenship behaviour); 3) written and oral communication proficiency; 4) demonstration of effort; 5) maintenance of personal discipline; 6) facilitation of personal and team performance; 7) supervision/leadership; and 8) management/administration.

Levels of individual performance are affected by a number of influences and factors as discussed below.

Influences on performance

Four major influences on performance were identified by Harrison (1997):

- the learner, who needs the right level of competence, motivation, support and incentives in order to perform effectively;

- the learner's work group, whose members will exercise a strong positive or negative influence on the attitudes, behaviour and performance of the learner;

- the learner's manager, who needs to provide continuing support and act as a role model, coach and stimulator related to performance;

- the organization, which may produce barriers to effective performance if there is no powerful, cohering vision; ineffective structure, culture or work systems; unsupportive employee relations policy and systems, or inappropriate leadership and management style.

Factors affecting performance

Vroom (1964) suggested that performance is a function of ability and motivation as depicted in the formula: Performance = f (ability × motivation). The effects of ability and motivation on performance are not additive but multiplicative. People need both ability and motivation to perform well, and if either ability or motivation is zero there will be no effective performance.

A formula for performance was originated by Blumberg and Pringle (1982). Their equation was:

Performance = individual attributes × work effort × organizational support

By including organizational support in the formula they brought in the organizational context as a factor affecting performance. This is in accordance with the later views of Deming (1986) who emphasized that differences in performance are largely due to systems variations, a view echoed by Coens and Jenkins (2002).

Research carried out by Bailey, Berg and Sandy (2001) in 45 establishments focused on another factor affecting performance – the opportunity to participate. They noted that: 'organizing the work process so that non-managerial employees have the opportunity to contribute discretionary effort is the central feature of a high performance work system.' (This was one of the earlier uses of the term discretionary effort.)

The 'AMO' formula put forward by Boxall and Purcell (2003) is a combination of the Vroom and Bailey *et al* ideas. This model asserts that performance is a function of Ability + Motivation + Opportunity to Participate (note that the relationship is additive not multiplicative).

All these formulas focus on individual performance but they neglect the effect of systems as discussed below.

Systems factors

Systems theory as formulated by Miller and Rice (1967) states that organizations should be treated as open systems that transform inputs into outputs within the environments (external and internal) upon which they are dependent. Systems theory is the basis of the input–process–output–outcome model of managing performance, which assesses the entire contribution that an individual makes within the system in carrying out his or her allotted tasks, not just the outputs. Inputs – the skills and knowledge that an individual brings to a job – together with process – which is how people actually perform their jobs – are measured to assess development and learning needs. Outcomes measure the scale of the individual's contribution to overall team, department and corporate performance, and are central to performance management. This method of managing performance is important because all the factors that influence performance, including the system and the context, can be taken into account when assessing it.

Individual performance is influenced by systems factors as well as person factors (Cardy and Dobbins, 1994). These will include the support they get from the organization and other factors outside the control of individuals. Jones (1995) proposes that the aim should be to 'manage context not performance' and goes on to explain that:

In this equation, the role of management focuses on clear, coherent support for employees by providing information about organization goals, resources, technology, structure, and policy, thus creating a context that has multiplicative impact on the employees, their individual attributes (competency to perform), and their work effort (willingness to perform). In short, managing context is entirely about helping people understand; it is about turning on the lights.

It was emphasized by Deming (1986) that differences in performance are largely due to systems variations. Gladwell (2008) also argues that success isn't primarily down to the individual, but to his or her context. Coens and Jenkins (2002) made the following comments on the impact of systems:

The impact of systems

An organizational system is composed of the people who do the work but far more than that. It also includes the organization's methods, structure, support, materials, equipment, customers, work culture, internal and external environments (such as markets, the community, governments), and the interaction of these components. Each part of the system has its own purpose but at the same time is dependent on the other parts…

Because of the interdependency of the parts, improvement strategies aimed at the parts, such as appraisal, do little or nothing to improve the system… Individual performance is mostly determined by the system in which the work is done rather than by the individual's initiative, abilities and efforts…

Because of these effects and the low yield benefit of improving the parts, it makes little sense to design organizational improvement systems around appraisal while the leveraging power of improving the system is ignored… The myopic focus on individual improvement equates to a religious dogma that is manifested through the rituals and rites of ranking and rating.

However, Coens and Jenkins also stated that: 'We do not advocate abandoning all strategies aimed at individual improvement, personal development and goal attainment. When combined with serious efforts toward improving the system and work environment, such initiatives can significantly bolster organizational transformation.'

Contextual factors

Systems operate within the context of the organization. Performance management is a method of influencing behaviour within a context in directions that will meet the needs of the stakeholders in the organization. It has been said by Nadler and Tushman (1980) that:

The manager needs to understand the patterns of behaviour that are observed to predict in what direction behaviour will move (particularly in the light of management action) and to use this knowledge to control behaviour over the course of time. Effective managerial action requires that the manager be able to diagnose the situation he or she is working in.

This point should be extended to include the people managers manage – they equally want to know and are entitled to know the situation they are working in.

The situation or context in which people work and the way performance can be measured can be described in terms of systems theory as described earlier. More specifically, the context includes the organizational culture, the employee relations climate, the people involved and the internal environment in terms of the organization's structure, its size and its technology and working practices.

Organizational culture

Organizational culture is the pattern of shared beliefs, norms and values in an organization that shape the way people act and interact and strongly influence the ways in which things get done. From the performance management viewpoint one of the most important manifestations of organizational culture is management style. This refers to the ways in which managers behave in managing people and how they exercise authority and use their power. If the prevailing management style in a command-and-control type structure is autocratic, directive, task orientated, distant and tough, then a 'caring and sharing' philosophy of performance management is not likely to work, even if it was felt to be desirable, which is unlikely. Alternatively, a non-directive, participative and considerate style is more likely to support a 'partnership' approach to performance management, with an emphasis on involvement, empowerment and ownership.

It is vital to take account of cultural considerations when developing and implementing performance management. The aim must be to achieve a high degree of fit between the performance management processes and the corporate culture when the latter is embedded and appropriate. However, performance management is one of the instruments that can be used in a cultural change programme where the focus is on high performance, engagement, commitment and involvement.

Employee relations climate

The employee relations climate of an organization represents the perceptions of employees and their representatives about the ways in which relationships between management and employees are maintained. It refers to the ways in which formal or informal employee relations are conducted and how the various parties (managers, employees and trade unions or staff associations) behave when interacting with one another. The climate can be good, bad or indifferent according to perceptions about the extent to which:

- The parties trust one another.
- Management treats employees fairly and with consideration.
- Management is open and honest about its actions and intentions.

- Harmonious relationships exist; management treats employees as stakeholders.
- Employees are committed to the interests of the organization.
- What management does is consistent with what it says it will do.

Clearly, a good climate will be conducive to the design and operation of effective performance management processes as long as these are developed jointly by the stakeholders and take account of the interests of all involved. An improved employee relations climate may also result from pursuing the development and implementation of performance management in accordance with the ethical principles set out in Chapter 4.

People

The development and application of performance management can be driven from the top, possibly forming part of a transformational programme incorporating cultural changes. There may be too much top-down control and change may go in the wrong direction, but if there is an enlightened approach that appreciates the need to involve stakeholders, then top management leadership will get things done and convey the message that performance management is important.

Performance management processes will vary in accordance with the composition of the workforce. For example, a firm employing mainly knowledge workers is likely to adopt a different approach from a manufacturing firm. Within the organization, approaches may vary between different groups of employees. In the Victoria and Albert Museum, for example, it is recognized that the way in which objectives are agreed by a curator will be different from how the standards of performance are agreed for security guards.

Structure

A hierarchical or functional structure with well-defined layers of authority is more likely to support a directive, top-down approach to setting objectives and reviewing performance. A flatter, process-based structure will encourage more flexible participative approaches with an emphasis on teamwork and the management of performance by self-directed teams.

A structure in which responsibility and authority are devolved close to the scenes of action will probably foster a flexible approach to performance management. A highly centralized organization may attempt to impose a monolithic performance management system, and fail.

Size

Research carried out by Beaver and Harris (1995) into performance management in small firms came to the conclusion that: 'the performance management systems of large firms simply cannot be scaled down to fit the smaller enterprise that often exhibits a radically different management process and operation.' They described the management process in small firms as likely to be characterized by the highly personalized preferences, prejudices and attitudes of the firm's entrepreneur or owner, who will probably work close to the operating process.

Technology and working practices

There is no conclusive evidence that advanced technology and working practices are correlated with sophisticated approaches to performance management. But it is reasonable to assume that high-technology firms or sophisticated organizations are more likely to innovate in this field. Another aspect of work practices is the extent to which the work is computer or machine controlled, or routine. Computerized performance monitoring (CPM) provides an entirely different method of measuring performance that is related directly to outputs and/or errors. As Bates and Holton (1995) noted as a result of their research, this can have detrimental effects: 'CPM can transform a helpful, less performance-orientated supervisory style into one that is more coercive and production orientated.'

However, research conducted by Earley (1986) found that employees trusted feedback from a computer more than feedback from a supervisor. He claimed that CPM could have a greater impact on performance because of higher self-efficacy (ie the individual's self-belief that he or she will be able to accomplish certain tasks).

Bureaucratic methods of working may also affect the design and operation of performance management. Organizations that function as bureaucracies, appropriately or inappropriately, are more likely to have a formalized performance management system. The system will probably be centrally controlled by HR and the emphasis will be on the annual appraisal carried out in accordance with strictly defined rules. The appraisal may be a top-down judgemental affair, often referring to personality traits. Performance and potential will be rated.

Organizations that work flexibly with an emphasis on horizontal processes and teamwork are more likely to have a less formal process of performance management, leaving more scope for managers and teams to manage their own processes in accordance with agreed principles.

The external environment

If the external competitive, business, economic and political environment is turbulent – which it usually is – organizations have to learn to respond and adapt rapidly. This will influence the ways in which business strategies and plans are developed and the sort of goals people are expected to achieve. Performance management has to operate flexibly in tune with the constant changes in demands and expectations to which the organization is subject. A business that operates in a fairly steady state as far as its external environment is concerned (rare, but they do exist) can adopt more structured and orderly performance management systems.

Performance management and motivation

The ways in which performance management processes can motivate people to improve their performance and develop their capabilities were explained in the theories summarized in the first section of this chapter, namely goal theory, control theory and social cognitive theory. Explanations are also provided by the theories concerned with reinforcement theory, expectancy, social learning and attribution as discussed below.

Reinforcement theory

Reinforcement theory as developed by Hull (1951) states that successes in achieving goals and rewards act as positive incentives and reinforce the successful behaviour, which is repeated the next time a similar need arises. Positive feedback therefore provides for positive reinforcement. Constructive feedback can also reinforce behaviours that seek alternative means of achieving goals.

Expectancy theory

Another key motivation theory underpinning performance management deals with the importance of expectations. The theory was originally formulated by Vroom (1964) in what he called the valency–instrumentality–expectancy theory. Valency stands for value, instrumentality stands for the belief that if we do one thing it will lead to another, and expectancy is belief in the probability that action or effort will lead to an outcome.

In accordance with expectancy theory, motivation is only likely when a clearly perceived and usable relationship exists between performance and outcomes, and the outcome is seen as a means of satisfying needs. This explains why extrinsic financial motivation provided by a pay-for-performance scheme will only work as a motivator if the link between effort and reward is clear and the value of the reward is worth the effort. It also explains why intrinsic motivation arising from the work itself can be more powerful than extrinsic motivation. Intrinsic motivation outcomes are more under the control of individuals who can place greater reliance on their past experiences to indicate the extent to which positive and advantageous results are likely to be obtained by their behaviour.

This theory was developed by Porter and Lawler (1968) into a model that explained the four factors that influence effort and task achievement:

- The value of rewards to individuals.
- The probability that rewards will result from effort, as perceived by individuals.
- Individual characteristics such as intelligence, know-how and skill.

- Role perceptions – what individuals want to do or think they are required to do. These are good from the viewpoint of the organization if they correspond with what it thinks the individual should be doing. They are poor if the views of the individual and the organization do not coincide.

Expectancy theory supports performance management processes designed to provide for intrinsic motivation by providing opportunities for growth and scope to use and develop abilities.

An expectancy-based motivational model for individual performance improvement was devised by DeNisi and Pritchard (2006). It is based on the belief that people allocate energy to actions in a way that will maximize their anticipated need satisfaction. The sequence is:

> actions > results > evaluation > outcomes > need satisfaction > performance

The key for performance management is to ensure that evaluations and outcomes are structured so that employees will focus their actions in the ways desired by the organization, resulting in the kind of performance that is needed and appropriate rewards. The stronger the links between each element in the motivation process, the greater will be the motivation of employees to improve their performance. The process should aim to strengthen the perceived connection between actions and outcomes.

Self-efficacy theory

Self-efficacy theory as developed by Bandura (1982) indicates that self-motivation will be directly linked to the self-belief of individuals that they will be able to accomplish certain tasks, achieve certain goals or learn certain things. An important aim of performance management is to increase self-efficacy by giving individuals the opportunity to consider and discuss with their managers how they can do more. But the onus is on managers to encourage self-belief in the minds of those with whom they discuss performance and development.

Social learning theory

Social learning theory, also developed by Bandura (1977), combines aspects of reinforcement and expectancy theory. It recognizes the significance of the basic concept of reinforcement as a determinant of future behaviour but also emphasizes the importance of internal psychological factors, especially expectations about the values of goals and the ability of individuals to reach them.

Attribution theory

Attribution theory is concerned with how people explain their performance. Five types of explanation may be used to account for either success or failure: ability, effort, task difficulty, circumstances and luck. If success or failure is explained in terms of effort, then high motivation may follow. If, on the other hand, failure to achieve is explained in terms of task difficulty, adverse circumstances or bad luck, the result may be a loss of motivation.

Incorrect attribution may result from inadequate feedback and managers can do much to influence attributions and therefore motivation by providing relevant feedback, discussing in a positive way precisely why certain results have been achieved or not achieved.

Role modelling

People can be motivated by basing their behaviour on a 'role model', that is, someone whose approach to work and ability to get things done is inspirational. This creates a desire to follow the example provided by the model. Managers and team leaders can function as role models, and performance management can enhance this process by dialogue and coaching.

Performance management and the psychological contract

The psychological contract is the set of reciprocal but unwritten expectations that exist between individual employees and their employers. A psychological contract is implied and inferred rather than stated and agreed. It cannot necessarily be spelt out in detail because it evolves over time. But performance management processes can be used to ensure that performance expectations are agreed and reviewed regularly. And this should contribute to the clarification of the psychological contract and the employment relationship.

3

Critiques of
Performance Management

Performance management has attracted a lot of critical attention from academics and other commentators. The aim of this chapter is to provide insight into some of the more problematic aspects of performance management by reviewing the literature and drawing conclusions from it. The chapter covers:

- a review of the critical arena;

- the views expressed by the more prominent writers and researchers who have been concerned with or about performance appraisal and management based on their research or experience;

- the implications of these views.

The critical arena

Criticisms fall broadly into two categories:

1. It's a good idea but it doesn't work (mainly practitioners and some academics).

2. It's a bad idea and it doesn't work (mainly academics).

It's a good idea but it doesn't work

Those who believe that it does not work assert that managers often don't like doing it because they see it as an imposed bureaucratic chore that has nothing to do with their real work. If they are forced to appraise according to the book they may do it badly. It is claimed that individuals either dread the appraisal meeting because it is potentially threatening (even though managers are notoriously unwilling to criticize openly), or because they perceive it as an irrelevant bore, with their managers 'going through the motions'. There is said to be general dissatisfaction amongst both managers and individuals with rating systems, which they see as being applied inconsistently and unfairly.

It is true that performance appraisal, old style, fails to work in the ways described above. Research has confirmed that many people – both managers and their staff – dislike or distrust rating and believe that performance-related pay can function unfairly. However, the Armstrong and Baron (1998) research revealed that most people approved of the performance review and personal development aspects of performance management and carried it out conscientiously (see Chapter 15).

It's a bad idea and it doesn't work

The severest, and in some ways, the most salutary criticisms have come from the academics, based on their research, together with the notorious attack by William Deming, the leading total quality management (TQM) guru backed up by his fellow quality guru, Philip Crosby. The main issues they identified were:

- The process is problematic because of the complexity and difficulties involved in one person attempting to sum up the performance of another.

- There is a problem in getting line managers to do it well, or at all.

- There are too many poorly designed or poorly administered performance management schemes.

- Managements tend to adopt a unitary frame of reference (we're all in it together, our interests coincide) when, in reality, organizations are more likely to be pluralistic in the sense that there are divergent interests that should be acknowledged.

- Managements indulge in rhetoric about development but often do not put their espoused views into practice.

- Appraisal ignores system factors.

- Appraisal is an inconsistent and fundamentally subjective process.

- Appraisal is a means of oppressive or coercive control.

Views of commentators

Barlow (1989)

'Institutionally elaborated systems of management appraisal and development are significant rhetorics in the apparatus of bureaucratic control.' They reward what is perceived to be successful performance and penalize deviance.

Appraisal systems impose artificial rationality. 'Ambiguity and complexity will not be eliminated from the pluralistic processes and alliances of organizational life as it actually is.'

The research established from managers that the appraisal system 'served neither to motivate nor control.' Managers saw the appraisal system as a bureaucratic ritual. The system institutionalized an ideology that sought to enlist participants' positive effort and continued compliance, despite the inegalitarian nature of business organizations. The following conclusion was reached.

Conclusions on appraisal (Barlow, 1989)

The dynamic of power relationships is bound up with their intangibility… Such relationships evolve from the myriad intangible observations and devices by means of which one person learns how to relate to and work with another. Formalized appraisal systems discount the influences of such dynamics because they cannot be enumerated satisfactorily. In doing so they ride roughshod over what frequently is precarious and tenuous.

Bowles and Coates (1993)

- Appraisal is shifting from concern with performance to concern for people in terms of their identification with the job and the organization. 'Believing in the organization is the criterion rather than performing for it.'

- Managers are mostly appraised by results, but results alone cannot reflect performance as it is affected by many other factors. Deming (1986) is right: job performance cannot be disentangled from systems effects.

- The emphasis given to collective effort and teamwork conflicts with the individualistic ethic of performance appraisal practice.

- The nature of performance appraisal, which involves one individual making judgements on another, 'tends to reinforce authority relations and defines dependency'.

A survey of 48 organizations in the Midlands established that the major benefit claimed by those with what they considered to be successful systems was its use in getting people to achieve work goals. The problems faced by some organizations were measuring performance and the extra demands made on managers.

Conclusions

- 'Performance appraisal requires subtle psychological and social skills which may not be acquired by many managers.'

- Performance appraisal seems to be often 'an opportunistic means to address performance issues', rather than 'a well thought out, coherent and systematic attempt to impart a new philosophy and practice of organizational relations'.

- 'The absence of clear indices of measurement will often cause images of performance to be exploited.' Performance may have less to do with physical outputs and more about exhibiting the correct 'mind set'.

- An ethic is required that 'conveys trust, integrity and faith in the ability of employees to contribute to a creative management practice'.

- Management should provide the 'enabling' conditions through which work is performed.

- 'The active involvement of employees in the management of performance potentially allows a constructive dialogue with management, to determine what factors foster performance.'

Carlton and Sloman (1992)

A review of the appraisal system in an investment bank revealed the following problems:

- Managers were hostile to what they perceived as bureaucracy and disliked form filling.

- Ratings linked to pay were disliked. As one line manager said: 'Performance appraisal is a load of rubbish. You decide on the rating you want to put in the box and then make up a few words of narrative in other sections to justify it.'

- Ratings drift occurred. Managers tended to over-rate people because of the link between appraisal and pay. As one manager commented when challenged: 'I knew that his performance did not justify the rating but I thought it would demotivate him if I marked him down.'

- The separation of appraisal and pay decisions was considered to be impossible because 'managers only fill in one form and if they do not perceive a clear link with salary, they will not do it'.

Coens and Jenkins (2002)

Throughout our work lives, most of us have struggled with performance appraisal. No matter how many times we redesign it, retrain the supervisors, or give it a new name, it never comes out right. Again and again, we see supervisors procrastinate or just go through the motions, with little taken to heart. And the supervisors who do take it to heart and give it their best mostly meet disappointment. Earnestly intending to provide constructive feedback and write good development plans and goals, they find that people with less than superior ratings are preoccupied with the ratings and not the message. Except for those receiving top ratings, the good conversation they had hoped for rarely happens. Employees tune out and politely complete the interview. Others become defensive and resentful, with shattered relationships sure to follow. Then the supervisors ask themselves, 'Where did I go wrong?' knowing they were only doing their job.

Crosby (1995)

The performance review, no matter how well the format is designed, is a one-way street. Someone the individual didn't select gets to perform a very personal internal examination. There are no certificates on the wall stating the qualifications of the reviewer. Yet the effect on the individual's present and future is as real as if everyone knew what he or she were doing... The reviews, which are supposed to give information to management about employees, do the reverse. The employees quickly realize that management has no way of knowing who is the fairest of them all, except through luck and instinct.

Deming (1986)

In the 12th of his 14 points, Deming made the following demand:

Remove the barriers that rob hourly workers and people in management of their right to pride in workmanship. This implies inter alia, abolition of the annual merit rating (appraisal of performance).

He also defined 'evaluation of performance, merit rating or annual review' as the third deadly disease of management. The further points he made were that:

- Rating the performance of individuals is unsound because differences in performance are largely due to systems variations.

- Targets and objectives for individuals damage customer-focused teamwork.

- Targets too often make no reference to the customer and results are limited if 'stretching' can only be achieved by sub-optimization, while, on the other hand, soft targets may be negotiated.

- Formal appraisal schemes reinforce managers' reluctance to engage in coaching and open, direct regular dialogue with people.

- Reliance on pay as a motivator destroys pride in work and individual creativity.

Furnham (1996)

The question posed was why the fundamental process of performance appraisal was frequently done so badly. The following reasons were suggested for this:

- Pusillanimity – managers are too scared to give negative or corrective feedback.

- Managers have not been trained in the skills of appraisal.

- Managers argue that rather than having a couple of specific hour-long meetings over the year, they give subordinates consistent feedback on a day-to-day basis. But what they fail to realize is that discussions about software, the sales figures and the strategic plan are not appraisal.

- The organization, despite much rhetoric, does not take the whole process seriously.

Furnham (2004)

'Although a basic management requirement in all types of organizations, nevertheless performance management systems almost universally work poorly and are negatively viewed by both managers and managed.'

Grint (1993)

There seems to be considerable, although not universal, dislike and dissatisfaction with all performance appraisal systems to some degree. Crudely speaking, human resource managers seem favourably inclined, line managers much less so.

The problems with appraisals are:

- the complexity of the variables being assessed;

- the subjective elements that confuse the assessment;

- the fact that rewards and progress are in the hands of a single 'superordinate' (ie appraiser/manager);

- the fact that individuals have to work with their appraisers after the appraisal;

- the fundamental issue relating to the appraisal by individuals of individuals who only act in social situations – the comment is made that a major aim of appraisal schemes is to limit the collective aspects of work and individualize the employment relationship. 'F W Taylor would indeed have been impressed.'

Reasons why assessments bear no close or, indeed any, relationship to reality

- The assessor only sees the assessed from one specific position.

- The impossibility of 'being able to reduce the complex nature of any individual to a series of scales in a tick list'.

- The multifaceted identity of people may lead to views about individuals varying widely – different people read each other very differently.

- As people ascend the hierarchy they are likely to be less and less aware of what their subordinates think about them and their performance.

- The possibility of ever achieving objective appraisals of a subordinate by a superior is remote.

The conclusion was that: 'Rarely in the history of business can such a system have promised so much and delivered so little.' But in spite of the relatively long and generally unhappy life of appraisal schemes they should not be abandoned. Instead they should be considered more sceptically – people might have to accept their 'subjective fate'.

Latham, Sulsky and Macdonald (2007)

> The answers required to move the field of performance management forward are much less straightforward than the questions. We know a great deal more about ways to manage the performance of an individual than about ways to manage a team. We know what to observe and how to observe an individual objectively. We are at a loss as to how to overcome political considerations that lead people not to do so. Advances in knowledge have been made with regard to technology that managers embrace to assist in the appraisal process, and that in the eyes of employees, their managers misuse. We know that making decisions is inherent in performance management, yet solutions to decision-making errors remain a mystery. Great strides in this domain include recognition that ongoing performance management is more effective than an annual appraisal in bringing about a positive change in an employee's behaviour, and that context must be taken into account in doing so.

Lee (2005)

Most traditional performance appraisal schemes are fundamentally flawed as they are counterproductive by design. The stated purpose of these systems is to measure and rate past performance when, in reality, the goal of any performance management system should be performance enhancement… No one has the power to alter the past, so it is far wiser to direct attention and efforts to the future.

Newton and Findlay (1996)

- Most writers on appraisal are over-influenced by the 'neo-human-relations' writers of the 1950s and 1960s (eg Douglas McGregor), who provide 'unitarist prescriptions that are generally insensitive to both context and outcome' and assume that appraisal will serve the supposed common interest of employer and employee.

- Appraisees are not going to view appraisal as a 'helping/counselling exercise' if there is the possibility that the data will be used in assessing promotion or demotion.

- Participative approaches to appraisal are suspect because they constitute 'a desire through which management control may be enhanced by appearing to disperse it'.

- Appraisal can be regarded as a management strategy 'aimed at eliciting a measure of voluntary compliance from employees' and encouraging workers to regulate and police their own behaviour.

'A greater understanding of the organizational context in which appraisal takes place and, consequently, of appraisal itself, requires an acknowledgement of the differences of interests between appraisers and appraisees.'

Pulakos, Mueller-Hanson and O'Leary (2008)

The main problems with performance management in the United States are:

- Performance management is regarded as an administrative burden to be minimized rather than an effective strategy to obtain business results.

- Managers and employees are reluctant to engage in candid performance discussions.

- Judgement and time factors impede accurate performance assessments.

Sparrow (2008)

Performance management issues in the UK include:

- the ability to produce higher levels of employee engagement as opposed to just more self-awareness (or measurement accuracy);

- the level of alignment between rewards (in their fullest sense) produced by the performance management system, and the varied needs of diverse employee segments, who may be working to very different psychological contracts;

- the extent to which stand alone performance management systems contribute directly to value creation in the organization or rather serve more to protect value by managing only marginal risks (extremely high or low performance, the identification and management of which may well be handled through other processes such as business performance modifications, team socialization processes or talent management/calibration exercises).

Stiles et al (1997)

A survey of three companies revealed that there was a considerable degree of managerial apathy and even scepticism about carrying out appraisal. The reasons were:

- the perceived bureaucracy of the appraisal system that diverted managers from their 'real job';

- the lack of positive outcomes in terms of both development and pay;

- variations between individual managers in judging performance;

- defensive use of appraisal – lumping everyone together in average or even high/low categories.

The research found the following problems in the way performance management was being used:

- Changes were driven in a top-down, systematic manner and the absence of consultation produced cynicism and a lack of trust among employees.

- Concern was expressed by employees over the fairness and accuracy of the performance management system – little or no negotiation in objective setting, question marks over the achievability of the targets, variability and inconsistency in appraisal, lack of opportunities for development, and a large degree of mystification about the workings of the appraisal were indicative of this concern.

- Employees believed changes to the performance management system had increased the transactional nature of the contract (eg emphasis on the link to pay, little concern about development).

- The manner of introducing the contract did little to restore the trust of employees – there was a lack of procedural justice (giving employees involvement in determining decisions about change, giving input during objective setting and performance evaluations).

Strebler, Bevan and Robertson (2001)

- The wholesale devolution of performance management responsibilities to line managers has meant that they have to grasp and deliver the often quite complex and subtle management skills required to set goals in line with a wider business plan, assess performance, give constructive feedback, identify training and development needs, and rate or rank performance for pay purposes. Not all have embraced this opportunity willingly or consistently, resulting in at best, performance review schemes of variable quality.

- Performance management assumes that line managers have the ability and motivation to perform somewhat conflicting roles of judge and coach. There is evidence that they fail to deliver on both counts. Most performance management is about control rather than development and most managers do not have the skills to make it work.

- Organizations come up with cunning, elegant and integrated designs for performance review linked to pay progression, team bonuses, personal development plans, competencies and 360-degree feedback (via their intranet). These designs frequently fail a number of tests, including the ability of line managers to assimilate and deliver the processes, the affordability of the training required, the quality of support needed from HR and doubts as to whether the benefits will justify the costs.

Townley (1990/1991)

An analysis of 30 university appraisal schemes generated the following general comments on appraisal:

- Appraisal is regarded as a technical function that is considered in isolation.

- Appraisal should be viewed as 'an assemblage of signs whose meaning is constructed dependent on the context of its introduction and operation'.

- A failure to contextualize appraisal will ignore the 'different, sometimes conflicting interests' that influence the form of appraisal adopted.

- Seeing appraisal in the context in which it operates 'points to the diversity of functions into which a single system may be invested'.

- Appraisal can become a 'mechanism around which interests are negotiated, counter-claims articulated and political processes expressed. Designers of appraisal schemes would do well to remember this.'

- The term appraisal usually implies a judgement by a superior of a subordinate, that is, a process that is unilateral and top down.

Townley (1993)

Management is 'institutionally empowered to determine and/or regulate certain aspects of the actions of others'. The concept of control is central to an understanding of management. Power is exercised through its intersection with knowledge: for example, methods of observation, techniques of registration – mechanisms for the supervision and administration of individuals and groups.

Appraisal is defined as a managerial activity – 'the provision of data designed to ensure that resources are used efficiently in accomplishing organizational objectives'. The role of appraisers is structured through setting the agenda. Management is inextricably linked to control over the labour process.

One of the inherent paradoxes of appraisal is that 'the information required to ensure effective work organization will not be forthcoming if it is thought that this will jeopardize the individual'.

Appraisal operates as a form of 'panopticon' (a concept for prison design originated by Jeremy Bentham in the 19th century that incorporates a central observation tower from which the activities of all the inmates can be seen). The process of appraisal takes this form because it combines hierarchy, unilateral observation and 'a normalizing judgement'. Anonymous and continuous surveillance is a method of articulating a monitoring role.

Appraisal is the 'exercise of control at a distance both spatially and temporally'. It 'illustrates how knowledge of the individual and the work performed articulates the managerial role as a directional activity'.

Winstanley and Stuart-Smith (1996)

Traditional approaches to performance management fail because they are flawed in implementation, demotivate staff and 'are often perceived as forms of control that are inappropriately used to "police" performance'. Performance management as a concept and a process can be criticized as follows:

- There is a lack of conclusive evidence that it leads to improved performance.

- It can produce undesirable side effects: demotivation on the one hand and over-bureaucratization on the other.

- It is difficult to set performance objectives that cover intangibles, are flexible in response to change and cover the whole job.

- Lack of time is given to the process.

- It is a form of 'Taylorism' – in the perception of appraisees, it can 'become akin to a police state' where evidence is collected, dossiers built up and 'supervision becomes a matter of spying through keyholes'.

- It is managerialist in that it takes a unitary view of the organization. This is referred to as the 'radical critique' of performance management, namely that 'it operates within a unitarist paradigm and is not able to treat organizations as pluralities of interests'.

- The question is asked: 'Are individuals in the process treated as "ends in themselves or merely means to other ends?"' (It is suggested that the latter approach is typical.)

- It reinforces modes of 'intrusive control'.

It is suggested that a stakeholder perspective should be adopted in the design of performance management systems that offers a wider role to individuals as 'creators' rather than 'victims' of performance management. Because pluralism is endemic in organizations, it should not only be the power holder's voice that is heard. 'Where consensus exists it can be built in, but where it does not, dissenters are not silenced.'

The approach should be one of 'stakeholder synthesis' that goes beyond the analysis of the interests of stakeholders to gaining their views about business strategy and incorporating these views in the system design.

Implications

The views expressed by these commentators provide a different perspective on performance management than is usually offered in prescriptive books and articles. And it is an interesting perspective. It penetrates beyond the rhetoric (a favourite term of abuse employed by the academics) to the forces that are actually at work when performance management systems are operated. It has to be recognized that in many organizations performance management, or rather appraisal, can be no more than a means of enlisting compliance, as these writers assert. It is also possible that much appraisal is carried out badly, although this was not confirmed by the focus groups conducted as part of the Armstrong and Baron (1998) research (see Chapter 15). And when appraisal schemes involve top-down judgement, they can be instruments through which unilateral power is exercised. It is also unrealistic to predicate managements' performance-improvement programmes on the assumption that everyone else will support them.

Systems factors must also be taken into account. If judgements about performance are made, they must consider not only what the individual has or has not achieved, but also the context in which this performance has taken place and the influence of the system of work and other extraneous factors on that performance. This will include the quality of leadership displayed by managers and their interest in the development of their staff.

There is a danger of performance management becoming bureaucratic, and if it includes performance ratings, these can be inconsistent and based on subjective opinions.

All these aspects of how performance management functions in organizations should be borne in mind when considering its introduction or amendment. When management says it wants to create 'shared understanding', does it really believe what is being said? And will something be done about the processes, including for example goal setting, feedback and coaching to ensure that it happens? If not, the accusation of many commentators that much of what is said about performance management is meaningless will be justified. And if management says it believes in a stakeholder approach, will something be done about it that does recognize that the organization is a community of interests, not all of which will necessarily coincide? The doubts expressed on the likelihood of this happening by the writers quoted in this chapter may well be justified in many organizations.

So there is much to be learned from these critiques.

Part II

The Practice of Performance Management

4

Performance Management Systems

This chapter describes performance management systems under the following headings:

- performance management defined;
- performance management as a system;
- the objectives of performance management;
- the principles of performance management;
- the characteristics of performance management;
- the performance management cycle and sequence;
- performance and development planning;
- performance measures;
- performance agreements;
- managing performance throughout the year;
- conducting formal performance reviews;
- analysing and assessing performance;
- the ethical dimension;
- issues in performance management;
- effective performance management.

Performance management defined

Performance management is a process for establishing shared understanding about what is to be achieved and how it is to be achieved, and an approach to managing and developing people that improves individual, team and organizational performance.

Performance management can also be described as a strategic and integrated approach to delivering sustained success to organizations that focuses on performance improvement and employee development. It is strategic in the sense that it is concerned with the broader issues facing the business if it is to function effectively in its environment, and with the general direction in which it intends to go to achieve longer-term goals. An important aim of performance management is to support the achievement of the business strategy. It is integrated in four senses: 1) vertical integration – linking or aligning business, team and individual objectives; 2) functional integration – linking functional strategies in different parts of the business; 3) HRM integration – linking different aspects of human resource management, especially organizational development, human capital management, talent management, learning and development, and reward, to achieve a coherent approach to the management and development of people; and 4) the integration of individual needs with those of the organization, as far as this is possible. It is focused on performance improvement in order to increase organizational, team and individual effectiveness. Organizations, as stated by Lawson (1995) have 'to get the right things done successfully'. Performance is not only about what is achieved but also about how it is achieved. Management is involved in direction, measurement and control. But these are not the exclusive concerns of managers – teams and individuals jointly participate as stakeholders. It is involved in employee development – performance improvement is not achievable unless there are effective processes of continuous development. This addresses the core competences of the organization and the capabilities of individuals and teams.

More specifically performance management is concerned with:

- aligning individual objectives to organizational objectives and encouraging individuals to uphold corporate core values;

- enabling expectations to be defined and agreed in terms of role responsibilities and accountabilities (expected to do), skills (expected to have) and behaviours (expected to be);

- providing opportunities for individuals to identify their own goals and develop their skills and competencies;

- motivating people by providing them with recognition and the opportunity to use and develop their skills and abilities.

The scope performance management gives to recognize achievements and provide opportunities for growth means that it is part of the total reward system. It can be used to generate ratings to inform performance pay decisions, but this is neither an inevitable nor a necessary part of the process. Performance management is essentially a developmental process that aims to improve the performance and potential of people through their own efforts and with the help of their managers and the organization.

Here are some other definitions:

Performance management is a means of getting better results from the organization, teams and individuals within an agreed framework of planned goals, objectives and standards (Armstrong and Murlis, 1994).

The performance management process is the process by which the company manages its performance in line with its corporate and functional strategies and objectives. The objective of this process is to provide a pro-active closed loop system, where the corporate and functional strategies are deployed to all business processes, activities, tasks and personnel, and feedback is obtained through the performance measurement system to enable appropriate management decisions (Bitici, Carrie and McDevitt, 1997).

Performance management is a range of practices an organization engages in to enhance the performance of a target person or group with the ultimate purpose of improving organizational performance (DeNisi, 2000).

Performance management is a broad set of activities aimed at improving employee performance (DeNisi and Pritchard, 2006).

A systematic approach to improving individual and team performance in order to achieve organizational goals (Hendry, Bradley and Perkins, 1997).

A clear focus on how each employee can contribute to the overall success of the organization lies at the heart of performance management systems (IDS, 1997).

The essence of performance management is the development of individuals with competence and commitment, working towards the achievement of shared meaningful objectives within an organization that supports and encourages their achievement (Lockett, 1992).

Performance management aims to improve strategic focus and organizational effectiveness through continuously securing improvements in the performance of individuals and teams (Philpott and Sheppard, 1992).

Performance management is a systematic approach to improving business and team performance to achieve business objectives (Strebler, Bevan and Robertson, 2001).

Performance management is about 'directing and supporting employees to work as effectively and efficiently as possible in line with the needs of the organization' (Walters, 1995).

These definitions frequently refer to performance management as a process of aligning or integrating organizational and individual objectives to achieve organizational effectiveness. It is interesting to note that only one definition mentions development and only three refer to teams. Yet in can be argued that development is the prime purpose of performance management. As Bones (1996) commented: 'performance does not need managing. It needs encouraging, developing, supporting and sustaining.'

It is sometimes assumed that performance appraisal is the same thing as performance management. But there are significant differences. Performance appraisal can be defined as the formal assessment and rating of individuals by their managers at or after a review meeting that usually takes place once a year. It has been discredited because it has traditionally operated as a top-down and largely bureaucratic system owned by the HR department rather than by line managers.

In contrast performance management is a continuous and wider, more comprehensive and more natural process of management that clarifies mutual expectations, emphasizes the support role of managers who are expected to act as coaches rather than judges, and focuses on the future.

Performance management as a system

It can be argued that performance management is essentially a process, one of managing performance. It can be regarded as a natural function of managing that involves the activities of planning, monitoring, analysing and reviewing. It is therefore legitimate to refer to the process of performance management where 'process' is defined as a way of doing things in order to achieve a purpose.

There are those who object to associating the word 'system' with performance management because of its connotations with the notion of a sort of mechanism. They contend that performance management can never be mechanistic. It is, they say, not a matter of going through the motions in order to execute a number of bureaucratic procedures such as completing appraisal forms. This may be indisputable but the term 'performance management system' is in general use. The justification for this is that it requires the application of a number of inter-related activities that are dealt with as a whole, which is what a system does. As Katz and Kahn (1966) wrote, systems are 'basically concerned with problems of relationship, of structure and of interdependence'. Williams (1998) took a systems view when he identified three models of performance management: 1) performance management as a system for individual performance; 2) performance management as a system for managing organizational performance; and 3) performance management as a system for managing individual and organizational performance. However, it is undeniable that the management of performance is largely concerned with process – how it is done. Performance management processes as described in Part 3 of this book consist of goal setting, feedback, performance reviews, analysing and assessing performance and coaching. They constitute the essential elements of performance management.

The following definition of the concept of a performance management system takes into account the considerations discussed above.

Performance management system defined

A performance management system is a set of interrelated activities and processes that are treated holistically as an integrated and key component of an organization's approach to managing performance through people and developing the skills and capabilities of its human capital, thus enhancing organizational capability and the achievement of sustained competitive advantage.

Objectives of performance management

The overall objective of performance management is to develop and improve the performance of individuals and teams and therefore organizations. It is an instrument that can be used to achieve culture change in the shape of the creation of a high-performance culture. It aims to develop the capacity of people to meet and exceed expectations and to achieve their full potential to the benefit of themselves and the organization. Performance management provides the basis for self-development but importantly it is also about ensuring that the support and guidance people need to develop and improve is readily available.

The following definition of what performance management systems are there to do was provided by Lee (2005).

What performance management systems exist to do (Lee, 2005)

The real goals of any performance management system are threefold – to correct poor performance, to sustain good performance and to improve performance… All performance management systems should be designed to generate information and data exchange so that the individuals involved can properly dissect performance, discuss it, understand it, and agree on its character and quality.

The respondents to the e-reward 2005 survey stated that their performance management objectives were:

- to align individual and organizational objectives – 64 per cent;

- to improve organizational performance – 63 per cent;
- to improve individual performance – 46 per cent;
- to provide the basis for personal development – 37 per cent;
- to develop a performance culture – 32 per cent;
- to inform contribution/performance pay decisions – 21 per cent.

The following is a typical statement of objectives from one respondent:

> *To support culture change by creating a performance culture and reinforcing the values of the organization with an emphasis on the importance of these in getting a balance between 'what' is delivered and 'how' it is delivered.*

A financial sector organization produced the following definition of the purpose of its performance management system.

The purpose of performance management: a financial sector organization

The aim is to improve performance. Rather than just saying that somebody's been very effective and ticking a box, the process is actually to sit down and have a discussion around the requirements of the role, dealing with what aspects are being done well and what aspects are not so good. Overall the purpose is to make it clear to people how their performance links in with the performance of the business.

Managing performance is about coaching, guiding, appraising, motivating and rewarding colleagues to help unleash potential and improve organizational performance. Where it works well it is built on excellent leadership and high-quality coaching relationships between managers and teams. Through all this our colleagues should be able to answer three straightforward questions:

- What is expected of me? How will I be clear about what is expected of me in terms of both results and behaviour?
- How am I doing? What ongoing coaching and feedback will I receive to tell me how I am doing and how I can improve?
- What does it mean for me? How will my individual contribution, potential and aspirations be recognized and rewarded?'

Principles of performance management

> ### *Guiding principles for performance management (Egan, 1995)*
>
> Most employees want direction, freedom to get their work done, and encouragement not control. The performance management system should be a control system only by exception. The solution is to make it a collaborative development system, in two ways. First, the entire performance management process – coaching, counselling, feedback, tracking, recognition, and so forth – should encourage development. Ideally, team members grow and develop through these interactions. Second, when managers and team members ask what they need to be able to do to do bigger and better things, they move to strategic development.

Characteristics of performance management

As Mohrman and Mohrman (1995) emphasized: 'Performance management practices must derive from and be tailored to fit each organization's changing requirements. This will lead to a wide diversity of practices.' But there are certain common characteristics as described below.

Performance management is a planned process whose five primary elements are agreement, measurement, feedback, positive reinforcement and dialogue. It is concerned with measuring outcomes in the shape of delivered performance compared with expectations expressed as goals or objectives. In this respect, it focuses on targets, standards and performance measures or indicators. It is based on the agreement of role requirements, goals, and performance improvement and personal development plans. It provides the setting for ongoing dialogues about performance that involves the joint and continuing review of achievements against objectives, requirements and plans, feedback, reinforcement and coaching.

However, it is also concerned with inputs and values. The inputs are the knowledge, skills and behaviours required to produce the expected results. Developmental needs are identified by defining these requirements and assessing the extent to which the expected levels of performance have been achieved through the effective use of knowledge and skills and through appropriate behaviour that upholds core values.

Performance is not just a top-down process in which managers tell their subordinates what they think about them, set objectives and institute performance improvement plans. It is not something that is done to people. As Buchner (2007) emphasizes, performance management should be something that is done for people and in partnership with them.

Performance management is a continuous and flexible process that involves managers and those whom they manage acting as partners within a framework that sets out how they can best work together to achieve the required results. It is based on the principle of management by contract and agreement rather than management by command. It relies on consensus and cooperation rather than control or coercion.

Performance management focuses on future performance planning and improvement and personal development rather than on retrospective performance appraisal. It functions as a continuous and evolutionary process, in which performance improves over time. It provides the basis for regular and frequent dialogues between managers and individuals about performance and development needs based on feedback and self-assessment. It is mainly concerned with individual performance but it can also be applied to teams. The emphasis is on development, although performance management is an important part of the reward system through the provision of feedback and recognition and the identification of opportunities for growth. It may be associated with performance or contribution-related pay but its developmental aspects are much more important.

The performance management cycle

A performance management system operates as a continuous and self-renewing cycle as shown in Figure 4.1.

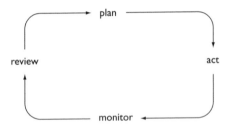

Figure 4.1   The performance management cycle

The performance management cycle closely resembles the cycle for continuous improvement defined by William Deming (1986). This is not a coincidence. Performance management is all about continuous improvement.

The performance management sequence

The sequence of processes carried out in this cycle and the likely outcomes are illustrated in Figure 4.2.

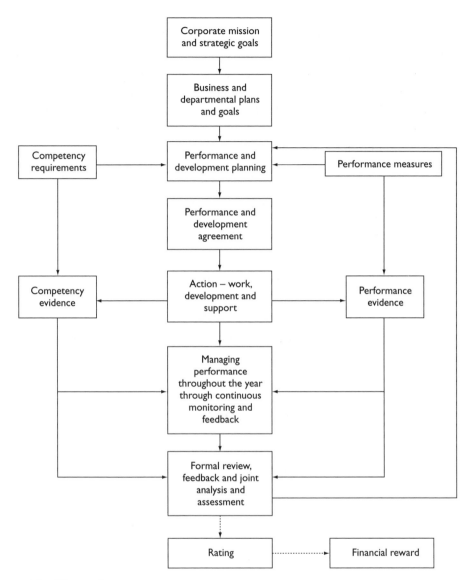

Figure 4.2 The performance management sequence

Note that ratings and financial reward are not an inevitable part of the sequence. Note also that this logical and linear model is unlikely to give a realistic picture of what actually happens in many organizations. It may represent the grand design but because the system is operated by people, who may be fallible, the reality is often different.

The key performance management activities

Within this sequence, the key performance management activities are performance and development planning, defining performance measures, concluding performance agreements, managing performance throughout the year and reviewing and analysing and assessing performance formally. These are described below in sequence as they take place in the performance management cycle. However, in practice, although interconnected, they do not take place in strict succession during the year and often overlap. For example, although performance review and performance planning are identified as separate activities they may take place at the same time; a review of past performance referenced to a role profile will lead directly to plans for the future, also linked to a role profile. A formal performance review may take place at an annual or twice-yearly meeting but it is a continuous process in that the methods used in a formal review meeting are also used in informal reviews during the year.

Performance management processes are largely concerned with interactions between the parties involved but they also relate to what individuals do about monitoring and improving their own performance, measuring and monitoring performance, and documenting the outcomes of performance management plans and reviews.

Examples of the performance management cycle as it exists in CEMEX, DHL and the Royal College of Nursing are given in Appendix B.

Performance and development planning

The performance planning part of the performance management sequence involves the agreement between the manager and the individual of how the latter is expected to perform in terms of results and behaviours. The expected results will be defined within the framework of a role profile as described below and in the form of goals or objectives as covered in Chapter 7. These objectives may have been cascaded down from the strategic objectives of the organization to achieve alignment, but in practice this may be difficult to achieve. In addition success criteria for each area of performance and methods of measuring performance against these objectives will be agreed. These should be precise, as advocated by Adrian Furnham.

Precision in defining and measuring performance dimensions (Furnham, 2004)

Define performance with a focus on valued outcomes. Therefore performance dimensions should be functions combined with aspects of value such as quantity, quality, timeliness, cost effectiveness, need for supervision or interpersonal impact.

Discussions take place between the manager and the individual on what the latter needs to do to achieve the agreed goals, raise standards, improve performance, develop the required competencies and, where appropriate, behave differently. It also establishes priorities – the key aspects of the job to which attention has to be given. The aim is to ensure that the meaning of the objectives, performance standards and competencies as they apply to everyday work is understood. They are the basis for converting aims into action. The framework for performance management is provided by the performance agreement, which is the outcome of performance and development planning.

The agreement is the basis for managing performance throughout the year and for guiding improvement and development activities. It is used as a reference point when reviewing performance and the achievement of improvement and development plans.

Role profile definition

Role profiles define a role in terms of the key results expected, what role holders are expected to know and be able to do, and how they are expected to behave in terms of behavioural competencies and upholding the organization's core values. Role profiles need to be updated every time a formal performance agreement is developed, and provide headings under which goals can be set. An example of a role profile is shown in Figure 4.3.

To develop a role profile it is necessary for the line manager and the individual to get together and agree key result areas, define what the role holder needs to know and be able to do, and ensure that there is mutual understanding of the behavioural competencies required and the core values the role holder is expected to uphold.

When introducing performance management it is probably best to abandon any existing job descriptions. They may well be out of date and probably go into far too much detail about what is to be done rather than focusing on what has to be achieved.

Defining key result areas

To define key result areas individuals should be asked by their manager to answer questions such as:

- What do you think are the most important things you have to do?
- What do you believe you are expected to achieve in each of these areas?
- How will you – or anyone else – know whether or not you have achieved them?

Role title: Database administrator

Department: Information systems

Purpose of role: Responsible for the development and support of databases and their underlying environment.

Key result areas
- Identify database requirements for all projects that require data management in order to meet the needs of internal customers.
- Develop project plans collaboratively with colleagues to deliver against their database needs.
- Support underlying database infrastructure.
- Liaise with system and software providers to obtain product information and support.
- Manage project resources (people and equipment) within predefined budget and criteria, as agreed with line manager and originating department.
- Allocate work to and supervise contractors on day-to-day basis.
- Ensure security of the underlying database infrastructure through adherence to established protocols and develop additional security protocols where needed.

Need to know
- Oracle database administration.
- Operation of Designer 2000 and oracle forms SQL/PLSQL, Unix administration, shell programming.

Able to:
- Analyse and choose between options where the solution is not always obvious.
- Develop project plans and organize own workload on a timescale of 1–2 months.
- Adapt to rapidly changing needs and priorities without losing sight of overall plans and priorities.
- Interpret budgets in order to manage resources effectively within them.
- Negotiate with suppliers.
- Keep abreast of technical developments and trends, bring these into day-to-day work when feasible and build them into new project developments.

Behavioural competencies
- Aim to get things done well and set and meet challenging goals, create own measures of excellence and constantly seek ways of improving performance.
- Analyse information from range of sources and develop effective solutions/recommendations.
- Communicate clearly and persuasively, orally or in writing, dealing with technical issues in a non-technical manner.
- Work participatively on projects with technical and non-technical colleagues.
- Develop positive relationships with colleagues as the supplier of an internal service.

Figure 4.3   A role profile

The answers to these questions may need to be sorted out – they can often result in a mass of jumbled information that has to be analysed so that the various activities can be distinguished and refined to seven or eight key areas. This process requires some skill, which needs to be developed by training followed by practice. It is an area in which HR specialists can usefully coach and follow-up on a one-to-one basis after an initial training session.

Defining what people need to know and be able to do

To define what people need to know and be able to do three questions need to be answered:

- To perform this role effectively, what has the role holder to be able to do with regard to each of the key result areas?

- What knowledge and skills in terms of qualifications, technical and procedural knowledge, problem solving, planning and communication skills etc do role holders need to carry out the role effectively?

- How will anyone know when the role has been carried out well?

Understanding behavioural competencies

The usual approach to including behavioural competencies in the performance agreement is to use a competency framework developed for the organization. The manager and the individual can then discuss the implications of the framework at the planning stage. The following is an example of a competency framework:

- Personal drive – demonstrate the drive to achieve, acting confidently with decisiveness and resilience.

- Business awareness – identify and explore business opportunities, understand the business concerns and priorities of the organization and constantly to seek methods of ensuring that the organization becomes more businesslike.

- Teamwork – work cooperatively and flexibly with other members of the team with a full understanding of the role to be played as a team member.

- Communication – communicate clearly and persuasively, orally or in writing.

- Customer focus – exercise unceasing care in looking after the interests of external and internal customers to ensure that their wants, needs and expectations are met or exceeded.

- Developing others – foster the development of members of his or her team, providing feedback, support, encouragement and coaching.

- Flexibility – adapt to and work effectively in different situations and carry out a variety of tasks.

- Leadership – guide, encourage and motivate individuals and teams to achieve a desired result.

- Planning – decide on courses of action, ensuring that the resources required to implement the action will be available and scheduling the programme of work required to achieve a defined end-result.

- Problem solving – analyse situations, diagnose problems, identify the key issues, establish and evaluate alternative courses of action and produce a logical, practical and acceptable solution.

Core values

Increasingly, performance management is being used by organizations to encourage people 'to live the values'. These values can include such concerns as quality, continuous improvement, customer service, innovation, care and consideration for people, environmental issues and equal opportunities. Discussions held when the performance agreement is being reached can define what these values mean as far as individual behaviour is concerned.

The Scottish Parliament emphasizes that assessing how well people uphold core values is an integral part of performance management, stating that: 'Our success depends on all of us sharing the common values set out in the management plan', ie:

Integrity	We demonstrate high standards of honesty and reliability.
Impartiality	We are fair and even-handed in dealing with members of the public and each other.
Professionalism	We provide high quality professional advice and support services.
Client focus	We are responsive to the needs of members, the public and one another.
Efficiency	We use resources responsibly and cost-effectively.
Mutual respect	We treat everyone with respect and courtesy and take full account of equal opportunities issues at all times.

Performance measures

Performance is measured at organizational level as described in Chapter 17 or at individual level as described below. Individual performance can be measured by reference to key performance indicators (KPIs) and metrics. KPIs define the results or outcomes that are identified as being crucial to the achievement of high performance. Strictly speaking, metrics are measurements using a metric system, but the term is used generally for any form of measure.

It can be argued that what gets measured is often what is easy to measure. And in some jobs what is meaningful is not measurable and what is measurable is not meaningful. It was asserted by Levinson (1970) that: 'The greater the emphasis on measurement and quantification, the more likely the subtle, non-measurable elements of the task will be sacrificed. Quality of performance frequently, therefore, loses out to quantification.'

Measuring performance is relatively easy for those who are responsible for achieving quantified targets, for example sales. It is more difficult in the case of knowledge workers, such as scientists. But this difficulty is alleviated if a distinction is made between the two forms of results – outputs and outcomes.

Outputs and outcomes

An output is a result that can be measured quantifiably, while an outcome is a visible effect that is the result of effort but cannot necessarily be measured in quantified terms.

There are components in all jobs that are difficult to measure quantifiably as outputs. But all jobs produce outcomes even if they are not quantified. It is therefore often necessary to measure performance by reference to what outcomes have been attained in comparison with what outcomes were expected, and the outcomes may be expressed in qualitative terms as a standard or level of competence to be attained. That is why it is important when agreeing objectives to answer the question: 'How will we know that this objective has been achieved?' The answer needs to be expressed in the form: 'Because such and such will have happened.' The 'such and such' will be defined either as outputs in such forms as meeting or exceeding a quantified target, completing a project or task satisfactorily (what is 'satisfactory' having been defined), or as outcomes in such forms as reaching an agreed standard of performance or delivering an agreed level of service.

Classification of output and outcome measures

Output measures or metrics include:

- financial measures – income, shareholder value, added value, rates of return, costs;
- units produced or processed, throughput; level of take-up of a service;
- sales, new accounts;
- time measures – speed of response or turnaround, achievements compared with time-tables, amount of backlog, time to market, delivery times.

Outcome measures include:

- attainment of a standard (quality, level of service etc);
- changes in behaviour;
- completion of work/project;
- acquisition and effective use of additional knowledge and skills;
- reaction – judgement by others (colleagues, internal and external customers).

Inputs – competency and upholding core values

However, when assessing performance it is also necessary to consider inputs in the shape of the degree of knowledge and skill attained and behaviour that is demonstrably in line with the standards set out in competency frameworks and statements of core values. Risher (2003) emphasizes that it is important to encourage behaviours such as the following:

- builds effective working relationships with others;

- takes the initiative to address problems;

- seeks knowledge related to emerging issues;

- shares know-how and information with co-workers;

- responds effectively to customer concerns.

The performance and development agreement

The performance agreement records the outcome of performance planning and also records how performance will be measured and the evidence that will be used to establish levels of competency. It is important that these measures and evidence requirements should be identified and fully agreed at this stage because they will be used by individuals as well as managers to monitor and demonstrate achievements. The development agreement can take the form of a personal development plan that sets out what needs to be learned and how that learning should be achieved.

Performance agreements define:

- Role requirements; these are set out in the form of the key result areas of the role; what the role holder is expected to achieve (outputs and outcomes).

- Objectives in the form of targets and standards of performance.

- Performance measures and indicators to assess the extent to which objectives and standards of performance have been achieved.

- Knowledge, skill and competency: definitions of what role holders have to know and be able to do (competences) and of how they are expected to behave in particular aspects of their role (competencies). These definitions may be generic, having been prepared for occupations or job families on an organization or function-wide basis. Role-specific profiles should, however, be agreed that express what individual role holders are expected to know and do.

- Corporate core values or requirements; the performance agreement may also refer to the core values of the organization for quality, customer service, team working, employee development and the like that individuals are expected to uphold in carrying out their work. Certain general operational requirements may also be specified in such areas as health and safety, budgetary control, cost reduction and security.

- A performance development plan: a work plan that specifies what needs to be done to develop and where necessary improve performance.

- A personal development plan that specifies what individuals need to do with support from their manager to develop their knowledge and skills.

- Process details: how and when performance will be reviewed and a revised performance agreement concluded.

Managing performance throughout the year

Perhaps one of the most important features of performance management is that it is a continuous process that reflects normal good management practices of setting direction, monitoring and measuring performance, and taking action accordingly. Performance management should not be imposed on managers as something 'special' they have to do. It should instead be treated as a natural function that all good managers carry out.

The main activities that take place during the course of managing performance throughout the year are providing feedback, updating objectives, and continuous learning on the job or through coaching as discussed below. Another requirement is to deal with under-performers. Managing performance throughout the year means continually monitoring outcomes against plans and ensuring that corrective action is taken when necessary. It involves individuals monitoring and managing their own performance, and managers providing feedback, support and guidance as necessary.

Performance management should be regarded as an integral part of the continuing process of management. This is based on a philosophy that emphasizes:

- the achievement of sustained improvements in performance;

- the continuous development of skills and capabilities;

- that the organization is a 'learning organization' in the sense that it is constantly developing and applying the learning gained from experience and the analysis of the factors that have produced high levels of performance.

Managers and individuals should therefore be ready, willing and able to work together and define and discuss how to meet development and improvement needs as they arise. As far as practicable, learning and work should be integrated. This means that encouragement should be given to all managers and employees to learn from the successes, challenges and problems inherent in their day-to-day work. This process of monitoring performance is carried out by reference to agreed objectives, success criteria and performance measures, and to work, development and improvement plans.

Managers accommodate the need for regular dialogue and feedback on performance in their everyday contacts with their individual team members. This is in addition to the established pattern of briefings and team or project review meetings.

Formal performance reviews

Although performance management is a continuous process it is still useful to have a formal review once or twice yearly. This provides a focal point for the consideration of key performance and development issues. The performance review meeting is the means through which the five primary performance management elements of agreement, measurement, feedback, positive reinforcement and dialogue can be put to good use. It leads to the completion of the performance management cycle by informing performance and development agreements. It involves some form of assessment.

Analysing and assessing performance

Performance management is concerned with analysing and assessing performance in achieving objectives and implementing development plans. Such assessment provides the basis for feedback and discussions on areas for further development or improvement. The analysis of performance will be concerned with hard measures of achievement against objectives and softer assessments of the behaviour of people as it has affected the results they achieved. It will be based on factual information so that the process can be described as 'evidence-based performance management'.

Many but not all performance management schemes include some form of rating that is usually carried out during or after a performance review meeting. The rating indicates the quality of performance or competency achieved or displayed by an employee by selecting the level on a scale that most closely corresponds with the view of the assessor on how well the individual has been doing. A rating scale is supposed to assist in making judgements and it enables those judgements to be categorized to inform performance or contingent pay decisions, or simply to produce an instant summary for the record of how well or not so well someone is doing.

The ethical dimension

Performance management should operate in accordance with agreed and understood ethical principles. These have been defined by Winstanley and Stuart-Smith (1996) as follows:

> *Ethical principles for performance management (Winstanley and Stuart-Smith, 1996)*
>
> - Respect for the individual – people should be treated as 'ends in themselves' and not merely as 'means to other ends'.
>
> - Mutual respect – the parties involved in performance management should respect each other's needs and preoccupations.
>
> - Procedural fairness – the procedures incorporated in performance management should be operated fairly in accordance with the principles of procedural justice.
>
> - Transparency – people affected by decisions emerging from performance management processes should have the opportunity to scrutinize the basis upon which decisions were made.

Procedural justice requires that performance management decisions are made in accordance with principles that safeguard fairness, accuracy, consistency, transparency and freedom from bias, and properly consider the views and needs of employees. Folger, Konovsky and Cropanzano (1992) set out the benefits of procedurally just performance management based on the components of due process. They labelled such systems 'due process performance management' and argued that they do not bring about gross reallocations of power between managers and employees, but rather require only that managers be open to employees' input and responsive to justifiable questions and concerns about performance standards and judgements. According to Taylor *et al* (1998) procedurally just performance systems may also increase managers' own positive outcomes.

Organizational researchers such as Taylor *et al* (1995) have gathered a strong body of evidence showing that employees care a great deal about the justice of performance management practices and staffing. This work generally has found that the more just or fair employees consider such systems to be, the more satisfied and accepting they are of the resultant outcomes, even when those outcomes are less than desirable. The strength of these findings has led some researchers such as Folger and Cropanzano (1998) to propose that the provision of fair procedures is a more powerful foundation for the management of employees than is the provision of financial rewards.

Issues in performance management

Eight issues in performance management have been identified by Kathy Armstrong and Adrian Ward (2005) of the Work Foundation. These are:

- Performance management is not a single intervention that can be implemented easily. It relies on a range of activities, involving several core HR processes, and requires these to be carefully integrated.

- A sophisticated 'process' does not always lead to effective performance management.

- It is difficult to improve management capability in managing performance.

- There is an enduring underlying belief that performance management is a good thing to do. However, there is a reluctance in organizations to evaluate the effectiveness of performance management systems and to harness the results of research.

- There is often a lack of understanding about the nature of the link between performance and organizational culture, and the implications for performance management. Performance management reflects the organizational culture and context.

- When the performance management system is not delivering, that is likely to be reflecting a deeper issue such as lack of organizational agreement about clarity of purpose, priorities or standards, or a mismatch between espoused values and actual behaviours.

- Aligning the performance management process with the direction of any desired organizational change is essential.

- It can support organizational change but may not be the only, or main driver of it.

Effective performance management

> ### Effective performance management (Rogers, 2004)
>
> An effective performance management system encourages managers and associates to work together, communicate openly and provide feedback regularly. Until people focus on communication, cooperation and collaboration skills, appraisal forms remain vehicles for failure and appraisals go on evoking fear and suspicion.

Performance management must achieve what it sets out to achieve in the manner in which it is expected to achieve it. But too often the reality does not match the vision, the rhetoric remains rhetoric – unfulfilled pledges and promises, no more. Sadly, the cynicism of many academics about performance management rhetoric (see Chapter 3) is justified. It can be said of some managements, who introduce performance management with a flourish of trumpets, what was said of Lloyd George: 'Count not his broken promises a crime, he meant them, how he meant them at the time.'

Performance management is difficult. Performance management is demanding. It is not an easy option. Grand designs can too readily produce edifices that soon crumble to dust. Engelmann and Roesch (1996) list the following negative consequences of poorly designed or poorly administered performance management schemes, or schemes that lack management commitment (and it could have been added, the ownership and support of other stakeholders):

- poor motivation and self-esteem because employees receive inadequate feedback on their work performance;

- little or no focused communication about performance between supervisors and employees;

- inefficient use of supervisors' time;

- litigation over alleged discriminatory actions.

The criteria for the successful design and operation of performance management to avoid these and other problems of lack of enthusiasm, positive dislike, or misunderstanding, are exacting.

As Lawler, Mohrman and Resnick (1984) stressed, performance management must focus on the process of performance review and on the organizational context in which the event takes place, not on the form or system. Too often, the system comes first and the process is neglected.

Strebler, Bevan and Robertson (2001) suggested that the principles set out below were required for performance management to work effectively.

Principles of effective performance management (Strebler, Bevan and Robertson, 2001)

1. Have clear aims and measurable success criteria.

2. Be designed and implemented with appropriate employee involvement.

3. Be simple to understand and operate.

4. Have its effective use core to all management goals.

5. Allow employees a clear 'line of sight' between their performance goals and those of the organization.

6. Focus on role clarity and performance improvement.

7. Be closely allied to a clear and adequately resourced training and development infrastructure.

8. Make crystal clear the purpose of any direct link to reward and build in proper equity and transparency safeguards.

9. Be regularly and openly reviewed against its success criteria.

An American perspective on achieving a satisfactory process of performance management, including performance pay and rating, was produced by Ed Lawler as reported by Risher (2005).

'Best practices' in performance management (Ed Lawler)

- Ownership of performance management by line managers. The way line managers handle performance management is a key to system effectiveness; they need to take control.

- Training for both managers and individuals being appraised. Both managers and employees need to understand the process, their roles and the skills and behaviours important to the process. The training also contributes to the accuracy of the ratings.

- Leadership by top management. Executives need to demonstrate their strong commitment to the performance system and the importance of high performance.

- Performance goals that are driven by business strategy. Most companies rely on individual goals with explicit ties to the strategy. The best practice relies on goals jointly set by managers and employees. The linkage helps to justify the ratings.

- Ongoing feedback from managers. Employees should receive regular feedback on results and their performance throughout the year.

- Use of competencies, development planning and how individuals achieve their results. The feedback should also focus on the individual's strengths and weaknesses and involve development planning to improve future performance.

- Ties between financial rewards and performance ratings. To manage the budget for salary increases, managers need to differentiate among their people.

- Calibration meetings for managers to compare and level ratings. When managers meet to discuss performance ratings, it strengthens the credibility and validity of ratings and reinforces the perceived importance of the process.

- Use of e-HR appraisal systems to integrate performance management. Web-enabled systems facilitate the integration of performance data with performance plans and ratings. E-HR systems also make the process more than a year-end event.

5
Managing Performance Management

Performance management is managing the business. It is what line managers do continuously, not an HR directed annual procedure. It is a natural process of management. But it is a natural process that can be enhanced if it is conducted systematically. That is why it is called a performance management system. The following questions will be answered in this chapter:

- How should performance management be managed?
- What should be managed?
- What approach should be adopted?
- What documentation is required?
- To what extent can the processes involved be computerized by the use of web-enabled performance management?
- What is the role of HR?

How should performance management be managed?

It is impossible to give a categorical answer to this question. It all depends upon the context, which includes culture, management style and approach (eg autocratic, bureaucratic) and organization structure (multinational, divisionalized, regionalized, centralized, devolved etc). In multinational organizations there may be a choice on the degree to which the approach should be convergent (eg the parent company's practices are replicated worldwide in order to achieve consistency in meeting universal standards) or divergent (eg HR policies and practices are tailored to meet local circumstances although adherence to certain guiding principles may be expected).

Dickmann, as reported by Welfare (2006), instanced organizations such as IBM and Oxfam that operate a model based on universal principles or values across the organization that are then implemented differently at regional or national level. He suggested that the extent of integration or convergence depends on the business model of the organization: 'If the company is basically a McDonald's, where there are only limited local variations but the product is essentially the same all over the world, then the approach is likely to be different to a company like Unilever, whose products and processes tend to be much more responsive to the local market.'

What needs to be managed?

The aspects of performance management that need to be managed are:

- the communication of the aims of performance management – how it works and the responsibilities of those involved;

- the performance agreement process – providing guidance on the use of role profiles and goal setting;

- the performance review process – ensuring that reviews are carried out properly and documented (this is a major administrative area that may be computerized as is considered in detail later in this chapter);

- personal development planning – providing guidance and support in preparing and implementing personal development plans;

- skills development – providing coaching, mentoring and training in developing performance management skills such as goal setting, providing feedback, coaching and conducting performance reviews;

- monitoring and evaluation – monitoring the application of performance management, evaluating its effectiveness and taking action to improve it when necessary.

The approach to managing performance management

It has often been said in this book – but it bears repetition – that it is the processes of performance management as practised by line managers that are important, not the content of the system and how it is administered – and the content often consists largely of paper forms or computer screens. The elegance with which forms and computerized systems are designed is relatively unimportant. Their purpose is no more than that of recording views and decisions; they are not ends in themselves.

Similarly, administrative procedures should not weigh down performance management. It is important to establish the principles of performance management and get everyone to buy into them, but administration and control procedures should be carried out with a light touch. There should be scope for managers to decide on their own detailed approaches in conjunction with their staff as long as they abide by the guiding principles. Performance management practice should indeed be monitored through the evaluation approaches described in Chapter 24. This may reveal the need for individual managers to receive more guidance or training. But oppressive control will only prejudice managers against a process that they will think has been imposed upon them. This is against the whole thrust of performance management, which is to get managers and their staff to recognize that this is an effective process of management from which all can benefit.

Performance management is not a form-filling exercise, as many traditional merit rating or performance appraisal schemes appeared to be. HR managers who spent their time chasing up reluctant line managers to complete their appraisal forms and return them to the personnel department often unwittingly defeated the whole purpose of the exercise. Managers tended to be cynical about their rating and box-ticking activities and often produced bland and unrevealing reports that could be prepared without too much effort. They became even more cynical if they had any reason to believe that the completed forms were gathering dust in personal dossiers, unused and unheeded. And, sadly, this was often what happened.

A case could be made for having no forms at all for managers to complete. They could be encouraged to record their agreement and the conclusions of their reviews on blank sheets of paper to be used as working documents during the continuing process of managing performance throughout the year.

But there is much to be said for having a format that can help in the ordering and presentation of plans and comments and act as an aide memoire for reference during the year. And the mere existence of a form or a set of forms does demonstrate that this is a process that managers and their staff are expected to take seriously. Consideration is next given first to traditional methods of documentation and then to more recent developments in web-enabled performance management.

Performance management documentation

Before designing performance management forms it is necessary to be quite clear about their purpose. The following questions need to be answered:

- To what extent are these working documents for use by managers and their staff?
- What information does the HR department need about the outcome of performance reviews?

- How is the quality of performance reviews to be assured?

- How can employees be reassured that they will not become the victims of prejudiced or biased reports?

Performance management forms as working documents

The main purpose of any performance management forms is to serve as working documents. They should be in continual use by managers and individuals as reference documents on objectives and plans when reviewing progress. They record agreements on performance achievements and actions to be taken to improve performance or develop competence and skills. They should be dog-eared from much use – they should not be condemned to moulder away in a file.

For this reason the forms should be owned by the manager and the individual (both parties should have a copy). Any information the HR department needs on ratings (for performance-related pay or career-planning purposes) or requests for training should be incorporated in a separate form for their use.

The employee can still be protected against unfair assessments and ratings by providing for the manager's manager (the 'grandparent') to see and comment on the completed report. These comments could be shown to the individual, who should have the right to appeal through a grievance procedure if he or she is still unhappy about the report.

There is, however, a good case for the HR department having sight of completed review forms for quality assurance purposes, especially in the earlier days of operating performance management.

Information for the HR department

The HR department may need to know:

- who the high flyers are – for development and career planning;

- who are the people who are performing badly – to consider with the line manager what action needs to be taken;

- performance ratings for performance-related pay decisions;

- recommendations on training to assess any common training needs and to initiate training action;

- about the performance of any individual who might be considered for promotion, transfer or disciplinary action.

Another factor that helps to persuade many organizations to hold copies of the review forms centrally is that a decision in an unfair dismissal case may depend on the quality of record keeping as well as the honesty of the performance review process – performance review forms may be required for evidence. This can create a problem if a manager who has produced bland, superficial but generally favourable reports on an employee is later allowed to take disciplinary action for incapability. Employment tribunals do not look with favour on this type of inconsistency. It is always necessary for the HR department to compare review reports with the picture painted by managers when the latter request disciplinary action and to question any inconsistencies.

The approach adopted by most organizations is to require at least a copy of the review form to be held centrally, together with a copy of the performance agreement if this contains training and development recommendations. Managers and individuals would, however, be encouraged to retain their own copies as working documents.

It is necessary to remember the provisions of the Data Protection Act, which give employees the right to inspect any documents or records that contain personal data.

Form design

When designing performance management forms, the aim should be to keep them as simple and brief as possible while allowing ample 'white space' for comments. Like all good forms, they should be self-explanatory, but they may be supplemented by notes for guidance.

Although documentation should be kept to a minimum, such documents as are used should be well designed and presented. A typical set of forms that do not include an overall performance rating section is illustrated below in Figures 5.1 and 5.2.

Variations on a theme

There are many varieties of performance management forms used by different organizations – some more elaborate with, for example, a special 'performance planner' form, and some simpler ones.

However, they generally have the same basic themes and may include spaces for:

- agreed objectives;
- agreed performance and personal development plans;
- review of performance against objectives;
- review of achievements against development plan.

If a competency framework exists, the form may include a section listing the competencies with space for comments.

PERFORMANCE AND DEVELOPMENT: AGREEMENT AND REVIEW SUMMARY	
Name:	Forename(s):
Job title:	Department:
Reviewer's name:	Job title:

PERFORMANCE AND DEVELOPMENT AGREEMENT	
Objectives	Performance measures
Competencies	Agreed actions

PERSONAL DEVELOPMENT PLAN			
Development need	How it is to be met	Action by	Target completion

Figure 5.1   Performance management form (part 1)

Forms in organizations with performance-related pay (PRP) will often have an overall rating section. Those without PRP may still retain ratings as a means of summarizing performance.

The Royal College of Nursing appraisal and appraisal preparation forms are illustrated in Appendix B.

Web-enabled performance management

The basic features of web-enabled or online performance management typically include the ability to capture performance ratings, including interfaces for displaying performance standards and rating-process information. More advance features include prompting managers and employees about performance management events, routing documents between employees, providing access to forms and providing automated reports.

PERFORMANCE AND DEVELOPMENT REVIEW	
Objectives	Achievements
Competencies	Actions taken
Development needs	Actions taken
Comments by reviewer:	
Comments by reviewee:	
Signed:	Date:

Figure 5.2   Performance management form (part 2)

Web-enabled performance management ensures widespread access and provides a standard-ized format for collecting and storing performance data. Web-based software can make it easy for managers and employees to record role profiles and performance agreements, including performance improvement and personal development plans and objectives, monitor progress against the plans, access performance documents online, and gather multi-source (360-degree appraisal) comments. All this data can be used to assist in performance reviews and record further agreements emerging from the reviews. The aim is reduce paperwork and simplify the process. A justification for 'e-appraisals' was provided by Barlow (2003).

The justification for e-appraisals (G Barlow)

The time-consuming process of administering old-style performance reviews no longer needs to exist within any organization. E-appraisals are an automated process that dramatically cuts the amount of time and effort that is spent on the administrative procedure by HR staff. The time and effort required to write professional appraisals by line managers can be greatly reduced by the more sophisticated e-appraisal programmes. They enable employees to gain access via the internet to their record of performance as it develops throughout the year instead of having to rely on their memory of their successes, failures and learning needs.

Summers (2005) claims that: 'In an internet-based performance management system, employees have "line-of-sight" visibility. They can set their goals to align with those of other managers, and they can see how these goals align all the way to the corporate goals.' The system provides 'the ability to pull information from multiple sources and aggregate it, to drive activity by interacting with users and to make information accessible and visible in truly meaningful ways'.

However, Pulakos, Mueller-Hanson and O'Leary (2008) comment that a problem with automated performance management systems is that in making evaluations easier to complete, they may result in a propensity for managers to get their performance management responsibilities done as quickly as possible and perhaps not spend the extra time in performance-related interactions with employees. And as Fletcher (2001) points out, the more impersonal nature of entering and communicating assessments via a computer could lead to greater objectivity but less sensitivity and tact in handling the situation – apart from anything else, there is no chance to observe the recipients' reactions directly.

Examples of web-enabled performance management systems

Raytheon

The Raytheon web-enabled system incorporates a 'performance screen' and a 'performance and development summary' as well as 360-degree assessment tools and details of how the Raytheon compensation system works. It enables goals to be cascaded down through the organization, although employees can initiate the goal-setting process using the performance screen as a tool. Employees can then document their accomplishments against their goals on their performance screen.

TRW Inc

As reported by Neary (2002) TRW Inc based their system on an 'output form' that included:

Page 1 Biographical data

- identification information;
- education;
- experience summary.

Pages 2–3 Performance summary

- accomplishments against previous year goals;
- TRW behaviours;
- TRW initiatives;

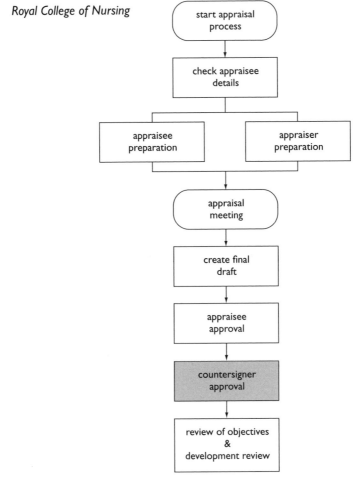

Figure 5.3 Royal College of Nursing: diagram of online performance appraisal scheme

- legal and ethical conduct – diversity and cultural sensitivity;
- previous year's professional development activities;
- employee comments;
- overall performance – manager's overall rating (four point scale) and comments.

Page 4 Development summary

- demonstrated strengths;
- improvement opportunities;
- performance goals for the upcoming year;
- professional development activities for the upcoming year;
- future potential/positions (employee perspective);
- future potential/positions (manager perspective);
- electronic sign off from both employee and manager.

Once managers have reviewed the employees' input, they are required to sit down with their reports and have a face-to-face dialogue about the employee's progress in the past year and plans for the coming year. To aid managers who may have many direct reports, a 'manage employees' function is included so that managers can see an on-screen overview of the status of each of their direct reports.

Each year, data from the previous year's system is transferred to this year's system, eliminating the need for additional data input.

The Zambon Group

Kathy Armstrong and Adrian Ward (2005) of the Work Foundation described how a multinational chemical and pharmaceutical company based in Italy with 2,300 employees developed a web-based performance management system.

A web-based performance management system at Zambon (Kathy Armstrong and Adrian Ward, 2005)

Consultants developed a blueprint for integrating the performance appraisal form with procedures to ensure a greater level of objectivity and transparency. Crucial to the success was the selection of technology. The overall approach was to separate development of the infrastructure from the business application, so each could be developed by IT and HR respectively. In other words, IT wanted to maintain control of the services and databases in order to guarantee full compatibility with existing IT systems, both at a central and user level. HR wanted to maintain the procedural software without the need for costly software development. The two technologies chosen were Decisionality DecisionFlows and Microsoft InfoPath. Microsoft InfoPath is an application that enables information workers to create dynamic forms that can help to share and manage data easily from different sources. DecisionFlows, in the form of web services, is designed to let business people create decisioning components without the need for software programmers. The tool is underpinned by decision-tree science, ensuring logical completeness (must join up the dots) and logic compliance (prevents recursive logic).

This combination of DecisionFlows and InfoPath enabled the rapid conversion of the existing performance appraisal forms and associated procedures into one integrated 'smart' form. This application development approach saves considerable time and costs, because the current systems become a 'black box' and InfoPath provides a state-of-the-art composite application. HR used DecisionFlows to develop procedural instructions and automatically generate web services. This means that HR is able to change its procedures at any time and deployment by IT ensures consistency. The result is that the rating outcomes are derived from a simplified series of questions and answers, thus enabling accurate, contextualized performance appraisal. HR supports the performance management process by providing training and coaching for managers and employees.

The role of HR

At one time, the personnel department tended to be not only the sponsor but also the custodian of performance appraisal schemes. As a result line managers regarded them as the preserve of personnel and therefore not their concern. They filled up the forms, often because they had to, but unenthusiastically.

The emergence of the 'business partner' concept of HR has led to a change in direction. HR no longer runs the performance appraisal scheme, but the danger of simply giving it away had to be recognized. Their role becomes that of encouraging and facilitating the sort of performance management processes described in this book. And this is an important role. They work alongside line managers, helping them as necessary to develop their skills and encouraging their use. They assemble teams of committed and experienced managers who can act as coaches and mentors and stimulate the creation of communities of practice, ensuring that performance management is on the agenda. More specifically, they run training events and conduct surveys to evaluate the effectiveness of performance management. In essence, HR specialists exist to support performance management rather than drive it. A comment on the role of HR in performance management based on research carried out by the Work Foundation is given below.

The role of HR in performance management (Kathy Armstrong and Adrian Ward, 2005)

HR's role in performance management is crucial. They tend to be the people that are in charge of designing and reviewing systems, convincing boards of a new approach, implementing new processes, running workshops for managers and staff, providing advice and support materials to staff and managers, and ensuring there is compliance with the system. However, they cannot be at every appraisal discussion; they can't ensure that managers and employees have 'quality' conversations; and they have a limited ability to improve the capability and engagement of managers in managing performance.

6

Managing
Under-performance

Performance management is a positive process that involves building on strengths. But it is also about helping people to improve. In many cases this will not be a big deal – the improvements required will be marginal and easily achieved. Sometimes, however, under-performance is a more serious problem that has to be managed. This chapter starts with an analysis of the problem and then describes ways of dealing with under-performers.

The problem of under-performance

A survey covering 139 organizations with a combined total of 300,000 staff conducted by IRS (Wolff, 2008) found that four-fifths had experienced under-performance to some extent while one in 10 had experienced it to a considerable extent. Only 8 per cent of respondents felt that their efforts to deal with poor performance had been successful and two-thirds of them did not consider that managers at their organization were capable of managing it.

Managers, as Schaffer (1991) points out, sometimes use a variety of psychological mechanisms for avoiding the unpleasant truth that performance gaps exist. These mechanisms include:

- Evasion through rationalization. Managers may escape having to demand better performance by convincing themselves that they have done all they can to establish expectations.

- Reliance on procedures. Management may rely on a variety of procedures, programmes and systems to produce better results. Top managers say, in effect, 'Let there be performance-related pay, or performance management or whatever' and sit back to wait for these panaceas to do the trick, which, of course, they will not unless they are part of a sustained effort led from the top and based on a vision of what needs to be done to improve performance.

- Attacks that skirt the target. Managers may set tough goals and insist that they are achieved, but still fail to produce a sense of accountability in subordinates.

Dealing with under-performers

Managing under-performers should be a positive process that is based on feedback throughout the year and looks forward to what can be done by individuals to overcome performance problems and, importantly, how managers can provide support and help. Note should be taken of the comment by Charles Handy (1989) that this should be about 'applauding success and forgiving failure'. He suggests that mistakes should be used as an opportunity for learning – 'something only possible if the mistake is truly forgiven because otherwise the lesson is heard as a reprimand and not as an offer of help'.

When dealing with poor performers the following comment by Howard Risher (2003) should be remembered: 'Poor performance is best seen as a problem in which the employer and management are both accountable. In fact, one can argue that it is unlikely to emerge if people are effectively managed.'

This is another way of putting the old Army saying: 'There are no bad soldiers, only bad officers.'

Poor performance may be wholly or partly the fault of the system. When looking at under-performance it is necessary to consider systemic as well as individual problems.

General approaches to managing under-performance

In general, respondents to the IRS survey (Wolff, 2008) suggested that the key to solving poor performance is communication, coupled with clarity about expectations and objectives, early intervention and ensuring managers have a clear view of the underlying problem before applying a solution. It is important to ensure that under-performing employees understand and acknowledge there is a problem when it can be attributed to them and accept some responsibility for achieving a solution. Depending on the cause, provision of support through training or coaching and regular contact with the line manager may also be important. But by far the most effective measure was to have competent and confident managers who were prepared to tackle the problem. Most organizations advocated an agreed improvement plan as the first step followed by regular but informal progress reviews.

Specific approaches to managing under-performance

The specific approaches adopted by respondents to the IRS 2008 survey were:

- The manager and employee jointly agree an improvement plan with timescales – 81 per cent.

- The manager and the employee agree to more regular, informal performance reviews – 68 per cent.

- A joint agreement on the provision of specific coaching or training – 61 per cent.

- The manager agrees to provide more coaching or guidance – 52 per cent.

- A joint re-evaluation of performance expectations – 52 per cent.

These are all valid ways of managing under-performance but they will be most effective if they are incorporated in a staged procedure as described below, which can provide a framework for managers and a basis for guidance and training.

The five basic steps

The five basic steps required to manage under-performers are:

1. Identify and agree the problem. Analyse the feedback and, as far as possible, obtain agreement from the individual on what the shortfall has been. Feedback may be provided by managers but it can in a sense be built into the job. This takes place when individuals are aware of their targets and standards, know what performance measures will be used and either receive feedback/control information automatically or have easy access to it. They will then be in a position to measure and assess their own performance and, if they are well-motivated and well-trained, take their own corrective actions. In other words, a self-regulating feedback mechanism exists. This is a situation that managers should endeavour to create on the grounds that prevention is better than cure.

2. Establish the reason(s) for the shortfall. When seeking the reasons for any shortfalls the manager should not crudely be trying to attach blame. The aim should be for the manager and the individual jointly to identify the facts that have contributed to the problem. It is on the basis of this factual analysis that decisions can be made on what to do about it by the individual, the manager or the two of them working together.

    It is necessary first to identify any causes that are due to weaknesses in the system or outside the control of either the manager or the individual. Any factors that are within the control of the individual and/or the manager can then be considered. What needs to be determined is first the extent to which the problem is due to a fault in the system itself or the way in which the system has been managed. If it is established that the individual is at least partly responsible for the poor performance, it can then be agreed whether this is because he or she:

    - did not receive adequate support or guidance from his/her manager;
    - did not fully understand what he/she was expected to do;
    - could not do it – ability;
    - did not know how to do it – skill;
    - would not do it – attitude.

3. Decide and agree on the action required. Action may be taken by the individual, the manager or both parties. This could include:

    – Taking steps to improve skills or change behaviour – the individual.

    – Changing attitudes; this is up to individuals as long as they accept that their attitudes need to be changed. The challenge for managers is that people will not change their attitudes simply because they are told to do so – they can only be helped to understand that certain changes to their behaviour could be beneficial not only to the organization but also to themselves.

    – Providing more support or guidance – the manager.

    – Clarifying expectations – joint.

    – Developing abilities and skills – joint, in the sense that individuals may be expected to take steps to develop themselves but managers may provide help in the form of coaching, additional experience or training.

    Whatever action is agreed both parties must understand how they will know that it has succeeded. Feedback arrangements can be made but individuals should be encouraged to monitor their own performance and take further action as required.

4. Resource the action. Provide the coaching, training, guidance, experience or facilities required to enable agreed actions to happen.

5. Monitor and provide feedback. Both managers and individuals monitor performance, ensure that feedback is provided or obtained and analysed, and agree on any further actions that may be necessary.

Use of a capability procedure

Every attempt should be made to deal with performance problems as they arise or at least consider them dispassionately at a review meeting. However, further action to deal with under-performers if all else fails may be necessary. But when confronted with such situations, many organizations have recognized that to go straight into a disciplinary procedure with its associations with misconduct is not the best way to handle them. They believe it is better to have a special capability procedure for performance issues, leaving the disciplinary procedure as the method used to deal with cases of misconduct. Such a procedure is typically staged as follows:

1. If a manager believes that an employee's performance is not up to standard an informal discussion is held with the employee to establish the reason and to agree the actions required by the employee and/or the manager to improve performance.

2. Should the employee show insufficient improvement over a defined period, a formal interview will be arranged with the employee (together with a representative if so desired).

The aims of this interview will be to: a) explain the shortfall between the employee's performance and the required standard; b) identify the cause(s) of the unsatisfactory performance and determine what – if any – remedial treatment (eg training, retraining, support, etc) can be given; c) set a reasonable period for the employee to reach the standard; and d) agree on a monitoring system during that period and tell the employee what will happen if that standard is not met.

3.   At the end of the review period a further formal interview will be held, at which time if the required improvement has been made: a) the employee will be told of this and encouraged to maintain the improvement; b) if some improvement has been made but the standard has not yet been met, the review period will be extended; c) if there has been no discernible improvement and performance is still well below an acceptable standard, consideration will be given to whether there are alternative vacancies that the employee would be competent to fill; if there are, the employee will be given the option of accepting such a vacancy or being considered for dismissal; d) in the absence of suitable alternative work, an employee who is clearly below an acceptable standard is liable to be dismissed.

4.   Employees may appeal against their dismissal.

Although capability action can be used as a means of overcoming performance problems, it should be treated as a separate procedure that is not regarded as part of the normal processes of performance management. These processes should help to identify performance problems that will be dealt with on the spot, if at all possible. Only if this fails are these problems transferred to the capability system for resolution.

This separation of performance management processes and capability procedures is important because of the serious harm that would be done to the positive performance improvement and developmental aspects of performance management if employees felt that the process was simply being used to collect evidence for use in taking disciplinary action. Performance reviews can become threatening affairs if they are perceived as placing sticks in the hands of management with which they can beat employees.

If the problem has to be transferred to the capability procedure, it is highly desirable to state what the problem is in full, with any supporting evidence that is available. Reference can be made to the fact that the problem was identified earlier as part of the continuing process of performance management but the content of any performance review form produced following a review meeting should not be used as evidence. The capability warning must be complete in itself.

In practice this may not cause much difficulty as long as the manager follows the guidelines for managing performance throughout the year as described in Chapter 4. These suggest that immediate action is taken to deal with performance problems; they should not be saved up to be discussed at a formal review meeting some time after the event. Raising problems immediately means that they are dealt with as a normal management process, and the capability procedure should only be resorted to when this process fails in spite of every effort to make it succeed.

Part III

Performance
Management Processes

7

Goal Setting

Setting goals or objectives (the terms are interchangeable) is the most important activity during the performance planning and agreement stages of performance management. It is covered in this chapter under the headings:

- principles of goal setting;
- goals and feedback;
- types of goals or objectives;
- how to set goals.

Principles of goal setting

Goal theory as originated by Latham and Locke (1979) stated that people perform better when they have specific and challenging but reachable goals. Acceptance of goals is achieved when:

- People perceive the goals as fair and reasonable and trust their managers.
- There are arrangements for individuals to participate in goal setting.
- Support is provided by the supervisor. A supportive supervisor does not use goals to threaten subordinates but rather to clarify what is expected of them.
- People are provided with the resources required to achieve their goals.
- Success is achieved in reaching goals that reinforces acceptance of future goals.

Locke and Latham (1990) held that specific and challenging goals lead to higher performance than no goals or generalized goals, such as 'try your best'. Also people who participate in setting their own goals are likely to set more difficult goals than others will set for them, and goal difficulty leads to increased commitment to achieving the goals. Feedback and competition have a similar effect on performance. Therefore, the extent to which goals lead to performance depends on participation, commitment and other elements of the performance management process such as feedback.

There are benefits arising from goal setting but also problems, as summed up by Latham and Locke (2006):

Benefits and problems of goal setting (Latham and Locke, 2006)

Benefits:	**Potential problems:**
Gives a sense of purpose.	Lack of sufficient knowledge for goal attainment.
Provides an unambiguous basis for judging success.	Goal conflict among group members.
Increases performance.	Fear of risk-taking.
Is a means for self-management.	Ignoring non-goal dimensions of performance.
Increases subjective well-being.	Demoralization because, following success, management may set higher, impossible goals.

Goals and feedback

Goals and feedback work together to affect goal accomplishment. Employees may provide their own feedback or receive it from others, such as supervisors or peers. Coaches are another source of feedback and support for participation in goal setting. Employees need feedback to help calibrate their progress toward a goal, as well as to suggest ways to adjust the level or direction of their efforts or to shift performance strategies. The combination of goals plus feedback is more effective than goals alone (Locke and Latham, 2002). Feedback and praise in the form of public recognition or by means of a monetary bonus do not affect performance unless they lead to setting of, and committing to, specific and difficult goals.

Types of goals

The different types of goals and how they are set are described below.

On-going role or work goals

All roles have built-in objectives that may be expressed as key result areas in a role profile. The definition of a key result area states that this is what the role holder is expected to achieve in this particular aspect of the role. For example: 'Identify database requirements for all projects that require data management in order to meet the needs of internal customers' or 'Deal quickly with customer queries in order to create and maintain high levels of satisfaction.'

Good role or work objectives will clearly define the activity in terms of the results and standards to be achieved. They may be supplemented by quantified targets or standards that may be quantified or qualitative. Although described as on-going, role objectives need to be reviewed regularly and as necessary, modified.

Targets

Targets are objectives that define the quantifiable results to be attained as measured in such terms as output, throughput, income, sales, levels of service delivery, cost reduction, reduction of reject rates. Thus a customer service target could be to respond to 90 per cent of queries within two working days.

Tasks/projects

Objectives can be set for the completion of tasks or projects by a specified date or to achieve an interim result. A target for a database administrator could be to develop a new database to meet the needs of the HR department by the end of the year.

Performance standards

A performance standard definition takes the form of a statement that performance will be up to standard if a desirable, specified and observable result happens. It should preferably be quantified in terms, for example, of level of service or speed of response. Where this is not possible, a more qualitative approach may have to be adopted, in which case the standard of performance definition would in effect state: 'This job or task will have been well done when (the following things happen).'

Behaviour

Behavioural expectations are often set out generally in competency frameworks but they may also be defined individually under the framework headings. Competency frameworks may deal with areas of behaviour associated with core values, for example teamwork, but they often convert the aspirations contained in value statements into more specific examples of desirable and undesirable behaviour that can help in planning and reviewing performance.

Values

Expectations can be defined for upholding the core values of the organization. The aim would be to ensure that espoused values become values in use.

Performance improvement

Performance improvement goals define what needs to be done to achieve better results. They may be expressed in a performance improvement plan that specifies what actions need to be taken by role holders and their managers.

Developmental/learning

Developmental or learning objectives specify areas for personal development and learning in the shape of enhanced knowledge and skills (abilities and competences).

Smart objectives

Many organizations use the following 'SMART' mnemonic to summarize the desirable characteristics of an objective:

S = Specific/stretching – clear, unambiguous, straightforward, understandable and challenging.

M = Measurable – quantity, quality, time, money.

A = Achievable – challenging but within the reach of a competent and committed person.

R = Relevant – relevant to the objectives of the organization so that the goal of the individual is aligned to corporate goals.

T = Time framed – to be completed within an agreed timescale.

Good objectives

The following is an expanded list of the characteristics of what a good objective should be:

- Consistent with the values of the organization and departmental and organizational objectives.

- Precise: clear and well-defined, using positive words.

- Challenging: to stimulate high standards of performance and to encourage progress.

- Measurable: related to quantified or qualitative performance measures.

- Achievable: within the capabilities of the individual. Account should be taken of any constraints that might affect the individual's capacity to achieve the objectives; these could include lack of resources (money, time, equipment, support from other people), lack of experience or training, external factors beyond the individual's control etc.

- Agreed by the manager and the individual concerned. The aim is to provide for the ownership, not the imposition, of objectives, although there may be situations where individuals have to be persuaded to accept a higher standard than they believe themselves to be capable of attaining.

- Time-related: achievable within a defined timescale (this would not be applicable to a role or work objective).

- Focused on teamwork: emphasize the need to work as an effective member of a team as well as individual achievement.

Integrating goals

A defining characteristic of performance management is the importance attached to the integration or alignment of individual goals with organizational objectives. The aim is to focus people on doing the right things in order to achieve a shared understanding of performance requirements throughout the organization.

The integration of organizational and individual/team objectives is often referred to as a process of 'cascading objectives'. However cascading should not be regarded as just a top-down process. There will be overarching corporate goals, but people at each level should be given the opportunity to indicate how they believe they can contribute to the attainment of team and departmental objectives. This is a bottom-up process and the views of employees about what they believe they can achieve should be noted and, as appropriate, higher-level objectives amended to take account of them. An approach along these lines increases 'ownership' of the objectives as well as providing a channel for upward communication on key issues affecting the achievement of business goals. Of course there will be times when the overriding challenge has to be accepted, but there will also be many occasions when the opinions of those who have to do the work will be well worth listening to.

Integration is achieved by ensuring that everyone is aware of corporate, functional and team goals and that the objectives they agree for themselves are consistent with those goals and will contribute in specified ways to their achievement. This process is illustrated in Figure 7.1.

Figure 7.2 illustrates how goals can be integrated in a specific area.

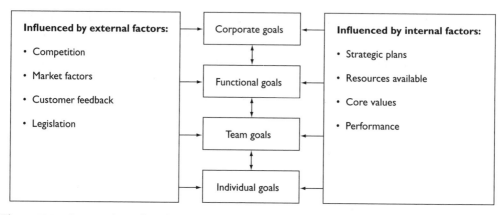

Figure 7.1   Integration of goals

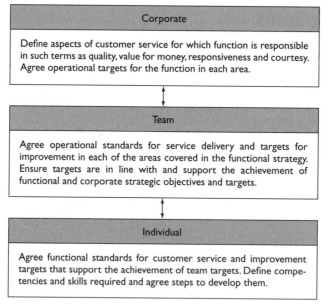

Figure 7.2   Two-way process of agreeing integrated goals

How to set goals

Goals are set by reference to an agreed role profile that should set out key result areas. Role profiles should be amended at the time any changes are made to these areas. But they should be formally reviewed and updated at the planning and agreement stage of the performance management cycle.

The following is an example of a goal-setting process used in a retail company. When setting staff objectives for the coming year, line managers are advised to start with their own objectives, going through each one and identifying what it is they need each team member to do in order to achieve his or her own targets. This helps employees understand how the process operates in a more detached manner before considering their own objectives. The number of objectives depends on the employee's role, and to assist in their design, set examples are provided for the various job levels for line managers to use and adapt. In addition, managers need also to identify when the objective needs to be achieved by: with a date, a recurring time or a time linked with another event. Further, internal guidance recommends that objectives need to be extremely clear so that there can be no ambiguity over whether or not they have been achieved at a later date.

The stages in the goal setting process as described by Mone and London (2002) are listed below.

Stages in the goal setting process (Mone and London, 2002)

1. Managers tell their employees that they are starting the goal setting process for the upcoming performance year and indicate the time frame in which they want to have the process completed. Managers outline the process for the employees.

2. In preparation, managers advise their employees to do the following to create a context for current goal setting: re-read the mission and vision for the company; re-read the department's mission and vision; review their job descriptions (role profiles); review their current goals, strategies and tactics; identify any new overarching goals; and develop a working draft of team goals for their departments, if necessary. Of course, this assumes that these documents exist, are readily available and are clear.

3. Managers share the overarching goals and department goals, if any, with their employees. They also share any other strategic messages that may be important for their employees to consider.

4. Using the above information, managers ask their employees to develop drafts of their performance goals, strategies and tactics, and development goals.

5. Managers meet with each of their employees to review and discuss their goals, strategies and tactics. During this meeting, managers will want to ensure that their employees' performance goals are aligned with the overall direction of the company and department, are challenging and meaningful, and are realistic. Managers will also want to ensure that each employee's development goals will help him or her to improve performance in the current job or acquire the skills or knowledge necessary to prepare for future jobs.

6. Once the goals, strategies and tactics have been finalized to the managers' requirements, managers ask their employees to develop the goal measures of success and goal measurements.

7. Managers meet with their employees to review, discuss and finalize measures.

8. Managers review their employees' goals, strategies etc as necessary.

9. Managers communicate and discuss any changes with their employees and revise as necessary.

10. Managers and each of their employees 'sign off' on the agreed goals, strategies, etc, and each keeps a copy for their files.

There are two issues with goal setting: predicting what is achievable and participation.

Predicting what is achievable

Schneiderman (1999) warned that:

> *Specific goals should be set based on knowledge of the means that will be used to achieve them. Yet the means are rarely known at the time the goals are set. The usual result is that if the goal is too low, we will underachieve relative to our potential. If the goal is too high, we will underperform according to other people's expectations. What's really needed is a means of predicting what is achievable if some sort of standard means for improvement were used.*

Participation in goal setting

Participation in goal setting is important, but, as noted by London, Mone and Scott (2004), it must be accompanied by an understanding of organizational goals, information about translating them into action, and support for meeting goals. The evaluation of individual goal setting and participation should begin with a review of the process that managers and employees follow throughout the organization to establish goals. As previously pointed out, participation in goal setting improves performance, not because participation by itself is inherently motivating, but because it provides the employee with an increased understanding of expectations and strategies for goal accomplishment.

8

Feedback

Feedback to individuals on how they are doing is one of the key performance management processes. It can be provided by managers informally during the year or formally at a performance review meeting in which it will play an important part. It can be given by colleagues, subordinates or customers as part of a 360-degree feedback system (see Chapter 9). Or it can be something that individuals do for themselves. This chapter deals with feedback under the following headings:

- feedback defined;
- the nature of feedback;
- use of feedback;
- how effective is feedback?
- guidelines on providing feedback;
- feedback expert systems.

Feedback defined

Feedback is the provision of information to people on how they have performed in terms of results, events, critical incidents and significant behaviours. Feedback can be positive when it tells people that they have done well, constructive when it provides advice on how to do better, and negative when it tells people that they have done badly. Feedback reinforces effective behaviour and indicates where and how behaviour needs to change.

In systems engineering, feedback transmits information on performance from one part of a system to an earlier part of the system in order to generate corrective action or to initiate new action. In this respect performance management has the characteristics of a system in that it provides for information to be presented (feedback) to people on their performance, which helps them to understand how well they have been doing and how effective their behaviour has been. The aim is for feedback to promote this understanding so that appropriate action can be taken. This can be positive action taken to make the best use of the opportunities the feedback has revealed, or corrective action where the feedback has revealed that something has gone wrong.

Systems engineers design self-regulating systems that generate their own feedback and respond to this information of their own volition. The same principle can be applied in performance management – individuals can be encouraged to understand the performance measures that are available for them to use in order to provide their own feedback and to develop their own plans for performance development and improvement.

Such self-generated feedback is a highly desirable feature of a full performance management process but there will always be a need for managers, colleagues and, sometimes, internal or external advisors to provide feedback based on their own observations and understanding.

The nature of feedback

Feedback in performance management is positive in the sense that its aim is to point the way to further development and improvement. Feedback can be positive when it recognizes success or constructive when it identifies areas for improvement that can lead to positive action. The latter can be regarded as negative feedback when perceived failings are dwelt on as matters for blame. If there have been mistakes or errors of judgement they should be treated as opportunities for learning so that they are less likely to be repeated in the future.

Evidence-based performance management depends on feedback that relies on facts not opinions. It refers to results, events, critical incidents and significant behaviours that have affected performance in specific ways. It compares what has actually happened with what was supposed to have happened. It refers to agreed objectives, success criteria and performance measures, and uses the latter to establish outcomes. The feedback should be presented in a way that enables individuals to recognize and accept its factual nature. Of course there will often be room for some interpretation of the facts but such interpretations should start from the actual situation as reported in the feedback not from the subjective views expressed by the provider of the feedback.

Use of feedback

Providing regular feedback as an important part of the continuous process of performance management was well described by Lee (2005) as follows.

> ### The use of feedback in reviewing and developing performance (Lee, 2005)
>
> Performance conversations should include a two-way exchange to ensure that the employee fully understands what is good, what is bad, and why the good performance is good and the bad is bad. With accurate descriptions of the nuances of performance the employee can better understand how his or her past actions or activities affected performance outcomes and how future efforts are likely to contribute to future performance. Accurate descriptions or diagnoses of performance are crucial, for understanding and improvement are possible only through timely feedback.
>
> The longer the gap between performance events and performance feedback, the greater the challenge of remembering with clarity the character and quality of the performance events... two semi-annual or one annual performance conversation cannot manage performance alone. They might be effective in documenting some performance parameters but they are not likely to be effective in managing, regulating and improving performance. Good supervision with ample feedback is good performance management.

Lee also pointed out that: 'Although many people confuse the two, feedback and appraisal are fundamentally different things. Feedback is information-based, whereas the basis of appraisal is judgement or evaluation. Furthermore, feedback is an ongoing activity, and appraisal is periodic and event-based (annual).'

As London, Mone and Scott (2004) comment, feedback plays a key role, along with goal setting, in the self-regulation of performance. Overall, feedback focuses attention on performance goals that are important to the organization, helps discover errors, maintains goal direction, influences new goals, provides information on performance capabilities and on how much more effort/energy is needed to achieve goals, and provides positive reinforcement for goal accomplishments

How effective is feedback?

Kluger and DeNisi (1996) cautioned that not all feedback interventions result in improvements. In their meta-analysis based largely on performance appraisal feedback they concluded that, in over a third of the cases, feedback actually resulted in decreased performance. The analysis suggested that there may be myriad factors that influence how individuals react to feedback, and who will improve following feedback and who will not. Research on performance appraisal feedback suggests that when individuals receive negative feedback they are often discouraged rather than motivated to improve.

What makes feedback effective?

DeNisi and Kluger (2000) commented that feedback interventions are more likely to be effective if they keep the employee's attention focused on goals at the task performance level, and least likely to be effective if they cause a shift of focus to a personal level.

Research by Gray (2001) identified two factors that influenced the extent to which receivers valued their feedback: 1) the extent to which the feedback was trustworthy, and 2) the extent to which it was constructive.

Guidelines on providing feedback

Build feedback into the job

To be effective feedback should be built into the job or provided soon after the activity has taken place.

Provide feedback on actual events

Feedback should be provided on actual results or observed behaviour. It should be backed up by evidence. It should not be based on supposition about the reason for the behaviour. You should, for example, say: 'We have received the following complaint from a customer that you have been rude, would you like to comment on this,' rather than: 'You tend to be aggressive.'

Describe, don't judge

The feedback should be presented as a description of what has happened; it should not be accompanied by a judgement. If you start by saying: 'I have been informed that you have been rude to one of our customers; we can't tolerate that sort of behaviour,' you will instantly create resistance and prejudice an opportunity to encourage improvement.

Refer to and define specific behaviours

Relate all your feedback to specific items of behaviour. Don't indulge in transmitting general feelings or impressions.

Define good work or behaviour

When commenting on someone's work or behaviour define what you believe to be good work or effective behaviour with examples.

Ask questions

Ask questions rather than make statements – 'Why do you think this happened?'; 'On reflection is there any other way in which you think you could have handled the situation?'; 'How do you think you should tackle this sort of situation in the future?'.

Select key issues

Select key issues and restrict yourself to them. There is a limit to how much criticism anyone can take. If you overdo it, the shutters will go up and you will get nowhere.

Focus

Focus on aspects of performance the individual can improve. It is a waste of time to concentrate on areas that the individual can do little or nothing about.

Provide positive feedback

Provide feedback on the things that the individual did well in addition to areas for improvement. People are more likely to work positively at improving their performance and developing their skills if they feel empowered by the process.

Provide constructive feedback

Focus on what can be done to improve rather than on criticism.

Ensure feedback leads to action

Feedback should indicate any actions required to develop performance or skills. The guidance on feedback provided by CEMEX is set out in Appendix B.

Feedback expert systems

As Van Fleet, Peterson and Van Fleet (2005) remark 'The dictums of "don't be judgemental" and "don't say anything at all if you can't say something nice" seem to be sufficiently ingrained to make many managers reluctant to provide performance feedback'. Giving feedback is, in fact, the most difficult task that managers face in operating performance management processes. Some are naturally good at it; many aren't.

The obvious solution to this problem, and one that is adopted by most organizations with performance management, is training. But this has its limitations. Research by Fink and

Longenecker (1997) showed that training produced little positive effect on feedback effectiveness. Training suffers from the transfer problem – in the limited time usually available, it often fails to provide managers with sufficient information and ways to apply the information in different situations. Too much time may elapse between the training and the opportunity to apply it, and managers will probably have no opportunity to practise any skills they have learned during this gap.

An alternative approach is to use an expert system. Such systems are meant to solve real problems that normally require specialized expertise. They are built by extracting the relevant knowledge from human experts and producing 'rules of thumb' for dealing with specific situations. The knowledge extracted in this way provides the system's knowledge base on a computer. Expert systems are provided by suppliers such as Oracle/PeopleSoft.

Performance feedback expert systems provide guidelines to managers on how to deal with the different types of people and situations they will meet when conducting performance reviews that involve the provision of feedback. They typically function by getting users to:

- profile themselves by responding to items dealing with such things as their experience in giving performance feedback;

- profile their workplace by providing information dealing with things such as nature of the performance management system;

- profile their staff in terms of personalities and previous interactions;

- input details for each situation for which feedback advice is sought – for example whether the feedback is positive or negative, what type of tasks are involved and the employee's experience;

- obtain suggestions from the expert system on how to handle the feedback in the circumstances described;

- query the system for more detailed explanations if they so wish.

Example of expert system advice on feedback (source: Van Fleet, Peterson and Van Fleet, 2005)

To demonstrate that you really understand the performance of… cite examples to illustrate what you mean when you make an evaluative comment. Also, stick to the facts and avoid any references to her personality. Finally, regarding any areas of poor performance, take the time to spell out what would have been good work, again giving examples.

The advantages of feedback expert systems are that: 1) they provide immediate expert practical advice on providing feedback that fits the situation faced by the manager; 2) they facilitate learning by doing; 3) they enable inexperienced managers to become effective rapidly; 4) the time and frequency of use can be controlled by the user; and 5) methods of using them can be learned quickly.

The disadvantages are that: 1) the advice may be too generalized to be applicable; 2) they rely on inputs from users on such factors as the personality of the individual to whom feedback is to be given, which may be subjective, inaccurate and misleading; 3) they over-formalize what is essentially an informal process and are in danger of mechanistically programming the provision of feedback; 4) it may be difficult to locate an appropriate package from a supplier; and 5) the cost of the package may be considerable (although this could be recovered in part at least by reduced training times).

9

360-degree Feedback

This chapter covers the practice of 360-degree feedback under the following headings:

- 360-degree feedback defined;

- the rationale for 360-degree feedback;

- use of 360-degree feedback;

- methodology;

- 360-degree feedback and appraisal;

- effectiveness of 360-degree feedback;

- advantages and disadvantages;

- introducing 360-degree feedback.

360-degree feedback defined

360-degree feedback, also known as multi-source feedback, was defined by Ward (1997) as 'the systematic collection and feedback of performance data on an individual or group derived from a number of the stakeholders on their performance'. It is a process in which someone's performance is assessed and feedback is given by a number of people, who may include their manager, subordinates, colleagues and customers. Assessments take the form of ratings against various performance dimensions.

The term 360-degree feedback is sometimes used loosely to describe upward feedback where this is given by subordinates to their managers. This is the most common approach and is more properly described as 180-degree feedback. Some organizations restrict feedback to individuals on the grounds that its main purpose is to help them to develop their performance. Some give it to both managers and individuals as the basis for appraisal, coaching and self-development. A few give it to managers to provide a basis for appraisal and pay decisions.

Coaching for individuals as a result of the feedback may be provided by a member of the HR department or an outside consultant. 360-degree feedback or a variant of it was used by 30 per cent of the respondents to the 2005 e-reward survey.

The rationale for 360-degree feedback

The rationale for 360-degree feedback has been expressed by Turnow (1993) as follows: 360-degree activities are usually based on two key assumptions: 1) that awareness of any discrepancy between how we see ourselves and how others see us increases self-awareness; and 2) that enhanced self-awareness is a key to maximum performance as a leader, and thus becomes a foundation block for management and leadership development programmes. Through feedback, recipients receive useful information about their strengths and weaknesses, which can guide their developmental planning. The feedback is valuable because it comes from multiple perspectives, the opinions are important, and each perspective may provide relevant yet different information. The feedback instruments provide an opportunity to a broader set of 'others', such as peers and subordinates, to provide feedback that traditionally has been the province of supervisors only.

London and Beatty (1993) have suggested that 360-degree feedback can become a powerful organizational intervention to increase awareness of the importance of aligning leader behaviour, work unit results and customer expectations, as well as increasing employee participation in leadership development and work unit effectiveness. It recognizes the complexity of management and the value of inputs from various sources – it is axiomatic that managers should not be assessing behaviours they cannot observe, and the leadership behaviours of subordinates may not be known to their managers. It also directs attention to important performance dimensions that may hitherto have been neglected by the organization.

Benefits of 360-degree feedback (The Feedback Project, 2001)

- Increased employee self-awareness.
- Enhanced understanding of behaviours needed to increase individual and organizational performance.
- The creation of development activities that are more specific to the employee.
- Increased involvement of employees at all levels in the hierarchy.
- Increased devolution of self-development and learning to employees.

Use of 360-degree feedback

360-degree feedback is used for a number of purposes. Research conducted by Handy, Devine and Heath (1996) found that typically, 360-degree feedback forms part of a self-development or management development programme. The 45 users covered by the survey fell into the following groups:

- 71 per cent used it solely to support learning and development.

- 23 per cent used it to support a number of HR processes such as appraisal, resourcing and succession planning.

- 6 per cent used it to support pay decisions.

An example of how 360-degree feedback is used in CEMEX is given in Appendix B.

360-degree feedback: methodology

360-degree feedback processes usually obtain data from questionnaires that measure from different perspectives the behaviours of individuals against a list of competencies. In effect, they ask for an evaluation: 'How well does... do...?' The competency model may be one developed within the organization or the competency headings may be provided by the supplier of a questionnaire. A typical questionnaire may cover aspects of performance such as leadership, teamwork, communication, organizational skills, decisiveness, drive and adaptability.

Ratings

Ratings are given by the generators of the feedback on a scale against each heading. This may refer both to importance and performance, rating the importance of each item on a scale of 1 (not important) to 6 (essential), and performance on a scale of 1 (weak in this area) to 6 (outstanding).

Feedback ratings are often accompanied by managers' self-ratings on the same items on which they are rated by their subordinates, peers and customers. Self-ratings help focus the manager's attention on the results and build motivation in establishing the direction of self-development efforts.

Data processing

Questionnaires are normally processed with the help of software developed within the organization or, most commonly, provided by external suppliers. This enables the data collection and analysis to be completed swiftly, with the minimum of effort and in a way that facilitates graphical as well as numerical presentation.

Graphical presentation is preferable as a means of easing the process of assimilating the data. The simplest method is to produce a profile as illustrated in Figure 9.1.

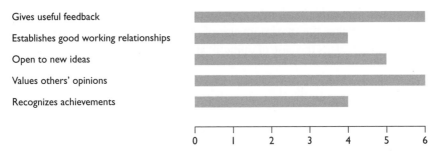

Figure 9.1   360-degree feedback graphic profile

Some of the proprietary software presents feedback data in a much more elaborate form.

Feedback

The feedback is often anonymous and may be presented to the individual (most commonly), to the individual's manager (less common) or to both the individual and the manager.

Action

The action generated by the feedback will depend on the purposes of the process: development, appraisal or pay. If the purpose is primarily developmental, the action may be left to individuals as part of their personal development plans, but the planning process may be shared between individuals and their managers if they both have access to the information. Coaches from inside or, commonly, outside the organization can review the feedback with the individual and discuss its implications and any development activities that may therefore be appropriate.

Even if the data only goes to the individual it can be discussed in a performance review meeting so that joint plans can be made, and there is much to be said for adopting this approach.

360-degree feedback and appraisal

An important issue to be addressed in developing a 360-degree feedback system is whether it should be used purely for development purposes (ie identifying learning and development needs) or whether it should be also or mainly used as part of the appraisal process (contributing to overall ratings and decisions on promotion, succession planning, pay or even retention). Research by Warr and Ainsworth (1999) established that 100 per cent of the organizations they studied used 360-degree feedback for development, 50 per cent used it as part of performance appraisal and only 7 per cent used it for determining pay.

Incorporating 360-degree feedback into appraisal can be attractive to organizations because they feel that: 1) it makes the maximum use of the data it provides so that they get their money's worth; 2) it widens the base of opinion; and 3) it offers a broader assessment of performance.

As noted by Fletcher (1998), the shift in the late 1990s from using 360-degree feedback for developmental purposes to making it part of the appraisal process took place because of the perceived failings of conventional top-down appraisals. These were often seen to be limited because they reflected the perspective of only one person and ratings have been shown to be prone to bias. Also, top down appraisals too often appeared to achieve little behavioural change.

According to Fletcher, including 360-degree feedback in appraisals seems to offer a solution to some of these problems. In theory, multiple levels and sources of data should lead to a more objective picture of an individual's contribution, strengths and development needs. It should consequently promote higher levels of trust in the fairness of the process. This in turn should make it more likely that changes in behaviour will ensue. Making feedback part of appraisal also indicates that the organization takes it seriously.

But as Fletcher pointed out, there are problems. People giving the ratings may be less inclined to be honest if they know that they can affect pay decisions or have negative effects on the person concerned. His research at Shell showed that when the purpose of ratings became evaluative rather than developmental, up to 35 per cent of those giving the ratings changed their assessments – and the changes could be in either direction. Furthermore, there is no guarantee that assessments by subordinates and peers will be free of bias. Fletcher concluded that his research findings should make people wary of grafting it onto appraisal systems. However, he did comment: 'This is not to say that it can't be used successfully, but it does need to be handled with care.'

Earlier research by Pollack and Pollack (1996) showed that the collection of 360-degree feedback data and the associated feedback process is more likely to be effective when the system is for developmental rather than appraisal purposes. Fletcher (1998) reported that organizations introducing 360-degree for appraisal purpose have, in many cases, dropped it within two years. It was noted by Silverman, Kerrin and Carter (2005) that raters in one organization they studied resisted using feedback for appraisal purposes because they were concerned about the impact their ratings would have on the receiver's pay or about issues of confidentiality. They commented that there was a substantial amount of research, for instance Handley (2001), that showed raters tended to be more lenient when feedback was associated with appraisal. As they emphasize: 'The findings strongly suggest that linking 360-degree feedback to administrative decisions can contaminate the whole process.' There is also a legal aspect to this: if anonymous ratings lead to administrative actions such as demotion or even termination, such actions may be difficult to support if challenged legally.

Effectiveness of 360-degree feedback

As shown below, research has produced varied conclusions about the effectiveness of 360-degree feedback. According to Bailey and Fletcher (2002) its benefits have been largely untested but rely on a number of assumptions – that individuals learn how effective task performance can be described, gain insight into how it is demonstrated and build the accuracy of self-perception and subsequent corrective behaviours. Their study of 104 managers receiving feedback on 50 behaviours over two years in an automobile breakdown service organization showed mixed benefits. The positive findings were that on average self-raters, first and second-level subordinates and bosses all saw improvements in competencies, development needs were perceived to decrease and there were dramatic changes in the perceptions of first and second-level subordinates in terms of the association of self and other ratings. Self-perceptions also became a more accurate predictor of actual appraisal scores over time. On the negative side, greater similarities in scores between peers, self and individual levels largely resulted from subordinates altering their assessment of target managers; the managers' self-perceptions did not change much over time.

Warr and Ainsworth (1999) reported that many organizations that have implemented 360-degree feedback said that it was considered to be a success. Indeed, short-term indicators of success were typically cited as being the initial resistance of employees changing to acceptance, and the fact that employees became willing to set aside time to use the system. Longer-term success was typically viewed as the system being rolled out across the organization, receivers reporting behavioural change as a result of the feedback, 360-degree feedback ideas becoming part of the employees' thinking about their development, and increased alignment between 360-degree processes and organizational strategy.

Mixed results were observed by Silverman, Kerrin and Carter (2005). In one of their case studies (a brewing company) they noted that:

> The 360-degree feedback process had not been effective in changing behaviour or performance and there was some concern that it may even have caused more harm than good. There were particular worries about having raised expectations regarding what was possible for individuals after the feedback had been given and then not being able to provide the resources for this activity.

In a local authority, feedback receivers found it difficult to cite concrete examples of behavioural change that could be attributed to the 360-degree feedback itself. However in a case researched by Silverman, Kerrin and Carter (a government office) it was established that 94 per cent of receivers had taken some action on the basis of the feedback and that there was evidence of positive, observable changes in behaviour. But feedback had more impact on some receivers than others. Another research project in a government office conducted by Morgan, Cannan and Culinane (2005) revealed a more negative situation. The findings were that at an organizational level the use of 360-degree feedback as a performance management tool failed to develop the awareness anticipated. Neither was it found to be aligned with other development plans or the organization's core competences. At an individual level, some individuals believed that they achieved little from the process overall.

Frisch (2001) commented that anonymous feedback is not necessarily a good thing: 'What happens in highly political, "out for yourself" organizational cultures is that anonymous feedback becomes an opportunity to get even or "take shots". Feedback that taps into power struggles and turf disputes can be personally damaging and yet hide behind the anonymity of the process.'

Maurer, Mitchell and Barbiette (2002) established that actual feedback ratings had only very weak relationships with subsequent involvement in development activity. What they found to be more important in predicting the uptake of development activity was a work environment in which employees are supportive of skills development, and the extent to which those involved believed that they could improve their skills.

360-degree feedback: advantages and disadvantages

Advantages:

Individuals get a broader perspective of how they are perceived by others than previously possible.

It gives people a more rounded view of their performance.

Increased awareness of and relevance of competencies.

Increased awareness by senior management that they too have development needs.

Feedback is perceived as more valid and objective, leading to acceptance of results and actions required.

Disadvantages:

People do not always give frank or honest feedback.

People may be put under stress in receiving or giving feedback.

Lack of action following feedback.

Over-reliance on technology.

Too much bureaucracy.

Can be time consuming and resource intensive.

The disadvantages can all be minimized, if not avoided completely, by careful design, involving stakeholders in the development programme, communication, training and follow-up.

Introducing 360-degree feedback

360-degree feedback is not an easy option. Silverman, Kerrin and Carter (2005) identified the following implementation issues that need to be addressed:

- The mission and scope of the use of 360-degree feedback is not clearly defined.
- Inadequate explanation of the whole process leads to a lack of understanding of why it is used.
- Organizational readiness for feedback is not evident.
- Sufficient resources are not made available. Unrealistic promises are made at the implementation stage, which leads to cynicism later on.
- The outcomes are not evaluated.

Guidelines produced by London and Beatty (1993) focus on 360-degree feedback as an operational procedure in the day-to-day activities of the organization. Their emphasis, appropriately, is on employee involvement at every stage – including development of job studies, identification and definition of areas for feedback and the design of feedback mechanisms. Implementation may require the study of specific organizational circumstances in relation to user acceptance and the ways in which 360-degree feedback may be of greatest short-term and long-term benefit for overall improvement of managerial competence.

Steps required

To develop and implement 360-degree feedback the following steps need to be taken:

1. Define objectives. It is important to define exactly what 360-degree feedback is expected to achieve. It will be necessary to spell out the extent to which it is concerned with personal development, appraisal or pay.

2. Decide on recipients who are to be at the receiving end of feedback. This may be an indication of who will eventually be covered after a pilot scheme.

3. Decide on who will give the feedback: the individual's manager, direct reports, team members, other colleagues or internal and external customers. A decision will also have to be made on whether HR staff or outside consultants should take part in helping managers to make use of the feedback. A further decision will need to be made on whether or not the feedback should be anonymous (it usually is).

4. Decide on the areas of work and behaviour on which feedback will be given. This may be in line with an existing competency model or it may take the form of a list of headings for development. Clearly, the model should fit the culture, values and type of work carried out in the organization. But it might be decided that a list of headings or questions in a software package would be acceptable, at least to start with.

5. Decide on the method of collecting the data. The questionnaire could be designed in-house or a consultant's or software provider's questionnaire could be adopted, with the possible option of amending it later to produce better fit.

6. Decide on data analysis and presentation. Again, the decision is on developing the software in-house or using a package. Most organizations installing 360-degree feedback do, in fact, purchase a package from a consultancy or software house. But the aim should be to keep it as simple as possible.

7. Plan the initial implementation programme. It is desirable to pilot the process, preferably at top level or with all the managers in a function or department. The pilot scheme will need to be launched with communications to those involved about the purpose of 360-degree feedback, how it will work and the part they will play. The aim is to spell out the benefits and, as far as possible, allay any fears. Training in giving and receiving feedback will also be necessary.

8. Analyse the outcome of the pilot scheme. The reactions of those taking part in a pilot scheme should be analysed and necessary changes made to the process, the communication package and the training.

9. Plan and implement the full programme. This should include briefing, communicating, training and support from HR and, possibly, the external consultants.

10. Monitor and evaluate. Maintain a particularly close watch on the initial implementation of feedback, but monitoring should continue. This is a process that can cause anxiety and stress, or produce little practical gain in terms of development and improved performance for a lot of effort.

360-degree feedback: criteria for success

- It has the active support of top management who themselves take part in giving and receiving feedback and encourage everyone else to do the same.
- There is commitment everywhere else to the process based on briefing, training and an understanding of the benefits to individuals as well as the organization.
- There is real determination by all concerned to use feedback data as the basis for development.
- Questionnaire items fit or reflect typical and significant aspects of behaviour.
- Items covered in the questionnaire can be related to actual events experienced by the individual.
- Comprehensive and well-delivered communication and training programmes are followed.
- No one feels threatened by the process – this is usually achieved by making feedback anonymous and/or getting a third party facilitator to deliver the feedback.
- Feedback questionnaires are relatively easy to complete (not unduly complex or lengthy, with clear instructions).
- Bureaucracy is minimized.

10
Performance Reviews

Performance management is a continuous process that involves informal reviews as required. As Plachy and Plachy (1988) explained: 'Performance review occurs whenever a manager and an employee confirm, adjust, or correct their understanding of work performance during routine work contacts.' It is the best way to manage performance. But it is still useful to have a formal review once or twice yearly. It is a focal point and a 'stocktaking' opportunity for the consideration of key performance and development issues and provides the basis for performance and development planning and agreements. This chapter covers:

- the process of reviewing performance;
- a description of the formal performance review process;
- problems with performance reviews;
- preparing for review meetings;
- self-assessment;
- conducting a performance review meeting.

The process of reviewing performance

Informal reviews are the process by which performance is managed throughout the year. Performance is reviewed as it occurs by the individual as well as the manager, comparing what happened with what should have happened. Informal feedback can take place whenever a manager comments on a piece of work or an action taken by an individual at work: 'Well done'; 'That's exactly what I wanted'; 'Could we discuss another way of doing this next time?'; 'Something seems to be going wrong. Let's discuss why and what can be done about it.'

Whenever appropriate, managers meet individual members of their teams to provide feedback, initiate coaching or other learning activities, and agree on revised goals or any corrective action required. The outcome of such meetings may not be formally documented unless action to deal with poor performance through a capability procedure is invoked. However, managers may take notes for reference when preparing to conduct a formal review meeting.

Formal reviews are meetings in which performance is analysed more systematically. They include an overview and analysis of performance since the last review, comparing results with agreed expectations and plans. Reference may be made to events that illustrate performance as discussed during the year (they shouldn't be brought up at a formal meeting for the first time). The level of performance achieved is assessed so that individuals know where they stand, and in many cases it is rated. Formal reviews are usually documented on paper or recorded on a computer. They can provide the basis for decisions on performance pay, promotion, inclusion in talent management development programmes, training, performance and development plans, and action to deal with poor performance (although the latter is best carried out at the time rather than waiting for an annual review).

All this happens on a one-to-one basis – a get-together of the manager and the individual. This should be a conversation involving dialogue and joint analysis of performance. It should be constructive and forward-looking, not a top-down judgemental affair. Ron Collard, as a Vice-President of the Institute of Personnel and Development, told the true story of an individual who, stopping his car next to that of his boss at a set of traffic lights one day, was surprised to see the boss gesticulating at him to wind down the car window. He duly did so and was even more amazed when the boss said: 'It's appraisal time – I'll put you down for a "3"… OK!' As Ron commented, it's no wonder that performance management gets such a bad name.

The performance review process (Strebler, Bevan and Robertson, 2001)

The performance review process should:

- have clear aims and measurable success criteria;
- be designed and implemented with appropriate employee involvement;
- have its effective use core to all managers' performance goals;
- allow employees a clear 'line of sight' between their performance goals and those of the organization;
- focus on clarity and performance improvement;
- be closely allied to a clear and adequately resourced training and development infrastructure;
- make crystal clear the purpose of any direct link to reward and build in proper equity and transparency standards;
- be regularly and openly reviewed against its success criteria.

The formal performance review meeting

The formal performance review meeting is the means through which the five primary performance management elements of agreement, measurement, feedback, reinforcement and dialogue can be put to good use.

The review should be rooted in the reality of the employee's performance. It is concrete, not abstract, and it allows managers and individuals to take a positive look together at how performance can be developed in the future and how any problems in achieving goals and meeting performance standards can be resolved. Individuals should be encouraged to assess their own performance and become active agents for change in developing that performance. Managers should be encouraged to adopt their proper enabling role: coaching and providing support and guidance.

There should be no surprises in a formal review if performance issues have been dealt with as they should have been – as they arise during the year. Traditional appraisals are often no more than an analysis of where those involved are now, and where they have come from. This static and historical approach is not what performance management is about. The true role of performance management is to look forward to what needs to be done by people to achieve the purpose of the job, to meet new challenges, to make even better use of their knowledge, skills and abilities, to develop their capabilities by establishing a self-managed learning agenda, and to reach agreement on any areas where performance needs to be developed and how that development should take place. This process also helps managers to improve their ability to lead, guide and develop the individuals and teams for whom they are responsible.

The most common practice is to have one annual review (65 per cent of respondents to the 2004 CIPD survey). Twice-yearly reviews were held by 27 per cent of the respondents. These reviews lead directly to the conclusion of a performance agreement (at the same meeting or later). It can be argued that formal reviews are unnecessary and that it is better to conduct informal reviews as part of normal good management practice to be carried out as and when required. Such informal reviews are valuable as part of the continuing process of performance management (managing performance throughout the year). But there is much to be said for an annual or half-yearly review that sums up the conclusions reached at earlier reviews and provides a firm foundation for a new performance agreement and a framework for reviewing performance informally, whenever appropriate.

Goal

In practice, when managers start to coach, most of the role involves asking questions that will help individuals work out for themselves what their goal is. To aid this process, a list of questions is usually provided, with the goal usually being one of the objectives or the performance criteria standard. Like the main objectives, all goals need to be SMART.

Other examples of how performance reviews are carried out in DHL, Hitachi UK and the Royal College of Nursing are given in Appendix B.

Problems with formal performance reviews

In traditional merit rating or performance appraisal schemes the annual appraisal meeting was the key event – in fact, in most cases the only event – in the system. Line managers were often highly sceptical about a process that they felt was imposed on them by the personnel department. A typical reaction was: 'Not another new appraisal scheme! The last three didn't work.' Managers felt that the schemes had nothing to do with their own needs and existed simply to maintain the personnel database. Too often the personnel department contributed to this belief by adopting a 'policing' approach to the system, concerning themselves more with collecting completed forms and checking that each box has been ticked properly than with helping managers to use the process to improve individual and organizational performance.

When McGregor (1957) took an 'uneasy look' at performance appraisal many years ago, he commented that managers shied away from it because they did not like sitting in judgement on their subordinates – 'playing at being God'. In his seminal book on the appraisal interview Maier (1958) suggested that for managers to attempt to give negative feedback and help subordinates develop their performance in the same interview could present difficulties unless very carefully handled.

Three main sources of difficulty in conducting performance reviews were identified in one of the earliest articles on performance management by Beer and Ruh (1976):

- the quality of the relationship between the manager and the individual – unless there is mutual trust and understanding the perception of both parties may be that the performance review is a daunting experience in which hostility and resistance are likely to emerge;
- the manner and the skill with which the interview is conducted;
- the review process itself – its purpose, methodology and documentation.

Performance review issues

- Why have them at all?
- If they are necessary, what are the objectives of reviewing performance?
- What are the organizational issues?
- On whom should performance reviews focus?
- On what should they focus?
- What criteria should be used to review performance?
- What impact does management style make on performance reviews?
- What skills are required to conduct reviews and how can they be developed?
- How can both negative and positive elements be handled?
- How can reviews be used to promote good communications?
- How should the outputs of review meetings be handled?
- To what extent is past performance a guide to future potential?
- When should reviews take place?
- What are the main problems in conducting reviews and how can they be overcome?
- How can their effectiveness be evaluated?

Why have performance reviews?

The answer to this question is, of course, that managers have no choice. Reviewing perform-ance is an inherent part of their role. The question should be rephrased as: 'Are formal reviews necessary as a performance management activity to supplement the continuous informal process of monitoring performance?'

The argument for a formal review is that it provides a focal point for the consideration of key performance, motivational and development issues. It is a means for considering the future in the light of an understanding of the past. It answers the two fundamental questions of 'Where have we got to?' and 'Where are we going?' It gives managers with their teams and the indi-vidual members of their staff the opportunity to pause after the hurly-burly of everyday life and reflect on the key issues of personal development and performance improvement. It is a means of ensuring that two-way communication on issues concerning work can take place, and it provides the basis for future work and development plans. Formal reviews do not sup-plement informal or interim progress reviews but they can complement and enhance them and therefore have an important part to play in performance management. In a sense, they are stock-taking exercises that take note of what has been happening in order to plan what is going to happen. A formal review is also necessary if performance has to be rated for performance-related pay purposes.

Objectives of performance reviews

The objectives of reviewing performance are as follows:

- Planning – to provide the basis for re-formulating the performance agreement and the performance and development plans incorporated in it.

- Motivation – to provide positive feedback, recognition, praise and opportunities for growth; to clarify expectations; to empower people by encouraging them to take control over their own performance, learning and development.

- Learning and development – to provide a basis for self-managed learning and the development through coaching and other learning activities of the abilities relevant both to the current role and any future role the employee may have the potential to carry out. Note that learning and development includes focusing on the current role, enabling people to enlarge and enrich the range of their responsibilities and the skills they require and be rewarded accordingly. This aspect of role development is even more important in flatter organizations where career ladders have shortened and where lateral progression is likely to be the best route forward.

- Communication – to serve as a two-way channel for communication about roles, expectations (objectives and competency requirements), relationships, work problems and aspirations.

Reviews can also provide the basis for assessing performance, especially if ratings are required for performance or contribution-related pay although there are arguments against over-mechanistic rating procedures (assessment and rating are discussed in Chapter 11).

Organizational issues

To have any chance of success the objectives and methodology of performance reviews should either be in harmony with the organization's culture or be introduced deliberately as a lever for change, moving from a culture of management by command to one of management by consent. Performance management and review processes can help to achieve cultural change, but only if the change is managed vigorously from the top and every effort is made to bring managers and staff generally on board through involvement in developing the process, through communication and through training.

If, however, an autocratic style of management is practised at the top and pervades the organization, a more circumspect approach might be necessary. Arguments have to be prepared to handle chief executives who say, firmly: 'I set the direction, I decide on the corporate objectives, only I am accountable for results to the shareholders, my word therefore goes. I am not in the business of managing by consent.' Remarks along these lines are not untypical, especially when the finance institutions are demanding a significant increase in the price/earnings ratio, or a hostile takeover bid is imminent. The best thing you can do is to argue as persuasively as possible that the achievement of corporate objectives is far more likely if people are fully committed to them, and that such commitment is more probable if they are given the opportunity of participating in setting their own objectives and even of influencing higher-level objectives if they can contribute to their formulation.

But if this argument fails you may have to accept that objectives will be cascaded down the organization as a top-down process. Even so, performance management can still operate effectively at the level of defining individual goals and competency levels and reviewing performance in relation to them, and at least it should give individuals some scope to comment on the objectives that have cascaded down as they apply to them. Some managers may continue to take an autocratic line, but others may accept the benefits of the joint approach that is fundamental to the philosophy of a complete process of performance management. This is where the HR function can foster cultural change by encouraging those who are moving in the right direction, pointing out the benefits to the laggards by reference to successful experiences elsewhere in the organization and finally, and importantly, convincing the head of the organization, if she/he needs to be convinced, that the whole process will add value and contribute significantly to bottom-line organizational performance.

In short, when introducing performance management you cannot work against the culture of the organization. You have to work within it, but you can still aspire to develop a performance culture, and performance management provides you with a means of doing so.

On whom should performance reviews focus?

Many performance management and review 'systems' seem to focus almost exclusively on the upper and lower extremes of the performance distribution, neglecting the core of middle-of-the-road performers on whom the organization relies to function effectively in its day-to-day operations and to sustain itself in the future.

This is illogical because exceptional performance is unlikely to go unrecognized and very poor performance should be equally obvious. From the point of view of both motivating and keeping people, the majority of employees who are in the middle of the performance distribution should be given equal if not more attention.

On what should the performance review meeting focus?

There are two focus issues in performance review meetings: first, the emphasis that should be placed on performance improvement as distinct from broader developmental needs; second, the degree to which the meeting should be forward rather than backward looking.

A single-minded focus on performance improvement at the expense of broader issues is unlikely to produce much motivation. The focus should also be on the individual's learning and development needs, bearing in mind that no one is simply being prepared for vertical movement up the hierarchy. This means helping people to widen their range of abilities (multi-skilling in shop floor terms) to enable them to meet the demands of future change and the additional activities they may be required to carry out. In this way employability both within and outside the organization can be enhanced. This particularly applies to the core of middle-of-the-road performers.

Performance review meetings that are used or are perceived as being there simply to generate ratings for performance-related pay purposes will almost inevitably fail to achieve what should be regarded as their most important objectives – to motivate and develop people.

The slogan that should be imprinted on the minds of all reviewers is that 'Yesterday is only useful if it teaches us about today and tomorrow.' The analysis of past performance is a necessary precursor to the preparation of performance and development plans for the future. But the tendency to dwell on the past rather than looking to the future must be avoided if the review is going to make any positive motivational impact.

What criteria should be used?

The criteria for assessing performance should be balanced between:

- achievements in relation to goals;
- the level of knowledge and skills possessed and applied (competences);
- behaviour in the job as it affects performance (competencies);
- the degree to which behaviour upholds the core values of the organization;
- day-to-day effectiveness.

The criteria should not be limited to a few quantified objectives, as has often been the case in traditional appraisal schemes. In many cases the most important consideration will be the job holders' day-to-day effectiveness in meeting the continuing performance standards associated with their key tasks. It may not be possible to agree meaningful new quantified targets for some jobs every year. As much attention needs to be given to the behaviour that has produced the results as to the results themselves.

The impact of management style

Most managers have their own management style and are reasonably well aware of what it is. If it has worked well for them in the past they will not want to change it in a hurry. But how do managers with a highly directive style adjust their behaviour when they are expected to conduct review meetings on a participative, two-way basis? With difficulty, if at all, in some cases. Guidance and coaching will be required if managers are to handle successfully the potential dilemma of inconsistency between their normal behaviour and how they are expected to behave when conducting performance reviews.

Performance review skills

Conducting an effective performance review, especially one in which problems of under-performance have to be discussed, demands considerable skill on the part of the reviewer in such areas as giving feedback, agreeing objectives, assessing performance and development needs, planning for performance improvement and carrying on a dialogue.

One advantage of introducing an element of formality into the review process is that it high-lights the skills required to carry out both formal and informal reviews and emphasizes the role of the manager as a coach. These skills come naturally to some managers. Others, probably the majority, will benefit from guidance and coaching in these key aspects of their managerial roles.

Outcome issues

If individual employees who have taken part in performance review meetings are to be motivated and retained, the outcomes of the meetings have to be relevant and put into action. All too often, review meetings have been seen as ends in themselves. It is necessary to be clear about the range of outcomes that are wanted and can be handled. Besides performance development plans, these can include personal development plans, lateral job moves, job restructuring and secondments.

Almost worse than no outcomes is the situation when outcomes are agreed and written up but not followed through. Raising expectations that are not subsequently met is a prescription for demotivation and disenchantment. Reviewers need to be certain that they do not over-commit themselves or the organization. They also need to be sure about their own commitment, as well as that of the individual, to agreed outputs.

Enacting agreed outputs is a powerful demonstration of the organization's commitment to the individual.

Dealing with positive and negative elements

This is probably the area of greatest concern to line managers, many of whom do not like handing out criticisms. Performance reviews should not be regarded as an opportunity for attaching blame for things that have gone wrong in the past. If individuals have to be shown that they are accountable for failures to perform to standard or to reach targets, that should have been done at the time when the failure occurred, not saved up for the review meeting.

And the positive elements should not be neglected. Too often they are overlooked or mentioned briefly then put on one side. The following sequence is not untypical:

- Objective number one – fantastic.

- Objective number two – that was great.

- Objective number three – couldn't have been done better.

- Now objective number four – this is what we really need to talk about, what went wrong?

If this sort of approach is adopted, the discussion will focus on the failure, the negatives, and the individual will become defensive. This can be destructive and explains why some people feel that the annual review meeting is going to be a 'beat me over the head' session.

To underemphasize the positive aspects reduces the scope for action and motivation. More can be achieved by focusing on positives than by concentrating on the negatives. People are most receptive to the need for further learning when they are talking about their achievements. Empowering people is a matter of building on success.

But this does not mean that under-performance should go unnoticed. Specific problems may have been dealt with at the time but it may still be necessary to discuss where there has been a pattern of poor performance. The first step, and often the most difficult one, is to get people to agree that there is room for improvement. This will best be achieved if the discussion focuses on factual evidence of performance problems. Some people will never admit to being wrong and in those cases you may have to say in effect: 'here is the evidence; I have no doubt that this is correct; I am afraid you have to accept from me on the basis of this evidence that your performance in this respect has been unsatisfactory.' It is often useful to give examples of what is considered effective performance in the area under review for comparative purposes. If at all possible, the aim is not to blame people but to take a positive view based on obtaining answers to questions such as these:

- Why do you think this has been happening?

- What do you think you can do about it?

- How can I help?

Using reviews as a communications channel

A well-conducted review meeting provides 'quality time' in which individuals and their managers can discuss matters affecting work and future developments. They also provide an extra channel of communication.

Properly planned review meetings allow much more time and space for productive conversation and communication than is generally available to busy managers – this is perhaps one of their most important purposes.

There should be ample scope for communication about the organization's or department's objectives and how individuals fit into the picture – the contribution they are expected to make. Information can be given on significant events and changes in the organization that will impact on the role of the department and its members.

One of the objections that can be made to this free flow of information is that some of it will be confidential. But the need for confidentiality is often overstated. If the feeling is conveyed to people that they cannot be trusted with confidential information, it will not do much for their motivation.

The review meeting often presents a good opportunity for upward communication. This is the time to find out about how people feel about their jobs, their aspirations and their relationships with their peers and their managers. The opportunity a review meeting gives to people to stand back from everyday pressures and consider matters that concern them with a sense of perspective is an important benefit.

Balancing past performance against future potential

Traditionally, line managers have been asked to predict the potential for promotion of their subordinates. That has put them in a difficult position unless they have a good understanding of the requirements (key dimensions and capabilities) of the roles for which their staff may have potential. This is unlikely in many cases, although the development of 'career maps' setting out the capabilities required in different roles and at different levels can provide invaluable information.

In general terms, past performance is not necessarily a good predictor of potential unless it includes activities related to dimensions that are also present in the anticipated role.

Because of these problems, assessments of potential are now less frequently included as part of the performance review meeting. They are more often carried out as a separate exercise in a talent management programme, sometimes by means of assessment centres.

When should reviews be held?

The usual practice is to have an annual formal review that provides a basis for a new performance agreement and performance rating, if that is required. Some organizations hold all reviews at the same time, especially if they need a performance rating for pay purposes. The timing of the review can be linked to the corporate business or operational planning programme to ensure that teams and individuals can contribute to the formulation of departmental, and ultimately corporate, objectives and to provide for these team/individual objectives to flow from those finally determined at corporate, functional and departmental levels. The model of the performance management system at the Royal College of Nursing (Figure 14.8 in Chapter 14) shows how this can be done.

There may be some scope allowed for separate business units or functions to align performance reviews to their own business planning cycle or to carry them out at the time most convenient to them. There is much to be said for allowing the maximum degree of flexibility in order to meet the needs of line management rather than to conform to the bureaucratic requirements of the HR department.

Some organizations have required performance reviews to be conducted on the individual's birthday (or thereabouts) or on the anniversary of their joining the organization. This spreads the load for managers but it makes it impossible to fit the review into the annual planning cycle, which is highly desirable if the integration of individual/team objectives and corporate objectives is to be achieved.

If the formal performance review is spread over the year, but the company still conducts pay reviews at the same time annually, a separate assessment for such reviews would have to be carried out.

Corporate guidelines to managers on performance management often suggest that they should hold interim formal progress reviews during the year, say once a quarter or half-way through the review year. Such reviews could be incorporated into the normal work or project review process (eg the supervisory meetings held by social service departments) or they would be held at focal points as decided when preparing the performance plan.

Managers should be allowed to choose their own times for conducting such interim or informal reviews, although the importance of carrying them out and not waiting until the end of the year could be emphasized in guidance notes and training. To underline the voluntary and informal nature of such progress reviews it is best not to ask managers to complete standard review forms. They should be left to document them as they feel fit.

Some organizations require a formal performance review for new starters at the end of, say, six months or a probationary period, if that has been stipulated.

Performance review problems

The main problems that arise in conducting performance reviews are:

- identifying performance measures and criteria for evaluating performance;
- collecting factual evidence about performance;
- the existence of bias on the part of managers;
- resolving conflict between reviewers and the people they review;
- defensive behaviour exhibited by individuals in response to criticism.

There are no easy answers to these problems, no quick fixes. It is wise never to underestimate how hard it is for even experienced and effective managers to conduct productive performance review meetings. It was the facile assumption that this is a natural and not too difficult process that has bedevilled many performance appraisal schemes over the years. This assumption has certainly resulted in neglect of the need to provide adequate guidance and training for reviewing managers and, importantly, those whom they review.

The approaches described in this chapter for preparing for and conducting performance reviews can alleviate the problems listed above even if they cannot guarantee to eliminate them. In summary, these approaches are to:

- Ensure that the criteria for evaluating performance cover agreed goals (quantified wherever possible), competencies based upon proper role analysis and measures of day-to-day effectiveness, preferably stated as standards of performance. Ensure also that success criteria have been agreed and specific performance measures identified.

- Monitor performance throughout the year in relation to performance plans and agreed goals, performance standards and behavioural requirements (competencies). Use the success criteria and performance measures as the basis for monitoring progress. Ensure that there is feedback at the time based upon evidence (techniques of providing feedback were discussed in Chapter 8) and record any critical incidents as they occur to assist in an overall assessment of performance.

- Take steps to eliminate bias. If the review process does not involve the delivery of judgements in the form of performance ratings bias may not appear so obviously, but it can still exist in subtle ways. Mentors and training can alert individuals to the risk of bias and assessments can be monitored by the manager's manager and HR.

- Ensure that both managers and their staff understand the positive nature of the process. Train managers in the virtues of building on positives as well as how to provide constructive feedback that is based on fact and not on opinions about the employee's personality traits.

- Encourage a positive approach by managers so that by using constructive criticism rather than attaching blame, they can reduce defensive behaviour. Briefing for all those involved on the benefits of the process to both parties should also help. Getting individuals to assess their own performance (self-assessment, as discussed later in this chapter) is another way of reducing defensive behaviour.

Evaluating formal performance reviews

There is no doubt that in spite of careful training and guidance some managers will be better at conducting performance review meetings than others. So how can their effectiveness as performance reviewers be evaluated as a basis for further training or guidance when necessary?

Traditionally, the personnel department had a policing role – checking that performance appraisal forms were completed on time and filled in properly. However, this will convey nothing about the quality of the meeting or the feelings of individuals after it; they may have signed the form stating they agree with its comments but this does not reveal what they really thought about the process.

Another approach is to get the manager's manager (the so-called 'grandparent') to review the form. This at least provides the individual who has been reported on with the comfort of knowing that a prejudiced report may be rejected or amended by a higher authority. But it still does not solve the problem of a negative or biased review process that would probably not be conveyed in a written report.

Space on the review form can be given to individuals to comment on the review, but many will feel unwilling to do so. If the interview has been conducted in an intimidating manner, how ready are they likely to be to commit themselves to open criticism?

Another, potentially more productive, approach is to conduct an attitude survey following performance reviews asking individuals in confidence to answer questions about their review meeting such as:

- How well did your manager conduct your performance review meeting?

- Are there any specific aspects of the way in which the review was conducted that could be improved?

- How did you feel at the end of it?

- How are you feeling at the moment about your job and the challenges ahead of you?

- How much help are you getting from your manager in developing your skills and abilities?

The results of such a survey, a form of upward assessment, can be fed back anonymously to individual managers, and possibly their superiors, and action can be taken to provide further guidance, coaching or formal training. A general analysis of the outcome can be used to identify any common failings that can be dealt with by more formal training workshops. Evaluation of performance management processes is dealt with more fully in Chapter 24.

Analysis of the issues

Effective performance review training and processes are not likely to happen unless the issues referred to above have been thoroughly analysed. This analysis should be used as the basis for designing training programmes and developing guidelines on preparing for and conducting reviews as described below.

Preparing for formal review meetings

Review meetings are likely to be much more effective if both parties – the manager and the individual – have prepared for them carefully. The extent to which detailed preparation is needed will vary according to the type of review. More care would need to be taken for a formal annual review, and the approach suggested below is aimed at such occasions. But the same principles would apply, albeit less formally, to interim reviews.

Preparation should be concerned with:

- the purpose and points to be covered at the meeting;
- what evidence on performance the manager should get ready for the meeting;
- what the individual should do in the way of self-assessment.

Purpose and points to be covered

The purpose of a review meeting would be defined as being to:

- provide an opportunity for a frank, open but non-threatening discussion about the individual's performance and learning and development needs;
- give the individual a chance to discuss her/his aspirations and any work problems;
- focus the attention of both the individual and the manager on objectives and plans for the future (ie provide the basis for the next performance agreement or plan).

The things to do at a performance review meeting (it is probably best not to over-formalize this list by calling it an agenda) are set out below.

What to do in a performance review meeting

- Discuss achievements in relation to objectives and performance/development plans.
- Assess the level of competence achieved against the headings and descriptors in the individual's role definition.
- Discuss the extent to which the individual's behaviour is in accord with the organization's core values.
- Identify any problems in achieving agreed objectives or standards of performance.
- Establish the reasons for such problems, including any factors beyond the individual's control as well as those that can be attributed to the individual's behaviour.
- Discuss any other problems relating to work and the individual's relationships with his/her manager, colleagues and, if appropriate, subordinates.
- Agree on any actions required to overcome problems.
- Agree on any changes to the role profile in terms of key result areas or key tasks and competency requirements that might be necessary.
- Review and revise performance measures (standards) as necessary.

Preparation for the meeting

The manager should initiate the main formal review meeting by letting the individual know some time in advance (two weeks or so) when it is going to take place. A period of about two uninterrupted hours should be allowed for the meeting.

The manager should discuss with the individual the purpose of the meeting and the points to be covered. The aim should be, as far as possible, to emphasize the positive nature of the process and to dispel any feelings of trepidation on the part of the individual. The manager should also suggest that the individual prepares for the meeting along the lines described below.

The basis for preparation by managers should be the objectives, standards, competency requirements and plans agreed at the last main review as amended during the year. Achievements should be assessed by the application of appropriate performance measures. Any other evidence of good or not-so-good performance should also be assembled. Reference should be made to any notes made during or following interim review meetings about the individual's performance. Alterations to the individual's role since the last review should be noted. Consideration should be given to any changes in internal organizational, divisional or departmental circumstances that may have affected the definition and achievement of objectives. External pressure that may have affected performance and outcomes should also be noted. A preparation checklist is given in the performance management toolkit in Appendix A.

Individuals should prepare for the meeting by carrying out a process of self-assessment as described below.

Self-assessment

Self-assessment is a process in which individuals review their own performance, using a structured approach, as the basis for discussions with their managers in review meetings. On the whole people are surprisingly realistic when they do this, as long as their assessment is not going to contribute directly to a performance-related pay decision. In fact, some people underestimate themselves, which makes it even easier for their manager to take a positive approach.

Self-assessment involves analysing performance and identifying successes and any problems in achieving goals. Individuals may attribute any problems to lack of skill or experience and should be encouraged to be specific so that a personal development plan can be prepared. They may also comment on a lack of adequate support from their manager or colleagues, insufficient resources, unattainable objectives or any other factor beyond their control that they believe has affected their performance. The structure for self-assessment can be provided by a self-assessment check list that is given to individuals before the review meeting. An example is provided in the performance management toolkit in Appendix A.

Advantages of self-assessment

The main advantage of using a self-assessment approach is that it reduces defensiveness by allowing individuals to take the lead in reviewing their own performance rather than having their managers' judgements thrust upon them. It therefore helps to generate a more positive and constructive discussion during the review meeting, which can focus on joint problem-solving rather than attaching blame. In addition, it encourages people to think about their own development needs and how they can improve their own performance, and provides for a more balanced assessment because it is based on the views of both the manager and the individual rather than those of the manager alone

Problems of self-assessment

Self-assessment can allow employees to take the lead but the aim of the review meeting remains that of achieving an agreed joint assessment and a development plan. Managers have therefore to contribute and, as necessary, add to the views expressed by employees. They should also be prepared to allow employees in effect to criticize them for lack of support, providing inadequate resources or setting unachievable standards. Many managers may be unwilling to accept such criticisms and many employees may be unwilling to make them for fear of their managers' reactions. Steps can be taken to overcome this problem by education, guidance and example, but realistically, this may be difficult.

There is still room for confrontation if managers bluntly disagree, and it may require considerable skill on their part to persuade employees to reconsider their self-assessment. This can be achieved by good reviewers, but it means taking care to handle the situation by asking further questions or presenting additional facts rather than simply expressing an adverse opinion that is unsupported by evidence.

As mentioned earlier, many people can be surprisingly realistic in assessing their own performance, but some will overestimate their abilities and they need to be handled carefully.

Requirements for success

Incorporating self-assessment as part of a performance management/review process is most likely to be successful when all concerned fully understand the purpose of self-assessment and both managers and employees understand their respective roles in the review meeting and how they should be carried out. Employees need guidance on how to carry out self-assessments, and both managers and employees need training in conducting reviews based on self-assessment, especially on joint problem-solving methods.

Self-assessment is directed to the future motivation and development of the employee and should not be used simply as the basis for raking over past problems, although it should be recognized that the analysis of any such problems will provide guidance on the way ahead.

Clearly, self-assessments should not be taken directly into account when making pay, promotion or disciplinary decisions.

Conducting a formal performance review meeting

There are golden rules for conducting formal performance review meetings:

- Be prepared. Managers should prepare by referring to a list of agreed goals and their notes on performance throughout the year. They should form views about the reasons for success or failure and decide where to give praise, which performance problems should be mentioned and what steps might be undertaken to overcome them. Thought should also be given to any changes that have taken place or are contemplated in the individual's role and to work and personal objectives for the next period. Individuals should also prepare in order to identify achievements and problems, and to be ready to assess their own performance at the meeting. They should also note any points they wish to raise about their work and prospects.

- Work to a clear structure. The meeting should be planned to cover all the points identified during preparation. Sufficient time should be allowed for a full discussion – hurried meetings will be ineffective. An hour or two is usually necessary to get maximum value from the review.

- Create the right atmosphere. A successful meeting depends on creating an informal environment in which a full, frank but friendly exchange of views can take place. It is best to start with a fairly general discussion that aims to put the individual at ease and create a non-threatening atmosphere and that covers the purpose of the meeting, emphasizing that it is a joint affair before getting into any detail.

- Provide good feedback. Individuals need to know how they are getting on. Feedback needs to based on factual evidence and careful thought should be given to what is said and how it is said so that it motivates rather than demotivates people. Techniques of giving feedback – a key aspect of the meeting – are described at the end of this chapter.

- Use time productively. The reviewer should test understanding, seek information, and seek proposals and support. Time should be allowed for the individual to express his or her views fully and to respond to any comments made by the manager. The meeting should take the form of a dialogue between two interested and involved parties both of whom are seeking a positive conclusion.

- Use praise. If possible, managers should begin with praise for some specific achievement, but this should be sincere and deserved. Praise helps people to relax – everyone needs encouragement and appreciation.

- Let individuals do most of the talking. This enables then to get things off their chest and helps them to feel that they are getting a fair hearing. Use open-ended questions (ie questions that invite the individual to think about what to reply rather than indicating the expected answer). This will encourage people to expand.

- Invite self-assessment. This is to see how things look from the individual's point of view and to provide a basis for discussion – many people underestimate themselves.

- Ask questions such as:
    - How well do you feel you have done?
    - What do you feel are your strengths?
    - What do you like most/least about your job?
    - Why do you think that project went well?
    - Why do you think you didn't meet that target?

- Discuss performance not personality – discussions on performance should be based on factual evidence, not opinion. Always refer to actual events or behaviour and to results compared with agreed performance measures. Individuals should be given plenty of scope to explain why something did or did not happen.

- Encourage analysis of performance – don't just hand out praise or blame. Analyse jointly and objectively why things went well or badly and what can be done to maintain a high standard or to avoid problems in the future.

- Don't deliver unexpected criticisms – there should be no surprises. The discussion should only be concerned with events or behaviours that have been noted at the time they took place. Feedback on performance should be immediate; it should not wait until the end of the year. The purpose of the formal review is to reflect briefly on experiences during the review period and on this basis to look ahead.

- Agree measurable objectives and a plan of action – the aim should be to end the review meeting on a positive note.

These golden rules may sound straightforward and obvious enough but they will only function properly in a culture that supports this type of approach. This is why it is essential to get and keep top management support and to take special care in developing and introducing the system and in training managers and their staff.

A problem-solving approach

The answers to these checklist questions provide an agenda for the review meeting in which individuals take the lead and managers respond as appropriate. The aim is to adopt a problem-solving approach. The role of managers is to comment on and sometimes add to the individuals' self-assessment. They should avoid confrontation – that is, total disagreement with the individuals' opinions – and should preferably ask exploratory questions such as those listed below.

Examples of questions posed by the manager during a review meeting

- Why do you feel like that?
- Why do you think that happened?
- Have you taken into account such and such an event?
- The information I have is that you have not consistently achieved the performance standard for this particular task we agreed last year. Here are some examples. How did this happen?
- Do you think there are any other causes of this problem?
- Do you think you have contributed to this problem?
- Are there any other issues or problems you have not mentioned?
- How are we going to make sure that this problem does not occur again in the future?

This approach enables the review to be constructive. It is conducted on a joint problem-solving basis, focusing on the identification and exploration of the key problems facing the employee and encouraging him or her to think through the issues involved. The manager will provide feedback, but this is constructive feedback in that it is aimed at encouraging the employee to work out for himself or herself what needs to be done, with the support or help of the manager.

11

Analysing and Assessing Performance

Performance management is forward-looking. It focuses on planning for the future rather than dwelling on the past. But it also takes into account when making these plans what has been achieved and, more importantly, how it has been achieved. Performance needs to be analysed prior to planning. And the analysis has to be based on reliable evidence, not opinion or hearsay.

Performance management is therefore an analytical process, especially when its purpose is developmental. But when its purpose is to provide an aid to decision making – on pay, promotion or retention – performance needs to be assessed and this often involves some form of rating. Much of this chapter therefore deals with rating through the use of rating scales but alternative approaches are also discussed. However, introductory sections examine the concept of evidence-based performance management and the analytical nature of performance management to provide a background to the more detailed review of assessment methods. These are followed by sections on:

- the process of rating;
- the rationale for rating;
- rating scales;
- forced distribution;
- behaviourally anchored rating scales;
- behavioural observation scales;
- problems with rating;
- alternatives to rating, namely: the critical incidence technique, visual methods of assessment and narrative assessment.

Evidence-based performance management

As defined by Rousseau (2006): 'Evidence-based management means translating principles based on best evidence into organizational practices. Through evidence-based management, practising managers develop into experts informed by social science and organizational research.' Founding performance management practices on the evidence obtained from research projects such as those quoted in this book is therefore in one sense evidence-based performance management. But in another broader sense, the practice of performance management at organizational, team or individual level is best carried out by reference to factual evidence on performance and the outcomes of behaviour. The purpose of performance analysis is to locate this evidence and draw inferences from it on the factors affecting performance and what needs to be done about them. Evidence may be available in the form of measures or metrics but these are not enough. It is necessary to penetrate behind the façade presented by the figures to elicit the facts, events and actions that underpin them.

Analysing performance

In his seminal article 'An uneasy look at performance appraisal', Douglas McGregor (1957) suggested that the emphasis should be shifted from appraisal to analysis. The article was written a long time ago but its message is just as relevant today, and the persistence of the concept of top-down judgemental appraisal in many organizations suggests that there is still much to be learnt from McGregor in this area, as in a lot of others.

Douglas McGregor on analysing performance

This [the shift to analysis] implies a more positive approach. No longer is the subordinate being examined by the superior so that his [sic] weaknesses may be determined; rather he is examining himself in order to define not only his weaknesses but also his strengths and potentials... He becomes an active agent, not a passive 'object'.

McGregor was also the first commentator to emphasize that the focus should be on the future rather than the past in order to establish realistic targets and to seek the best means of reaching them.

The problem of performance analysis

Assessments require the ability to judge performance, and good judgement is a matter of using clear standards, considering only relevant evidence, combining probabilities in their correct weight and avoiding projection (ascribing to other people one's own faults).

Most managers think they are good judges of people. One seldom if ever meets anyone who admits to being a poor judge, just as one seldom meets anyone who admits to being a bad driver, although accident rates suggest that bad drivers do exist and mistakes in selection, placement and promotion indicate that some managers are worse than others in judging people. Different managers will assess the same people very differently unless, with difficulty, a successful attempt to moderate their views is made. This is because managers assessing the same people will tend to assess them against different standards. Managers may jump to conclusions or make snap judgements if they are just required to appraise and rate people rather than to conduct a proper analysis of performance. Other problems include poor perception (not noticing things or events for what they are), selectivity (relying on partial data and noticing only things one wants to see) and poor interpretation (putting one's own, possibly biased, slant on information). This can lead to what O'Malley (2003) refers to as Type I and Type II errors. A Type I error occurs when the conclusion is that there are no differences in employees' performance when in fact there are. Conversely, a Type II error is concluding that there are differences when there are none.

Overriding all these problems is the likelihood that managers and employees are unsure what good or poor performance looks like and cannot recognize either when they meet them. The notion of performance is a vague one. Is it simply what some one produces – their output? Or is it how they produce it – their behaviour? Or is it both? It is, in fact, both, but this is not recognized by everyone, which results in suspect assessments.

The approach to performance analysis

To overcome these problems it is necessary to:

- ensure that the concept of performance is understood by all concerned, managers and employees alike, which means appreciating what constitutes good and not so good performance and how it should be measured and analysed;

- encourage managers to define and agree standards and measures of effectiveness beforehand with those concerned as a basis for analysis;

- encourage and train people to avoid jumping to conclusions too quickly by consciously suspending judgement until all the relevant data available has been analysed;

- provide managers with practice in exercising judgements that enable them to find out for themselves where they need to improve their performance analysis techniques;

- adopt an evidence-based management approach.

Analysis leads to some form of assessment, which is typically carried out by rating as described below although there are other approaches as considered later in the chapter.

The process of rating

The e-reward 2005 survey of performance management found that 70 per cent of respondents used overall ratings. Since the days of merit rating and then performance appraisal rating still reigns supreme. To many people it was and is the ultimate purpose and the final outcome of performance appraisal. Academics, especially American academics, have been preoccupied with rating – what it is, how to do it, how to improve it, how to train raters – for the last 50 years. Many problems with rating have been identified but it doesn't seem to have occurred to them that these could readily be overcome if rating weren't used at all.

The theory of rating

The theory underpinning all rating methods is that it is possible as well as desirable to measure the performance of people on a scale accurately and consistently and categorize them accordingly. As DeNisi and Pritchard (2006) comment: 'Effective performance appraisal systems are those where the raters have the ability to measure employee performance and the motivation to assign the most accurate ratings.'

Murphy and Cleveland (1995) distinguished between judgement and ratings. A judgement is a relatively private evaluation of a person's performance in some area. Ratings are a public statement of a judgement evaluation that is made for the record. But ratings do not always correspond with judgements and raise other issues as discussed later.

A theory of the rating process (Wherry and Bartlett, 1982)

- Raters vary in the accuracy of ratings given in direct proportion to the relevancy of their previous contacts with the person being rated.

- Rating items that refer to frequently performed acts are rated more accurately than those that refer to acts performed more rarely.

- The rater makes more accurate ratings when forewarned of the behaviours to be rated because this focuses attention on the particular behaviours.

- Deliberate direction to the behaviours to be assessed reduces rating bias.

- Keeping a written record between rating periods of specifically observed critical incidents improves the accuracy of recall.

Research conducted on rating has produced a number of findings that supplement this theory. Pulakos, Mueller-Hanson and O'Leary (2008) noted that ratings for decision making (eg on performance pay) tend to be higher than ratings for development, which tend to be variable, reflecting both employee strengths and development needs. They also commented that if the system is used for decision making, numerical ratings are important. If a system is strictly developmental, there is less need for ratings and in fact they may detract from development. This is because employees tend to be more concerned about their 'score' than their understanding of their development needs. From a development perspective, narratives tend to provide more useful information than numerical ratings. Even when performance is rated against defined standards the ratings do not convey what the employee did or did not do in sufficient detail. Jawahar and Williams (1997) reported that performance evaluations such as ratings obtained for administrative purposes (eg pay or promotions) are more lenient than those for research, feedback or employee development purposes.

One of the issues concerning assessment is the degree to which receivers accept what the reviewer says about them. Research by Roberts (1994) indicated that acceptance is maximized when the performance measurement process is perceived to be accurate, the system is administered fairly, the assessment system doesn't conflict with the employee's values and when the assessment process does not exceed the bounds of the psychological contract.

What reviewers should do to increase acceptance of assessments (Roberts, 1994)

- Pay less attention to mechanics and place more emphasis on process.
- Avoid basing conclusions on a small number of instances.
- Learn to seek information on external factors that may influence performance.
- Document employee performance.
- Involve individuals in the process through a genuine invitation to participate.
- Appreciate that reviewers do not have all the relevant performance information and that the employee is an important source.
- Encourage self-appraisal.
- Provide regular informal feedback bearing in mind that once-a-year performance appraisal is unlikely to meet employee feedback requirements.

Silverman, Kerrin and Carter (2005) reported that many studies have demonstrated that performance ratings become more positive over time, which was confirmed by Fletcher (2001). However, although this may suggest performance improvement it could simply arise because raters become complacent or careless or both.

Strebler, Bevan and Robertson (2001) commented that: 'The psychometric properties of the rating process – ie whether achieved ratings are valid and a true measure of actual performance – is the most researched aspect of performance assessment.' Their research established in one care organization that people became focused around the review headings (a little like wasps around jam) for the sole purpose of getting points (and points mean prizes) rather than improving the quality of care they delivered.

Rating scales

Rating scales indicate the level of performance or competency achieved or displayed by an employee. This is done by selecting the point on a scale that most closely corresponds with the view of the assessor on how well the individual has been doing. A rating scale is supposed to assist in making judgements and it enables those judgements to be categorized to inform performance or contribution pay decisions or simply to produce an instant summary for the record.

Types of rating scales

Rating scales can be defined alphabetically (a, b, c etc), or numerically (1, 2, 3 etc). Initials (ex for excellent etc) are sometimes used in an attempt to disguise the hierarchical nature of the scale. The alphabetical or numerical scale points may be described adjectivally, for example, a = excellent, b = good, c = satisfactory and d = unsatisfactory.

Alternatively, scale levels may be described verbally as in the following example:

- Exceptional performance: Exceeds expectations and consistently makes an outstanding contribution that significantly extends the impact and influence of the role.

- Well-balanced performance: Meets objectives and requirements of the role, consistently performs in a thoroughly proficient manner.

- Barely effective performance: Does not meet all objectives or role requirements of the role; significant performance improvements are needed.

- Unacceptable performance: Fails to meet most objectives or requirements of the role; shows a lack of commitment to performance improvement, or a lack of ability that has been discussed prior to the performance review.

Positive–negative definitions

Traditionally, definitions have regressed downwards from a highly positive, eg 'exceptional', description to a negative, eg 'unsatisfactory', definition as in the following typical example:

A. Outstanding performance in all respects.

B. Superior performance, significantly above normal job requirements.

C. Good all round performance that meets the normal requirements of the job.

D. Performance not fully up to requirements. Clear weaknesses requiring improvement have been identified.

E. Unacceptable; constant guidance is required and performance of many aspects of the job is well below a reasonable standard.

Positive definitions

An alternative and increasingly popular approach is to have a rating scale that provides positive reinforcement or at least emphasizes the need for improvement at lower levels. This is in line with a culture of continuous improvement. The example given below emphasizes the positive and improvable nature of individual performance.

- Very effective: Meets all the objectives of the job. Exceeds required standards and consistently performs in a thoroughly proficient manner beyond normal expectations.

- Effective: Achieves required objectives and standards of performance and meets the normal expectations of the role.

- Developing: A contribution that is stronger in some aspects of the job than others, where most objectives are met but where performance improvements should still take place.

- Basic: A contribution that indicates that there is considerable room for improvement in several definable areas.

Positive definitions aim to avoid the use of terminology for middle-ranking but entirely acceptable performers such as 'satisfactory' or 'competent', which seem to be damning people with faint praise.

Some organizations use the term 'improvable' for the 'basic' category on this list. Others have included 'learner/achiever' or 'unproven/too soon to tell' categories for new entrants to a grade for whom it is too early to give a realistic assessment.

This scale deliberately avoids including an 'unacceptable' rating or its equivalent on the grounds that if someone's performance is totally unacceptable and unimprovable this should have been identified during the continuous process of performance management and corrective action initiated at the time. This is not an action that can be delayed for several months until the next review when a negative formal rating is given, which may be too demotivating or too late. If action at the time fails to remedy the problem, the employee may be dealt with under a capability procedure and the normal performance review suspended unless and until the problem is overcome. However, the capability procedure should still provide for performance reviews to assess the extent to which the requirements set out in the informal or formal warnings have been met. Note also that in order to dispel any unfortunate associations with other systems such as school reports, this 'positive' scale does not include alphabetic or numerical ratings.

Number of rating levels

There is a choice of the number of levels – there can be three, four, five or even six levels as described below. The e-reward (2005) survey found that the most popular number of levels was five (43 per cent of respondents).

Advocates of three grades contend that people are not capable of making any finer distinctions between performance levels. They know the really good and poor performers when they see them and have no difficulty in placing the majority where they belong, namely in the middle category. The following is an example of a three-category scheme used by a large financial services company in which the definitions of levels are more comprehensive than usual.

A three-category rating scheme

Fulfilling expectations

In order to fulfil the expectations agreed for your role, you and your manager will agree at your review how you have:

- worked with others and developed yourself;
- followed through processes and made improvements;
- met the needs of internal/external customers;
- achieved key financial and business results.

The expectations are stretching and demanding and if you achieve them you will have done well and made a full and balanced contribution that has delivered the requirements of the business.

The majority of staff achieve what we expect of them and are currently assessed at this level – we expect this to continue in the future.

Exceeding expectations

People who exceed the expectations agreed for their role will be exceptional for two reasons:

- Expectations of all of us are generally stretching and rise over time, so to have exceeded them denotes an approach that has added value beyond these normal high standards.
- Performance is assessed not only in the job but also compared to colleagues doing similar jobs, so a clearly differentiated contribution will have been made.

People who exceed expectations can therefore expect higher pay awards and faster salary progression.

Not fulfilling expectations

We hope that there will not be many people who do not fulfil expectations. Such people will be counselled and supported to improve their performance but if, in the end, their contribution has not met the requirements of the business, they can expect to receive a smaller pay rise or no pay rise at all.

Those who prefer more than three grades take the opposite but equally subjective view that raters do want to make finer distinctions and feel uncomfortable at dividing people into superior (average or above average) sheep, and inferior (below average) goats. They prefer intermediate categories in a five-point scale or a wider range of choice in a four- or six-point scale.

The advocates of a larger number of points on the scale also claim that this assists in making the finer distinctions required in a performance-related pay system. But this argument is only sustainable if it is reasonably certain that managers are capable of making such fine distinctions (and there is no evidence that they can) and, where relevant, that these can be equitably reflected in meaningful pay increase differentials.

Five-level scales are the most common arrangement. Typically, they provide for two superior performance levels, a fully satisfactory level and two shades of less than capable performance. The rationale is that raters prefer this degree of fineness in performance definition and can easily recognize the middle grade and distinguish those who fall into higher or lower categories. It is also in accord with the typical way in which the normal curve of distribution is expressed, where the middle category includes 60 per cent of the population, the next higher or lower categories each comprise 15 per cent of the population and the remaining 10 per cent is distributed equally between the highest and lowest category. This normal curve was originally applied to the distribution of intelligence in the form of IQs (intelligence quotients). It was believed that general ability is also distributed in the same pattern. However, this is a highly questionable assumption, which has not been substantiated by research. When confronted with a five-level scale raters can be tempted to over-concentrate on the middle rating and avoid discriminating sufficiently between superior and inferior performers. Alternatively, five-level scales can lead to 'rating drift' – a tendency to push ratings into higher categories. This can only be avoided by carefully wording the level descriptions to ensure that the middle category is used appropriately and by training managers in rating methodology.

Four-level scales are sometimes used, often with positive definitions as in the example given above. They provide for finer distinctions than a three-level scale while helping to avoid the problems inherent in five-level scales of either central tendency or rating drift.

The rationale for a six-level scale is that it gives a wider range and, like the four-level scale, eliminates the tendency in five-level scales either to pick mainly the central rating or to give in to the temptation to drift upwards from it. Another perceived benefit of having six levels is that the core of competent performers who are given a third level are aware that there are three levels below them. This is assumed to have a greater motivational value than being placed in the third of five grades with only two lower categories. But this number of levels presumes that managers are capable of consistently making the fine distinctions necessary and there is no evidence that this is the case.

Conclusions on the number of levels

The format to use is a matter of choice and judgement. Many organizations have five levels and some are settling for three levels but there is no evidence that any single approach is clearly much superior to another, although the greater the number of levels the more is being asked of managers in the shape of discriminatory judgement. It does, however, seem to be preferable for level definitions to be positive rather than negative and for them to provide as much guidance as possible on the choice of ratings. It is equally important to ensure that level definitions are compatible with the culture of the organization and that close attention is given to ensuring that managers use them as consistently as possible.

Forced distribution

Forced distribution, also known as forced ranking, the vitality curve or differentiation, means that raters have to conform to a laid-down distribution of ratings at different levels. It can be described as an indicative range or quota system. The aim is to get what is believed to be a 'proper' distribution of ratings and overcome the central rating tendency of managers who do not like committing themselves to very low ratings, or even high ones. It can be used by organizations to highlight their best performers so that they can be included in a management development or talent management programme, or it can identify their worst performers so that action can be taken by invoking a capability procedure or discarding them.

The pattern of forced distribution may correspond to the normal bell-shaped curve that has been observed to apply to IQ scores, although there is no evidence that performance in an organization is distributed normally – there are so many other factors at work such as recruitment and development practices. Employees subjected to forced distribution have to be allocated to sections of the curve in accordance with performance assessments or rankings. For example, as illustrated in Figure 11.1, the highest-level performers would be placed in category A – the first 15 per cent of the curve. The middle 70 per cent would be placed in category B in the centre of the curve and the bottom 15 per cent would be placed in category C.

Other distributions can be adopted, for example, 15 per cent A, 75 per cent B and 10 per cent C, on the assumption that a company's recruitment and development activities produce more top players than also-rans. Three categories are the most common although a five-level A to E system is used in some organizations; a less popular choice because it requires more refinement of judgement than is likely to be possible and creates an underclass of Ds who have been forced into that group whether or not they are below par.

Forced distribution can also be based on forced ranking (the two terms are sometimes used interchangeably). In the UK senior civil service this involves comparing and ranking the performance of individuals against colleagues in similar roles and then placing them in one of

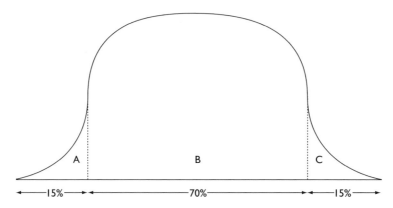

Figure 11.1 Forced distribution of employees

three performance tranches, the top tranche consisting of 25 per cent of the civil servants, the next 65 to 70 per cent and the lower 10 to 15 per cent.

Forced ranking, so called, first achieved fame when it was used by Jack Welch at GE to identify high flyers and poor performers. He argued that 20 per cent of any group of managers were top performers, 70 per cent were average and 10 per cent were not worth keeping. The latter were 'let go', hence the term 'rank and yank' for this procedure. Supporters of forced ranking say it is a good way of weeding out unsatisfactory employees as well as identifying and rewarding the top players. But it doesn't always work. Arkin (2007) noted that: 'before imploding, thanks to the actions of its own top performers, Enron used a complicated system to rank and yank its employees.'

Forced distribution achieves consistency of a sort but managers and staff rightly resent being forced into this sort of straightjacket. Only 8 per cent of the respondents to the CIPD 2004 survey (Armstrong and Baron, 2004) used forced distribution while 12 per cent of respondents to the e-reward survey did.

The problem with forced distribution and other overall rating systems is that the notion of performance is vague. In the case of ranking it is therefore unclear what the resulting order of employees truly represents. If used at all, ranks must be accompanied by meaningful performance data.

The 'rank and yank' approach has its advocates, but Meisler (2003), in an article tellingly called 'Dead man's curve', thought that: 'For most people – especially those with outmoded concepts of loyalty and job security – the prospect of Darwinian struggle at the work place is not a happy one.' O'Malley (2003), in an article on forced ranking, described it as a 'gross method of categorizing employees into a few evaluative buckets'.

Kathy Armstrong and Adrian Ward (2005) of the Work Foundation noted from their case study research that using indicative ranges, quotas or forced distribution systems pushes managers to make 'relative' assessments of their staff – often as part of a moderation process with other managers that can often resemble crude 'horse-trading'. They are making ranking decisions to ensure that the score profile in their team or department broadly fits the indicative ranges. The consequence of this can be that an individual may score a box 2 when assessed against their objectives, but be given a box 3 rating because there are already 'too many' box 2 performers in the team. This can be confusing for everyone and demotivating for those staff who are 'moderated' down to a lower rating. They can work earnestly towards their objectives all year in the expectation that if they meet or exceed them, then they will be assessed and rewarded appropriately. However, imposing a ranking mechanism means that two people who are equally effective in meeting their objectives can receive different ratings and performance pay.

A survey of 200 HR professionals by the Novations Group (2006) found that they reported a range of negative outcomes, including reduced productivity and collaboration and damage to morale and employee engagement.

Forced distribution (Pfeffer and Sutton, 2006)

We couldn't find a shred of evidence that it is better to have just a few alpha dogs at the top and treat everyone else as inferior. Rather, the best performance comes in organizations where as many people as possible are treated as top dogs. If you want people to keep working together and keep earning together, it is better to grant prestige to many rather than few, and to avoid big gaps between who gets the most rewards and kudos.

Research conducted by Garcia as reported in *Machine Design* (2007) established that in forced ranking systems individuals will care less about performing well on a given task and instead shift their focus to performing relatively better on a scale. Those ranked highest on the scale are more competitive and less cooperative than those ranked lower.

If an organization does adopt a forced distribution approach it will only work if employees understand what is expected of them, if there are fair procedures for reviewing and classifying levels of performance and if employees trust their managers to use these procedures to assess their performance correctly. A mechanistic 'rank and yank' system will only create a climate of fear and will at best inhibit and at worst destroy any possibility that performance management is perceived and used as a developmental process.

It is better to have good processes for identifying performance problems and helping under-performers to improve, coupled with effective capability procedures as described in Chapter 6.

Behaviourally anchored rating scales

Behaviourally anchored rating scales (BARS) as originally conceived by Smith and Kendall (1963) are graphic performance-rating scales with specific behavioural descriptions defining points against each scale (ie 'behavioural anchors'), which represents a dimension, factor or work function considered important for performance. They are designed to reduce the rating errors that it was assumed are typical of conventional scales. They include a number of performance dimensions such as teamwork, and managers rate each dimension on a scale as in the following example:

A. Continually contributes new ideas and suggestions. Takes a leading role in group meetings but is tolerant and supportive of colleagues and respects other people's points of view. Keeps everyone informed about own activities and is well aware of what other team members are doing in support of team objectives.

B. Takes a full part in group meetings and contributes useful ideas frequently. Listens to colleagues and keeps them reasonably well informed about own activities while keeping abreast of what they are doing.

C. Delivers opinions and suggestions at group meetings from time to time, but is not a major contributor to new thinking or planning activities. Generally receptive to other people's ideas and willing to change own plans to fit in. Does not always keep others properly informed or take sufficient pains to know what they are doing.

D. Tendency to comply passively with other people's suggestions. May withdraw at group meetings but sometimes shows personal antagonism to others. Not very interested in what others are doing or in keeping them informed.

E. Tendency to go own way without taking much account of the need to make a contribution to team activities. Sometimes uncooperative and unwilling to share information.

F. Generally uncooperative. Goes own way, completely ignoring the wishes of other team members and taking no interest in the achievement of team objectives.

It is believed that the behavioural descriptions in such scales discourage the tendency to rate on the basis of generalized assumptions about personality traits (which were probably highly subjective) by focusing attention on specific work behaviours. But there is still room for making subjective judgements based on different interpretations of the definitions of levels of behaviour.

Behaviourally anchored rating scales take time and trouble to develop and are not in common use except in a modified form as the dimensions in a differentiating competency framework. It is the latter application that has spread into some performance management processes.

Behavioural observation scales

Behavioural observation scales (BOS) as developed by Latham and Wexley (1977) are summated scales based on statements about desirable or undesirable work behaviour. These are compete behavioural statements, for example 'Conducts performance reviews on time', 'Conducts the performance review as a dialogue with the employee'. The headings are devised through the factor analysis of critical incidents. The assessor records the frequency with which an employee is observed engaged in a specified behaviour on a five-point Likert scale, an example of a behavioural item for appraising a sales representative on a five-point rating scale is:

Knows the price of competitive products.				
Never	Seldom	Sometimes	Generally	Always
1	2	3	4	5

Managers simply record the frequency (0–19 per cent, 20–39 per cent, 40–59 per cent, 60–79 per cent, 80–100 per cent) with which they have actually observed the employee engaging in the relevant behaviour.

According to Latham, Sulsky and Macdonald (2007) behavioural observation scales were regarded as the most practical rating method by users. Like behaviourally anchored rating scales, they produce fewer rating errors than other methods as long as raters have been trained in their use. Their superiority to other scales arises from the fact that they are based on Wherry and Bartlett's (1982) theory of rating (summarized earlier in this chapter).

However, Kane and Bernardin (1982) detected what they called a fatal flaw in this system. They pointed out that:

This scale is used to rate the observed occurrence rates of selected behaviours identified as being illustrative of desirable and undesirable ways of carrying out job functions. Each rating interval is assumed to connote a constant degree of performance satisfactoriness, regardless of the behaviour it is used to characterize (allowing, of course, for its transformation to its scale complement in the case of undesirable behaviours). The problem that this scale design raises is that a given occurrence rate interval does not, in fact, connote a constant level of performance satisfactoriness for all job behaviours.

Arguments for and against rating

Rating is used by the majority of organizations with performance management or appraisal systems and there are good arguments for doing so. But there are also persuasive arguments against rating. The pros and cons are discussed below.

Arguments for rating

The arguments for rating are that:

- It satisfies a natural wish from people to know where they stand. But this is only desirable if the manager's opinion is honest, justified and fair, and the numbers or letters convey what is really felt and are meaningful.

- It provides a convenient means of summing up judgements so that high or low performances can easily be identified (as long as the judgements are consistent and fair).

- It motivates people by giving them something to strive for in the shape of higher ratings (as long as they know what they have to do to get a better assessment).

- It is not possible to have performance-related pay without an overall rating (assuming performance-related pay is wanted or needed).

- It can provide a basis for identifying high flyers for a talent management programme or for generally predicting potential. But past performance is only a predictor of future performance when there is a connecting link, ie there are elements of the present job that are also important in a higher-level job.

Arguments against

Ratings are largely subjective and it is difficult to achieve consistency between the ratings given by different managers (ways of achieving consistent judgements are discussed below). Because the notion of 'performance' is often unclear, subjectivity can increase. Even if objectivity is achieved, to sum up the total performance of a person with a single rating is a gross over-simplification of what may be a complex set of factors influencing that performance – to do this after a detailed discussion of strengths and weaknesses suggests that the rating will be a superficial and arbitrary judgement. To label people as 'average' or 'below average', or whatever equivalent terms are used, is both demeaning and demotivating. The whole performance review meeting may be dominated by the fact that it will end with a rating, thus severely limiting the forward-looking and developmental focus of the meeting, which is all-important. This is particularly the case if the rating governs performance or contribution pay increases.

Furnham (2004) raised a number of questions about the rating process including the issue of what should be observed and recorded, the availability of reliable performance standards, the evaluative and judgemental nature of the process

There are also many well-known rating errors. Grote (1996) lists nine as follows:

- Contrast effect. The tendency of a rater to evaluate people in comparison with other individuals rather than against the standards for the job.

- First impression error. The tendency of a manager to make an initial positive or negative judgement of an employee and allow that first impression to colour or distort later information.

- Halo or horns effect. Inappropriate generalizations from one aspect of an individual's performance to all areas of that person's performance.

- Similar-to-me effect. The tendency of individuals to rate people who resemble themselves more highly than they rate others.

- Central tendency. The inclination to rate people in the middle of the scale even when their performance clearly warrants a substantially higher or lower rating.

- Negative and positive skew. The opposite of central tendency: the rating of all individuals as higher or lower than their performance actually warrants.

- Attribution bias. The tendency to attribute performance failings to factors under the control of the individual and performance successes to external causes.

- Recency effect. The tendency of minor events that have happened recently to have more influence on the rating than major events of many months ago.

- Stereotyping. The tendency to generalize across groups and ignore individual differences.

Powerful attacks on rating were made by Coens and Jenkins (2002) and Lee (2005) as set out overleaf.

Attacks on rating

Coens and Jenkins

Ratings are not a good idea because of the 'unintended consequences – the insidious, destructive and counterproductive effects of giving people ratings about their work performance. Whether accurate or not, people are psychologically affected by ratings. And except for people rated at the highest end of the scale, the impact is usually negative… Our ability to fairly measure the performance level of an individual is severely hampered by the unknowable effects of systems and random variations.'

Lee (2005)

- The rating process is actually a by-product of the attempt to measure performance outcomes. An excessive emphasis on measurement can be misguided. The desired end that is lost in measuring performance is not measurement at all, but rather description.
- Poor ratings can stigmatize performance and cause unnecessary resistance to the acceptance of feedback.
- The goal is to have the employee assist us in describing, interpreting and redirecting performance feedback, not reacting to the ratings. Feedback can accomplish the same positive goal as a rating without the negative side effects.
- If the goal is performance improvement, then feedback – not labelling past efforts – is the preferred tool.
- Although ratings can be positive they can also be punitive and focus attention on the negative rather than the possible. The only message the employee gets from a poor rating is: 'Stop doing what you have been punished for doing.' This kind of rating may not even be an adequate description, since many ratings are a summary of a number of activities collected over time. It does not focus attention on what to do to get better.
- Ratings are feedback but feedback of the worst kind.

Conclusions on rating

There are strong arguments both for and against rating. But the majority of organizations favour rating for three main reasons: 1) it informs performance pay decisions; 2) it identifies high flyers for talent management purposes or poor performers for remedial action or dismissal; and 3) it tells employees where they stand. Some either ignore the cons or are unaware of them. But many are concerned with the real problems of inaccuracy and inconsistency and ways of tackling these are discussed below. Some organizations have adopted alternative approaches, as described in the next section of this chapter.

Achieving accuracy in ratings

Murphy and Cleveland (1995) suggested that rating accuracy is improved when:

- Good and poor performance are clearly defined.

- The principle of distinguishing among workers in terms of their levels of performance is widely accepted.

- There is a high degree of trust in the system.

- Low ratings do not automatically result in the loss of valued rewards.

- Valued rewards are clearly linked to accuracy in performance appraisal.

Achieving consistency in ratings

The following methods are available for increasing consistency.

Training

Training can take place in the form of 'consistency' workshops for managers who discuss how ratings can be objectively justified and test rating decisions on simulated performance review data. This can build a level of common understanding about rating levels. This is sometimes called 'frame of reference training' (Bernardin *et al*, 2000). The purpose of frame of reference training is to calibrate trainers so that they agree on: 1) how to match the specific behaviours of the behaviour of those they are rating to the appropriate performance; 2) the effectiveness levels of alternative behaviours; and 3) the rules for combining individual judgements into a summary evaluation for each performance dimension.

Peer reviews

Groups of managers meet to review the pattern of each other's ratings and challenge unusual decisions or distributions. This process of moderation or calibration is time consuming but is possibly the best way to achieve a reasonable degree of consistency, especially when the group members share some knowledge of the performances of each other's staff as internal customers.

Monitoring

The distribution of ratings is monitored by a central department, usually HR, which challenges any unusual patterns and identifies and questions what appear to be unwarrantable differences between departments' ratings.

Consistency at a price can also be achieved by forced distribution or ranking as described earlier.

Alternatives to rating

Many organizations retain ratings because they perceive that the advantages outweigh the disadvantages – people need to know where they stand – or because they believe they are an essential part of a performance pay system. But those businesses that want to emphasize the developmental aspect of performance management and play down, even eliminate, the performance pay element, may be convinced by the objections to rating and will want to use other methods of analysing and assessing performance. As discussed below, the alternatives are the critical incident technique, visual forms of assessment and the overall analysis of performance.

The critical incident technique

The critical incident technique was developed by Flanagan (1954). On the basis of his research he concluded that to avoid trait assessment (merit rating) and over-concentration on output (management by objectives) appraisers should focus on critical behaviour incidents that were real, unambiguous and illustrated quite clearly how well individuals were performing their tasks. Flanagan advocated that managers should keep a record of these incidents and use them as evidence of actual behaviour during review meetings, thus increasing objectivity. He defended this proposal against the suggestion that he was asking managers to keep 'black books' on the grounds that it was positive as well as negative examples that should be recorded and that it would be better to make a note at the time rather than rely on memory, which is selective and may only recall recent events.

The critical incident technique did not gain much acceptance, perhaps because the 'black book' accusations stuck, but also because it seemed to be time-consuming. In addition, the problem was raised of converting the incident reports into an overall rating.

But the concept of critical incidents has had considerable influence on methods of developing competency frameworks, where it is used to elicit data about effective or less effective behaviour. The technique is used to assess what constitutes good or poor performance by analysing events that have been observed to have a noticeably successful or unsuccessful outcome, thus providing more factual, 'real' information than by simply listing tasks and guessing performance requirements. Used in this way the critical incident technique will produce schedules of 'differentiating competencies' that can form the basis for assessing and, if desired, rating competency levels. Differentiating competencies define the behavioural characteristics that high performers display, as distinct from those characterizing less effective people: ie the performance dimensions of roles. The critical incident method is also used to develop behaviourally anchored rating scales as described earlier.

Even if the Flanagan concept of critical incidents has not survived as a specific assessment technique, it does provide the basis for evidence-based performance management – analysis and assessment processes that rely on factual evidence rather than opinion.

Visual methods of assessment

An alternative approach to rating is to use a visual method of assessment. This takes the form of an agreement between the manager and the individual on where the latter should be placed on a matrix or grid as illustrated in Figure 11.2, which was developed by Ann Cummins of Humanus Consultancy for a client in the financial services sector. A 'snapshot' is thus provided of the individual's overall contribution, which is presented visually and as such provides a better basis for analysis and discussion than a mechanistic rating. The assessment of contribution refers both to outputs and to behaviours, attitudes and overall approach.

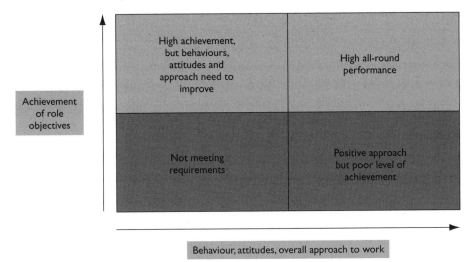

Figure 11.2   A performance matrix

The review guidelines accompanying the matrix are as follows:

You and your manager need to agree an overall assessment. This will be recorded in the summary page at the beginning of the review document. The aim is to get a balanced assessment of your contribution through the year. The assessment will take account of how you have performed against the responsibilities of your role as described in the role profile; objectives achieved and competency development over the course of the year. The assessment will become relevant for pay increases in the future.

The grid on the annual performance review summary is meant to provide a visual snapshot of your overall contribution. This replaces a more conventional rating scale approach. It reflects the fact that your contribution is determined not just by results, but also by your overall approach towards your work and how you behave towards colleagues and customers.

The evidence recorded in the performance review will be used to support where your manager places a mark on the grid.

Their assessment against the vertical axis will be based on an assessment of your performance against your objectives, performance standards described in your role profile, and any other work achievements recorded in the review. Together these represent 'outputs'.

The assessment against the horizontal axis will be based on an overall assessment of your performance against the competency-level definitions for the role.

Note that someone who is new in the role may be placed in one of the lower quadrants but this should be treated as an indication of development needs and not as a reflection on the individual's performance

A similar 'matrix' approach has been adopted in a financial services company. It is used for management appraisals to illustrate their performance against peers. It is not an 'appraisal rating' – the purpose of the matrix is to help individuals focus on what they do well and also any areas for improvement.

Two dimensions – business performance and behaviour (management style) are reviewed on the matrix, as illustrated in Figure 11.3, to ensure a rounder discussion of overall contribution against the full role demands rather than a short-term focus on current results.

This is achieved by visual means – the individual is placed at the relevant position in the matrix by reference to the two dimensions. For example a strong people manager who is low on the deliverables would be placed somewhere in the top left-hand quadrant but the aim will be movement to a position in the top right-hand quadrant.

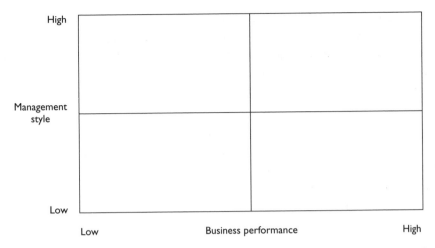

Figure 11.3   Performance matrix in financial services company

A performance matrix used in Unilever is shown in Figure 11.4. This measures the 'how' of performance on the vertical axis and the 'what' on the horizontal axis. The matrix model also contains guidelines on the possible actions that can be taken for each assessment quadrant.

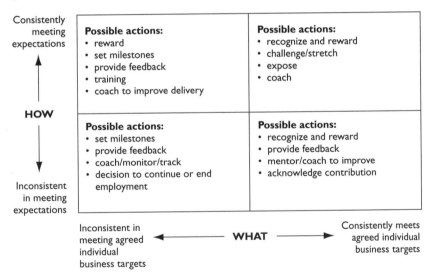

Figure 11.4   Assessment and action matrix – Unilever

Overall analysis of performance

Those who do not believe in ratings argue that performance management is essentially about analysis rather than evaluation. The aim is to reach agreement about future action rather than to produce a summarized and potentially superficial judgement. The aim of overall analysis is to reveal strengths and any areas for development or improvement. Managers are expected to reach an understanding with their team members as a result of the analysis that will ensure the latter will appreciate how well or not so well they are doing. The analysis should also identify the high flyers and those who are failing to meet acceptable standards.

Businesses with performance or contribution-related pay schemes may disagree with this overall approach on the grounds that ratings are necessary to inform pay decisions. The majority (73 per cent) of the respondents to the e-reward 2004 contingent pay survey depended on performance ratings to indicate the size of an increase or whether there was to be an increase at all. Even those without such pay schemes like to follow the traditional path of summarizing performance by ratings 'for the record', although they are not always clear about what to do with the record.

An overall assessment may be recorded in a narrative consisting of a written summary of views about the level of performance achieved. This at least ensures that managers have to collect their thoughts together and put them down on paper. But different people will consider different aspects of performance and there will be no consistency in the criteria used for assessment so it is therefore necessary to have a framework for the analysis. This could be provided on a 'what' and 'how' basis. The 'what' is the achievement of previously agreed objectives related to the headings on a role profile. The 'how' is behaviour in relating to competency framework headings. The results for each 'what' and 'how' heading could be recorded following a joint analysis during a review meeting. This approach could usefully be based on a performance matrix assessment as described earlier. But it should always be remembered that the purpose is to generate information that will lead to planned development or performance improvement actions. It is these that must be recorded but this should include statements of why they are necessary and what they are expected to achieve.

Coens and Jenkins (2002) asserted that performance is largely driven by the system and questioned the ability of anyone to distinguish adequately an individual's performance from the situational constraints. They pointed out that: 'In a given year some people perform better and some worse. A single individual's performance may be better one year, worse the next and somewhere in the middle in the year following. These differences, however, may not be the result of some people trying harder or anything else significant. It may just be the random happenstance of events and factors that impact individual performance.' They therefore argue that: 'Rather than think we can rank or effectively rate people we change our assumptions, we accept that while results are measurable, discrete differences in what can be directly attributable to individuals [are] not measurable. We may only be able to recognize, with a healthy scepticism, people who "stand out" in various settings, thereby warranting special attention.'

It is not necessary to agree with all these rather challenging statements, but there is something in the conclusion that we can recognize people at either extreme but cannot accurately distinguish performance differences in the bulk of people lying between those extremes. Managers can in effect tell an individual that s/he has done exceptionally well and that s/he will therefore be included in the talent management programme, or they can inform another individual that s/he has not done very well and that they must discuss what needs to be done about it. The others can be told that they are doing a perfectly good job and discussions can take place on how they can build on their strengths or on any learning activity (preferably self-directed) that might help them to do even better.

Conclusion

Analysis and assessment is a necessary and inevitable performance management activity but it is one of the most difficult ones to get right. Attempts to use mechanistic method-ologies involving ratings or rankings often prove of doubtful value. There is much to be said for the overall analysis approach, possibly supplemented with a visual assessment. Approaches to making performance or contribution pay decisions without ratings are described in Chapter 20.

12

Coaching

Coaching is a fundamental performance management activity that takes the opportunities presented by the work itself and uses them to develop the knowledge, skills, competencies and therefore the performance of people. Coaching opportunities arise in two ways: informally on a day-to-day basis, and after a formal performance review that identifies learning and development needs. The CIPD learning and development 2008 survey found that 44 per cent of organizations offer coaching to all employees and the most important providers of coaching were line managers.

Research by Graham, Wedman and Garvin-Kester (1994) showed that specific coaching behaviours have been directly correlated with net increases in sales. Research by Ellinger (2003) indicated that improvements in systems and cost savings may be directly attributed to coaching interventions by managers. Ellinger, Ellinger and Keller (2003) conducted research in a distribution centre and found that supervisory coaching behaviour was a highly significant predictor of employee job satisfaction and performance.

This chapter focuses on the line manager's responsibility for coaching under the following headings:

- coaching defined;
- the process of coaching;
- the approach to coaching;
- techniques of coaching;
- the skills of coaching.

Coaching defined

Coaching is a personal (usually one-to-one) on-the-job approach to helping people to develop their skills and levels of competence. The need for coaching may arise from formal or informal performance reviews but opportunities for coaching will emerge during normal day-to-day activities. Every time a manager delegates a new task to someone, a coaching opportunity is created to help the individual learn any new skills or techniques needed to get the job done. Every time a manager provides feedback to an individual after a task has been completed, there is an opportunity to help that individual do better next time.

Coaching was defined by Ellinger, Ellinger and Keller (2003) as a day-to-day, hands-on process of helping employees recognize opportunities to improve their performance and capabilities; a form of facilitating learning. Jarvis (2004) stated that coaching usually lasts for a short period and focuses on specific skills and goals.

As Lee (2005) explained: 'The coaching model of performance management redefines the relationship between the supervisor and the subordinate. The two work together to help the subordinate perform at his or her very best.' Coaching involves short-term interventions designed to remedy problems that interfere with the employee's performance but it is also concerned with longer-term development and continuous learning.

Coaching can be distinguished from mentoring and counselling. Mentoring describes a relationship in which a more experienced individual uses his or her greater knowledge and understanding of the work or workplace to support the development of a more junior or inexperienced colleague. Counselling addresses the employee's emotional state and the causes of personal crises and problems. It is usually conducted by trained counsellors and involves short-term interventions designed to remedy problems that interfere with the employee's job performance.

The process of coaching

As described by the CIPD (2007) coaching is essentially a non-directive form of development. Evered and Selman (1989) defined the following essential characteristics that define good coaching: developing a partnership, commitment to produce a result, responsiveness to people, practice and preparation, a sensitivity to individuals, and a willingness to go beyond what has already been achieved.

Woodruffe (2008) suggested that coaching should aim to:

- amplify an individual's own knowledge and thought processes;

- improve the individual's self-awareness and facilitate the winning of detailed insight into how the individual may be perceived by others;

- create a supportive, helpful, yet demanding, environment in which the individual's crucial thinking skills, ideas and behaviours are challenged and developed.

Coaching as part of the normal process of management consists of:

- Making people aware of how well they are performing by, for example, asking them questions to establish the extent to which they have thought through what they are doing.

- Controlled delegation: ensuring that individuals not only know what is expected of them but also understand what they need to know and be able to do to complete the task satisfactorily. This gives managers an opportunity to provide guidance at the outset – guidance at a later stage may be seen as interference.

- Using whatever situations may arise as opportunities to promote learning.

- Encouraging people to look at higher-level problems and how they would tackle them.

Approach to coaching

Coaching can provide motivation, structure and effective feedback if managers have the required skills and commitment. As coaches, managers believe that people can succeed, and that as their managers they can help people to identify what they need to do to develop and grow their skills. When coaching, managers look for the best in people and try to build on their strengths, rather than dwelling on their weaknesses. The aim is to help people to help themselves. Coaching encourages self-directed learning using any resources such as e-learning that are available. It is not a matter of spoon-feeding people.

Coaching may be informal but it needs to be planned. It is not simply checking from time to time on what people are doing and then advising them on how to do it better. Nor is it occasionally telling people where they have gone wrong and throwing in a lecture for good measure. As far as possible, coaching should take place within the framework of a general plan of the areas and direction in which individuals will benefit from further development. Coaching plans should be incorporated into the personal development plans set out in a performance agreement.

Thompson, Purdy and Summers (2008) listed five coaching stages: 1) developing a relationship with the client; 2) collecting and analysing diagnostic information; 3) processing feedback and planning actions; 4) taking action; and 5) evaluating progress.

Woodruffe (2008) recommended a three-part approach to coaching:

1. Discovery. The aim of the first meeting – or meetings – is to focus on discovery. In this stage, individuals being coached find out about themselves. Personality inventories may be used to facilitate discussions concerning the individual's self-perception. Career expectations and career development are explored. 360-degree feedback tools are used to introduce the views of others. The goal of the discovery phase is to heighten self-awareness.

2. Action Plan. Once individuals have a clear picture of their strengths, weaknesses and how they come across to others, they are encouraged to set goals and objectives to develop and challenge themselves. The goals will be set within the context of career development and will take advantage of current business issues or projects.

3. Review and recommit. At this point individuals review their performance against the goals they had set. Action plans can be updated and altered if necessary. The sessions are used to discuss and build upon successes, as well as examining how obstacles and difficulties can be overcome.

Coaching will be most effective when the coach understands that his or her role is to help people to learn and individuals are motivated to learn. Employees who are doing well should be keen to learn more in order to do even better. Employees who are aware that their present level of ability needs to be improved if they are going to perform their work satisfactorily should recognize that they will benefit from an opportunity to enhance their knowledge and skills through coaching. Individuals should be given guidance on what they should be learning and feedback on how they are doing and, because learning is an active not a passive process, they should be actively involved with their coach who should be constructive, building on strengths and experience.

Techniques of coaching

Good coaching is about encouraging people to think through issues, getting them to see things differently, enabling them to work out solutions for themselves that they can 'own', and empowering them to do things differently. Hallbom and Warrenton-Smith (2005) recommend the following coaching techniques:

- Ask high-impact questions – 'how' and 'what' open-ended questions that spur action rather than 'why' questions that require explanations.

- Help people to develop their own answers and action plans.

- Identify what people are doing right and then make the most of it rather than just trying to fix problems – coaching is success driven.

- Build rapport and trust – make it safe for employees to express their concerns and ideas.

- Get employees to work out answers for themselves – people often resist being told what to do, or how to do it.

A common framework used by coaches is the GROW model:

'G' is for the goal of coaching – this needs to be expressed in specific measurable terms that represent a meaningful step towards future development.

'R' is for the reality check – the process of eliciting as full a description as possible of what the person being coached needs to learn.

'O' is for option generation – the identification of as many solutions and actions as possible.

'W' is for wrapping up or 'will do' – when the coach ensures that the individual being coached is committed to action.

The following is an example of a 'GROW' coaching process used in a retail company.

Goal

In practice, when managers start to coach, most of the role involves asking questions that will help the individuals work out for themselves what their goal is. To aid this process, a list of questions is provided, with the goal usually being one of the objectives or the performance criteria standard. Like the main objectives, all goals need to be SMART.

Reality

The second stage, 'Reality', examines the current situation and what the individual has been doing and achieving. To aid this process, managers collect together examples to use in the coaching process. In addition, the company's guidance notes give a list of questions to ask to gain a perspective on the individuals' views and understanding of various situations. Among the list of questions are:

- What is the situation at the moment?
- Who else is or could be involved?
- What is their perception of the situation?
- What would be happening/what would it look like if it were perfect?
- On a scale of 1 to 10, what is it like now? What improvement do you want?
- What are the barriers to moving from X out of 10 to Y out of 10?
- What is holding you back?
- What have you tried so far? What were the results?

Options

'Options', the third stage, attempts to encourage employees to come up with ideas on what they could do to achieve their objectives or reach the performance criteria standard. Again, a list of guidance questions is given to managers to help with the process, but this time there is an attempt to explore some of the more unconventional solutions that staff might have. The company stresses that the session should allow employees to think quite broadly and that managers should not criticize any ideas that emerge. Once employees run out of ideas, then managers provide their own.

Will

The final stage of the coaching process is to formulate an action plan, outlining what the individual is going to do. The plan, the company says, should be specific with clear deadlines. Once more, the company provides a number of questions to inform thinking, including:

- What are the next steps?

- Precisely when will you do them?

- What might get in the way?

- What support do you need?

- How and when will you get that support?

- What further help do you want from me?

In addition, managers need to identify possible obstacles and agree what can be done about them, as well as agreeing the support the individual will need and how it will be provided via coaching and training. Managers are advised to focus on the individual's behaviour and what the individual needs to do differently, but are told that this should not relate to their personality. Nevertheless, it can mean focusing on small, manageable pieces of behavioural change. This stage could also involve explaining fully and specifically what the individual needs to do, while picking examples of when people did do well in the past can sometimes prove useful and can be built on. What is important at this stage, the company says, is involving the individual in developing the solution to make it more likely that they are committed to the action plan.

Coaching skills

A good coach is one who questions and listens. Coaching will be most effective when the coach understands that his or her role is to help people to learn, and when individuals are motivated to learn. They should be aware that their present level of knowledge or skill or their behaviour needs to be improved if they are going to perform their work to their own and to others' satisfaction. Individuals should be given guidance on what they should be learning and feedback on how they are doing, and, because learning is an active not a passive process, they should be actively involved with their coach, who should be constructive, building on strengths and experience.

To do all this good coaches have listening, analytical and interviewing skills and the ability to use questioning techniques, give and receive performance feedback, and create a supportive environment conducive to coaching. These are demanding requirements and managers need encouragement, guidance, training and, indeed, coaching to meet them.

Developing a coaching culture

On the basis of CIPD research, Clutterbuck and Megginson (2005) described a coaching culture as one where 'coaching is the predominant style of managing and working together and where commitment to improving the organization is embedded in a parallel commitment to improving the people'. A culture of coaching is linked to the basic performance management processes of providing feedback and reinforcement as the following quotation explains.

A culture of coaching (Lindbom, 2007)

A culture of coaching is one in which the regular review of performance and just-in-time feedback is expected. Employees depend on reinforcement when they have done things correctly, and understand that a constructive critique of their work when it needs improvement helps them to be more effective. For managers, this culture sets the standard for recognition for jobs well done. The culture of coaching also sets the expectation for feedback – positive or for improvement – that is specific, behavioural and results based. This type of culture is self-reinforcing as it leads to improved performance, which encourages employees to seek more feedback and managers to see the value of coaching as the key requirement of their job.

Evered and Selman (1989) made huge claims for the importance of developing a coaching culture when they argued that good coaching was the essential feature of really effective management. They advocated a paradigm in which 'the process of creating an organizational culture for coaching becomes the core managerial activity', and where coaching is viewed 'not as a subset of the field of management but rather as the heart of management'.

In a coaching culture managers believe that people can succeed, that they can contribute to their success and that they can identify what people need to be able to do to improve their performance. They recognize that coaching can provide motivation, structure and effective learning and see performance management as an enabling, empowering process that focuses on learning requirements. Hamlin, Ellinger and Beattie (2006) commented on the basis of their research: 'Truly effective managers and managerial leaders are those who embed effective coaching into the heart of their management practice.'

Developing a coaching culture in which managers have the skills and commitment to coach informally as well as on more formal occasions is difficult. It takes time and is a matter of guidance, training, encouragement and the example provided by senior managers and colleagues. As Lindbom (2007) emphasizes: 'Coaching must become part of the organization's identity by including it in core competencies and behaviour expectations.' HR or learning and development specialists have an important role. They can act as mentors (or establish a team of mentors) to provide guidance and emphasize the added value that can be obtained from coaching to the benefit not only of the individual but also the manager and the organization.

Part IV
Performance
Management in Action

13

Performance Management Surveys

Performance management surveys provide evidence on the approaches adopted to performance management, opinions about performance management and insight into the issues that are being or need to be addressed. The surveys summarized in this chapter were conducted by:

- the CIPD;
- e-reward;
- Houldsworth and Jirasinghe;
- Lawler and McDermott;
- the Institute of Employment Studies;
- the Work Foundation.

CIPD

The CIPD survey of performance management conducted by Armstrong and Baron (2004) covered 506 respondents. The key data emerging from the survey were as follows:

- 87 per cent operated a formal performance management process (36 per cent of these were new systems).
- 71 per cent agreed that the focus of performance management is developmental.
- 62 per cent used objective setting.
- 31 per cent used competence assessment.
- 14 per cent used 360-degree feedback.
- 62 per cent used personal development plans.
- 59 per cent gave an overall rating for performance; 40 per cent did not.

The number of rating levels used:

3: 6 per cent;

4: 28 per cent;

5: 47 per cent;

6+: 17 per cent.

- 8 per cent used forced distribution to guide ratings.

- 55 per cent disagreed that pay contingent on performance is an essential part of performance management.

- 42 per cent used ratings to inform contingent pay decisions; 52 per cent did not.

- 31 per cent had performance-related pay.

- 46 per cent separate performance management reviews from pay reviews; 26 per cent did not.

- 75 per cent agreed that performance management motivates individuals; 22 per cent disagreed.

- 80 per cent agreed that line managers own and operate the performance management process; 20 per cent disagreed.

- The extent to which buy-in to performance management is obtained from line managers is:

  - completely and actively in favour: 15 per cent;

  - most generally accept that it is useful: 62 per cent;

  - most are indifferent but go through the motions: 22 per cent;

  - most are hostile: 1 per cent.

- 61 per cent of line managers believe that performance management is very or mostly effective; 37 per cent believe it is partly effective or ineffective.

- 37 per cent of other staff believe that performance management is very or mostly effective; 58 per cent believe it is partly effective or ineffective.

- 71 per cent agreed that the focus of performance management is developmental; 27 per cent disagreed.

- 42 per cent agreed that pay contingent on performance is an essential part of performance management; 55 per cent disagreed.

- 42 per cent of respondents agreed that performance management should be distanced as far as possible from payment systems; 56 per cent disagreed.

E-reward

The outcomes of the e-reward survey of performance management held in April 2005 covering 181 respondents are summarized below.

Incidence of performance management

- 96 per cent had performance management.
- Over half had operated performance management for more than five years.
- In 91 per cent of respondents' organizations, performance management covered all jobs.

Principal features of performance management processes

- Almost all respondents used objective setting and performance review.
- Personal development plans were used in 89 per cent of organizations and performance improvement plans in 74 per cent.
- 24 per cent of respondents reported that they were using or developing competence frameworks as part of the process.
- 30 per cent used 360-degree feedback.

Objectives of performance management

The six top objectives of performance management were:
- to align individual and organizational objectives – 64 per cent;
- to improve organizational performance – 63 per cent;
- to improve individual performance – 46 per cent;
- to provide the basis for personal development – 37 per cent;
- to develop a performance culture – 32 per cent;
- to inform contribution/performance pay decisions – 21 per cent.

Training

Formal training for line managers was provided by 86 per cent of respondents, 45 per cent used coaching and 46 per cent of respondents offer formal training to both line managers and staff.

Web-based methods of administering performance management

A relatively small number of respondents (16 per cent) used web-based methods of adminis-tering performance management.

Impact of performance management

- Very significant – 32 per cent.
- Fairly significant – 36 per cent.
- Insignificant – 10 per cent.
- Not known – 22 per cent.

Houldsworth and Jirasinghe (2006)

A survey of the views of line managers on performance management was conducted by Houldsworth and Jirasinghe (2006). The findings as summarized below present an encourag-ing picture of attitudes to performance management.

- A considerable degree of satisfaction with performance management – 68 per cent indicated that performance management was very effective to excellent in their organ-ization (this contradicts the often expressed view that line managers do not like per-formance management).
- 75 per cent of managers believed that performance measures keep people focused on what is important.
- 83 per cent claimed that they were clear about what constituted good performance in their organization.
- 46 per cent felt that the main driver in performance management was motivation.
- 65 per cent believed that their goals were aligned to organizational strategy.
- 67 per cent thought that performance management focused on career development.
- 55 per cent reported that rating of performance was important in their organization.
- 69 per cent reported a link between performance and pay.
- 46 per cent thought that pay was really differentiated on the basis of performance.
- 62 per cent said that their organizations held calibration meetings to support the fair-ness of the process and reward links.

Lawler and McDermott

Lawler and McDermott carried out a survey in 2003 of 55 HR managers from large and medium-sized US organizations with questions about the nature of their performance management systems and their effectiveness. In 86 per cent of the organizations there were consistent and company-wide performance management practices. The main findings were as follows:

- Business strategy-driven performance goals and jointly set individual goals that formed parts of the approach adopted by the majority of organizations make a positive contribution to performance management.

- Ongoing feedback by managers is strongly related to performance management effectiveness, as stated by the researchers: 'The results strongly suggest that organizations should build ongoing feedback into their systems.'

- There was a particularly strong relationship between effectiveness and using measures of how individuals accomplish their results. The comment made by the researchers was that: 'This strongly suggests that systems work when people are appraised on both their results and how they obtain them.'

- The results of the survey also suggested that using competencies and developmental planning makes a significant impact in terms of creating an effective performance management system.

- Effectiveness is higher when rewards are tied to appraisals.

- 360-degree appraisal was not widely used and was not likely to be used for financial reward purposes.

- If the performance management system is going to be tied into business strategy, it is critical that senior management make that tie.

- It is important that line managers own the performance management system.

- The correlation between the presence of training and the effectiveness of performance appraisals was very high.

- Web-enabled (e-HR) systems were used in 57 per cent of the organization (this contrasts with the mere 16 per cent of UK organizations using such systems as established by the 2005 e-reward survey).

- Individual performance management practices need to be driven by the business strategy and fit with one another and with the overall human resource management system of the organization.

The Institute of Employment Studies

Research by Strebler, Bevan and Robertson (2001) of the Institute of Employment Studies on performance management showed that:

- It lacks strategic focus.

- It gives conflicting messages between encouragement and control.

- It has a limited impact on business performance.

- It stretches managers who often lack the skills and motivation to deliver it effectively.

- It is participation in the review meeting that matters most to employees rather than its outcomes.

- The importance of employee commitment is increasing.

- There is an emphasis on development and increased disillusion with the link to pay.

Other findings

- Reviewees want feedback on tangible outcomes and results rather than broad traits.

- A manager commented: 'The performance review is good. However, it falls over because there is no feedback during the year, so if one's performance is below par, there would be no feedback until the end of the year thus not giving the individual a chance to improve.'

- Another comment: 'Any system is only as good as the individuals operating it.'

- Satisfaction with the performance review meeting:

Satisfied and very satisfied with:	*Dissatisfied and very dissatisfied with:*
– the extent to which they had a say: 78 per cent;	– coaching by line manager to improve performance: 33 per cent;
– the time allocated to process: 62 per cent;	– discussion of long-term objectives: 30 per cent;
– the preparation undertaken by the manager: 49 per cent.	– discussion of training needs in current job: 24 per cent.

- Reviewees were satisfied with the review process delivered by their managers rather than its contribution to performance improvement and development. This resulted from a poor delivery of coaching and training and development.

Comments about objectives from managers

- Setting of targets and performance measures is a top-down process with little room for input. Targets are as a result imposed and unrealistic.

- There remains the problem of arbitrary objectives and staff being unfairly treated when factors outside of their control impact upon attainment of so-called SMART objectives.

- I am a lawyer in the senior civil service and the work I do is predominately legal. It is difficult to set objectives for me that are meaningful, because the work I do (along with about 1,000 other government lawyers) is demand led. The priorities that have to be met are the client's not mine.

The Work Foundation

The Work Foundation research carried out by Kathy Armstrong and Adrian Ward in 2005 was based on six detailed case studies. It was concluded that the variety of approaches taken by the case study organizations shows that when it comes to performance management, one size does not fit all. Performance management can be used to achieve a range of aims. It is important for organizations consciously to adopt whatever aim suits the culture and its business strategy. It is also important not to expect performance management to be a panacea for all kinds of organizational ailments. Organizations need to be clear about the purpose of performance management. The challenge is for performance management to retain a strategic role rather than tending towards tactical activities, such as the process.

The common themes from the case studies were synthesized into a framework of seven elements that organizations must discuss and, more importantly, get right when looking to maximize the effectiveness of performance management in their organizations. These seven elements are:

- Process: the means by which individual performance is directed, assessed and rewarded.

- People management capability: the skills, attitude, behaviours and knowledge that line managers need in order to raise the performance standards of those around them.

- Motivation: the extent to which the organization's approach to PM unlocks discretionary effort among its employees.

- Measurement and reward: the indicators or 'dials on the dashboard' that are used to assess individual performance and the organizational effectiveness of the whole PM system, and the way these are used to allocate rewards.

- Role of HR: the extent to which HR leaders demonstrate subject matter expertise, draw on relevant theory and research evidence, and influence thought leaders in organizations to focus on the aspects of performance management that make the most difference to performance.

- Learning organizations: the extent to which organizations are able to reflect objectively and learn from their own performance management experience, building on what works and refining where necessary.

- Role of culture and clarity of purpose: the extent to which an approach to performance management resonates and is congruent with the broader culture of the organization in which it is being applied.

14

Performance Management Models

Models of performance management systems provide a useful means of summing up how performance management works that can be communicated to employees and provide the basis for education and training activities. The models illustrated are those used by the following organizations:

- Astra-Zeneca company;
- CEMEX;
- Centrica;
- DHL;
- HalifaxBoS;
- Pfizer Inc;
- Raytheon;
- Royal College of Nursing;
- Standard Chartered Bank;
- Victoria and Albert Museum;
- Yorkshire Water.

A model used in BP Lubricants as part of their performance management system that they call the communication and engagement value tree is also illustrated.

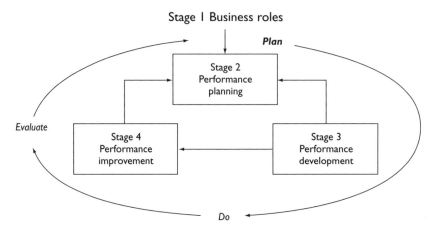

Figure 14.1 Model of the performance management system in Astra-Zeneca

WHAT IS PERFORMANCE MANAGEMENT?

Performance management is the foundation of CEMEX's talent management model

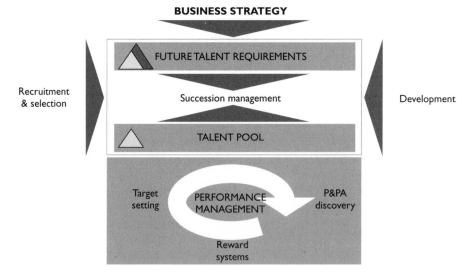

Figure 14.2 Model of the performance management system in CEMEX

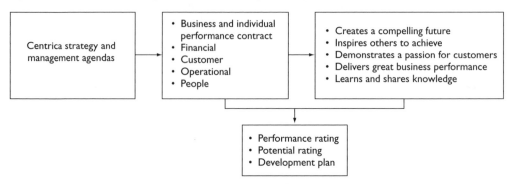

Figure 14.3 Model of the performance management system in Centrica

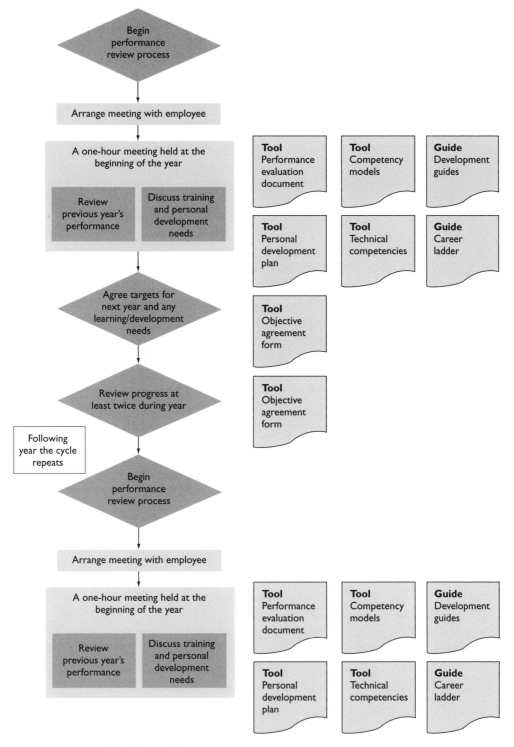

Figure 14.4   Model of the performance management system in DHL

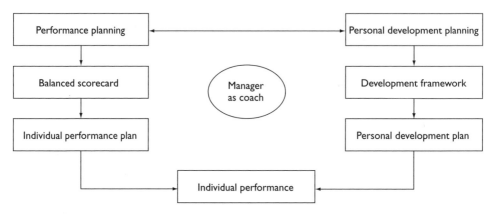

Figure 14.5   Model of the performance management system in HalifaxBOS

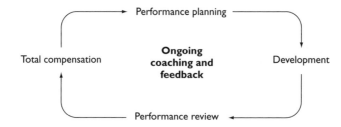

Figure 14.6   Model of the performance management system in Pfizer Inc

Figure 14.7   Model of the performance management system in Raytheon

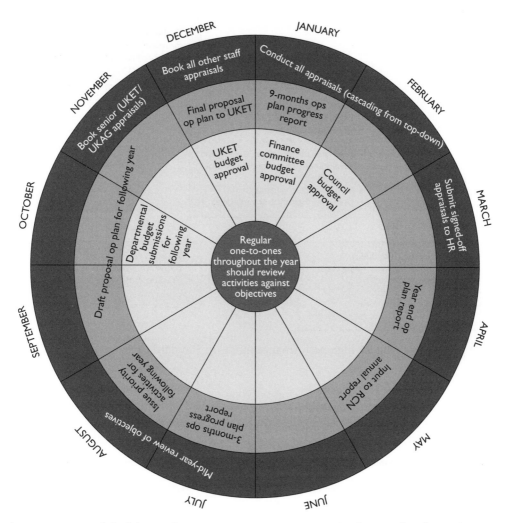

Figure 14.8 Model of the performance management system in the Royal College of Nursing

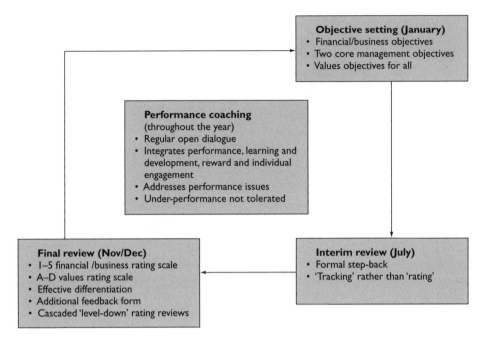

Figure 14.9 Managing for high performance model in Standard Chartered Bank

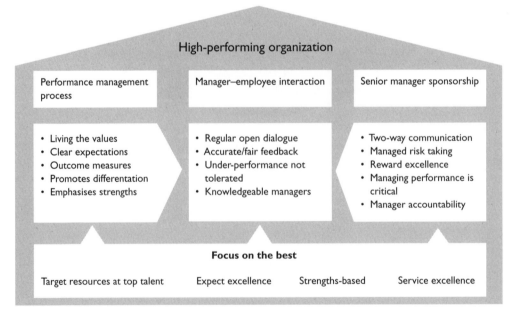

Figure 14.10 Managing for future high-performance model in Standard Chartered Bank

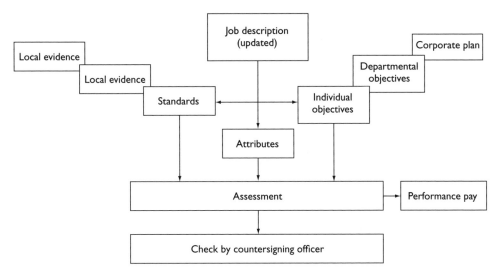

Figure 14.11 Model of the performance management system in The Victoria and Albert Museum

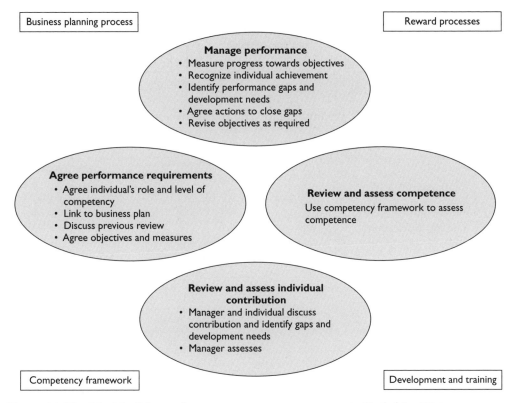

Figure 14.12 Model of the performance management system in Yorkshire Water

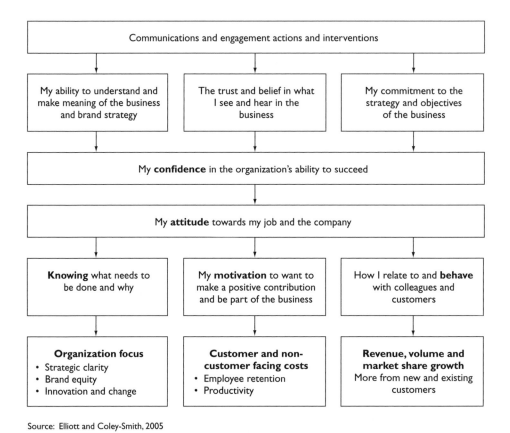

Source: Elliott and Coley-Smith, 2005

Figure 14.13   BP Lubricants' communication and engagement value tree

15

Reactions to Performance Management

As stated by Armstrong and Baron (1998), one of the main objectives of their research was to get people 'to tell us how it is'. Research projects into performance appraisal and performance management held before or since have generally relied on questionnaires, interviews with HR managers and, additionally, in the 1992 IPM survey, the use of attitude surveys. Some academic researchers, as referred to in Chapter 3, have made contacts with individuals but there has been no systematic in-depth attempt to find out from those who experience performance management what they actually think about it. As this chapter shows, the Armstrong and Baron research produced rich material that is still revealing today. The research took the form of 12 focus groups held in six organizations: one in financial services, one in the manufacturing sector, a call centre, an oil exploration company, a local authority and a charity.

The focus groups

In each of the organizations in which focus group meetings were held, a sophisticated form of performance management had been introduced within the last year or two accompanied by comprehensive communication and training for those concerned. They had all taken deliberate steps to increase line management and employee ownership of the processes. Two organizations had performance-related pay (PRP) for managers and staff, although in one example the aim had been to distance pay from performance management. One had performance pay only for managers and two did not have PRP. Another had team pay and pay that was influenced by performance and competence achievements but was not directly geared to a rating system.

The researchers asked for the focus groups to be composed of volunteers, and this was the case, with the exception of two groups for managers to which the whole management team had been invited. A standard checklist was used for all focus groups but inevitably the discussion often veered away from the checklist points. The focus groups were recorded in full and contents analysis techniques were used to analyse the data.

In analysing the results of the focus groups the researchers were aware that these were simply snapshots taken of a small and selected sample of organizations. Any inferences (not conclusions) had to be qualitative.

Two other factors were taken into account in the analysis of focus group discussions. The first factor is that the members are responding to questions put by a facilitator. With the best will in the world, facilitators sometimes set the tone of the meeting, however hard they work at not asking leading questions and however much they sit back and let the discussion flow, with only an occasional prompt or grunt. The second factor is that any focus group can be dominated by forceful or articulate members and there is always a possibility of other members simply following their leader in response to the dynamics of the group situation they find themselves in. So far as could be judged, although there were indeed some highly articulate participants, they did not suppress other people's views and there was usually sufficient diversity of opinion to lead to the conclusion that group cohesion factors had not overwhelmed individuality. But forces affecting the contribution of individual members and leading to choruses of approval or disapproval that were joined in by all may have been at work below the surface.

For all these reasons the researchers were cautious about offering any firm and final conclusions from the focus groups. They were simply indicative of the sort of reactions people can have to performance management. The fact that in some organizations these reactions were more favourable than might be expected may be coincidental. Reactions in other organizations with a much less sophisticated approach to performance management might have been much more hostile. But at least there were real people telling the researchers, as far as could be judged, what they really thought (all contributions were recorded anonymously). And, in the view of the researchers, this does provide some insight into possible reactions to particular aspects of performance management that are well worth considering by all those involved in the design, development and operation of performance management processes.

The focus groups were held for managers and team leaders or staff to obtain different perspectives in all the organizations except the charity, which had a mix of team leaders and support staff. The analysis in the first part of this chapter deals separately with these categories in each of the organizations in which focus groups were held. The quotations are verbatim but only a selection is given below that seemed to represent a significant point of view. A balanced set of quotations is given to represent different opinions. Quotations immediately following another quotation are from different people. Brief comments are provided at the end of each focus group discussion summary. These comments attempt to capture the general tone and direction of the discussion but they are inevitably impressionistic.

Focus groups: organization A (a financial services company)

Managers' group

The rating system

- Subjectivity is inevitable. The art is to take subjectivity out through cross-team bench-marking and training.

- Numbers are more important to individuals than the amount of money they get.

- How do you get consistency? How do you make sure that the effort that's put into getting a grade 3 is consistent across the business?

- What doesn't seem to be clear is what the top executives think is the difference between a 3 and a 4.

- What does Audit or what does Finance have to do to get a 4, and what do they have to do to get a 3?

Objective setting

- You shouldn't need to wait until the year-end to decide how someone is performing. You should be reviewing objectives at least monthly.

- People have their objectives on a piece of paper and they know their money is based on these objectives. And as a result of that, they compromise other areas of the [organization] in terms of the whole picture, to meet those objectives, because they are not actually measured on whether they have messed somebody else up.

- It's short-termism. I've seen it where different departments are actually messing each other up consciously to achieve their individual objectives, and that's a real problem for me.

Developing staff

- It's a joint thing between them and us. Helping people identify what they should be focusing on – nothing to do with performance.

- We've got to develop people to move on to something without really knowing what they are moving on to. Therefore you can only give general advice because no career progression advice is available.

- We don't manage under-performers. We just like to push it under the carpet because we want to avoid a conflict situation. We're not very good, perhaps, at developing people that need to be developed.

Link to pay

The whole process is an absolute nightmare.

Comments on managers' focus group

These comments and other unquoted contributions were almost wholly hostile, with the focus being on the managers' perceptions of the unfairness of the reward system. Objective setting, rating and pay systems issues dominated the discussion. Relatively few comments, favourable or unfavourable, were made about other aspects of performance management.

Staff focus group

Comments about performance management

- You need appraisal to get the best out of people and develop them.

- What we've moved away from is people's perceptions, just marking someone depending on how they felt about them. Whereas now there's evidence.

- It's subjective between the manager and the appraisee. It's OK if you are doing your objectives, but if your manager doesn't agree there's nothing you can do about it.

- The managers, they're not managing the performance of the individual. You've got to look at each individual and their targets and objectives within the team, and if they are not coming up to scratch, you need to counsel them and get them back to a satisfactory level.

- If you've got an under-performer, people are not dealing with these people in the correct way. They are moving on somewhere else and people are not being addressed properly.

Comments about rating

- Performance management, if it worked right it would be good. But there's too much inconsistency. You've got different managers marking in different ways.

- Wherever you move, people are going to manage, and motivate and mark you in different ways. And that's something that we all need to be aware of.

Comment on objective setting

- Everybody's individual plans go towards the big team plan and sometimes that isn't communicated as it should be because we all should be working for one big goal. All our little bits and pieces should add up.

Link to pay

- Performance and money, different things. People link their level to the percentages all the time; they have to come away from that, don't they?

- That's what I'm saying about the performance culture, it just doesn't happen. The idea is there and we've kind of got halfway there, but having got only halfway it could possibly be more destructive than doing good... It's not the truth that if you perform well you'll be rewarded.

- The system might be right but the implementation is absolutely terrible.

Comment on the ability of managers to manage pay

Line managers are used to being told what to do, and we are trying to move away from that and give them free rein. They can't actually deal with that, they can't cope with that.

Comments on the staff focus group

Although some of the commentators welcomed the concept of performance pay, quite a lot of dissatisfaction was expressed about the way it was administered.

Focus groups: organization B (a manufacturing company)

Summary of points made by members of the group (comprised of both managers and team leaders)

- Self-analysis by staff was realistic – Manager: 'They didn't differ from me with what they came up with.'

- Meetings were realistic – Manager: 'Because they were comfortable where they were, knowing their role.'

- Review meeting went well – Manager and team leader 'Because we work well together and it's easier to communicate the information across.'

- Team leader – 'Providing the dialogue flows and it's open, everything falls into place.'

- Manager – 'When I first started in management you would get an overall view of someone – they're good or they're not so good – but it is difficult to say what they are not so good at. You've got nothing to measure it against. Now I have, and that's what it's about for me.'

- Manager – 'It gives you the opportunity to provide focus – to look into a particular area and to be able to say more development is needed in that area.'

- Team leader – 'So it's actually tying it down and saying, OK, let's focus on these three points for the next six months. Once they're developing, then we'll pull in a few more.'

- Team leader – 'It takes the vagueness away and puts the specifics in.'

Observations

This was an organization that had taken considerable pains with the development of a competency framework as a basis for performance management. Extensive training had also taken place that contributed to the generally favourable response. The single comment about ratings was echoed by other people and ratings have since been discontinued.

Focus groups: organization C (a call centre)

Managers

General comments on the performance review process

- It gives our staff a sense of direction and feedback.

- It focuses your attention on the fact that you should be spending some quality time with your staff.

- It gives me something to aim for, short term and long term.

- I think it's an opportunity to consolidate all the feedback you've given on a more informal basis.

- When you have six-monthly reviews it formalizes and pulls together everything else that has been on an ongoing basis.

- You give continuing attention to your team members one way and another so they don't get any surprises at the review.

- It is an ideal management discipline to have in place because it does ensure that you have a structured discussion between yourself and your manager or whoever.

- It gives staff the chance to discuss with their managers any problems they've got that they can't discuss at any other time.

- My staff falls into two categories. Some are very keen, look forward to the review and are well prepared. Then you get the other group who will listen to what the line manager has to say to them and they will have a little input but will not have prepared in advance. About 40 per cent are well prepared, 20 per cent reasonably well prepared and 40 per cent not really prepared.

- I think it is right that there should be some form of appraisal but I have some problems with the content and I have heaps of problems managing to cope with it because of the volumes of paper etc.

- The potential problem is that you are asking some managers to conduct 20 or 30 reviews. And staff feel it is something they should have but the manager is not paying enough attention to it because of other pressures.

- The time involved for mangers is definitely an issue.

Comments on objective setting

- We do link individual objectives with business objectives, so that staff can quite clearly see their impact on what the business is doing – we are all working in the same direction.

- It depends where you are. It's more difficult to tie the two things together [business and personal objectives] if you are pushing a trolley around the building. But it is much easier where people can say that if I increase my volume and if I can get my quality right, then I can see what I am doing towards the business objectives.

- The gap remains of trying to translate these generic objectives to the individual who has to achieve X, Y and Z. They may be small cogs in a big machine.

Observations

These managers were generally supportive. A crude measure of the degree of support can be obtained by an analysis of the number of favourable comments (the meetings were recorded in full). In this case, 71 per cent of the remarks supported the process because, essentially, those present thought it provided 'quality time' and the opportunity to consolidate feedback and 'pull everything together'. This organization has well-developed competency frameworks and the favourable comment about their use is interesting. There were some complaints about the time taken for reviews and doubts were expressed about the possibility of cascading objectives.

Team leaders

General comments on the performance review process

- It gives you a structure for where you're going. You agree what you need to pick up on. It's a two-way discussion. And you're responsible for setting these objectives with your line manager. You're not just told what to do. And you go through and decide on which you want to concentrate on in the next six months. It gives you a sense of responsibility for your own future.

- I think you get quality time with your manager. And it's very difficult to get that time in the working environment.

- The majority of my staff like the performance review. They like to know how they are doing and where they are going in the future. The ones who don't like it are those who want to do the minimum of what they can get away with.

- People like feedback. They like to know how they are doing. They like to discuss their development. Even if they are not performing up to standard, they want to know how they can progress.

- If you have a member of staff who is not doing so well and you sit down to talk about it, at first they say: 'Well, I don't know about that.' But when you give them particular instances and you talk it through, at the end of it they do say: 'Well yes, you're right, I did do that.' It makes them reflect positively on the negative aspects as well.

- What my staff get out of it is communication. Someone is interested in what they are saying, just for once.

Comments on ratings

- For me, the rating is something to work for.

- It makes it a lot better when someone says: 'If you do this or that, you can have that.'

- If you are being subjective you have to justify the rating. And it leaves you as an assessor wide open when someone asks: 'Why has someone got that when I've got this?'

- The only time that rating helps is when it comes to the pay.

- Different managers have different expectations. Even when my performance remains just the same, one manager may not like my style, and another manager might, so it's subjective.

Comment on objective setting

- The generic objectives were fine for us, but when they were applied to the staff – cascaded down to everybody – there was a lot they couldn't do or accomplish.

Comments on development

- It makes you realize where your areas of improvement lie.

- The performance review process makes you think 'I have all these individuals and some like to do this and some like to do that' and you tailor-make the training to what they want to do.

Comment on pay

If anything, it [performance-related pay] is the negative side of the scenario.

Observations

As in the case of their managers, the team leaders generally approved of performance management – 61 per cent of the comments were favourable. They liked the structure it provided for discussions on performance and development, the 'quality time' it provided and the opportunity it gave for them and their staff to get to know each other better. But some concern was expressed about the problems of achieving objectivity. Doubts were also cast about the rating and objective-setting processes. If reactions to the review meeting are isolated, the proportion of favourable comments increases from 61 per cent to 84 per cent.

Staff

General comments on the performance review process

- They can tell us what they want just as we can tell them what we want!

- In a one-to-one meeting people can bring things out to their supervisors who say: 'I've never been aware of that – why didn't you tell us before?' That's definitely an advantage.

- If you want to go ahead, if you want to work yourself up, then it's good because you find out what your needs are. You can discuss the issues rather than being told: 'This is what you need to do.' You can then go away happy, thinking: 'I know what I want to know about that.'

- I think my team leader carries out the review very well. You get everything across and she listens to it and then she tells me what I've got to do to get where I want to get.

- Some do the job well; others just do the job to get it over.

- Our line manager has 20 or 30 people to look after, and that's an awful lot of people.

Comments on rating

- I go in prepared to do battle. I always know what mark I'm going to get before I go in, so I go in and I'm going to say exactly what I want to say.

- The principle is good – if you do a good job you get rewarded. But the fact is that it's your immediate superior. It's their interpretation – how they class your work, good or bad – that determines how much you get paid.

- My team leader doesn't know us. And he marks us down on things. But he doesn't speak to anyone on the section. So how can he mark you personally when he doesn't know you?

Comments on objective setting and review

- I think it's fine to define the critical success factors broadly: 'This is what we want to achieve,' and everybody's job links into the whole lot really.

- You've got to have your own targets and every individual has them and knows what they have to do. But there has to be one target for the company. Everything is linked.

- I know what my job is but I couldn't tell you what my objectives are.

- I don't think anyone here could really link their objectives to the critical success factors.

- If anything goes wrong in my area, it's always not: 'How shall we fix it?' but: 'Who did it?'

Comments about development

- If the personal development plans are done properly they are probably the greatest benefit of the performance review process – you get your say about your career.

- It helps you to understand where you want to get to and how you're going to get there.

- I'd rather do my training at work than going out of the office and with a pen and paper writing it down. I'd rather be there, doing it, learning from my mistakes.

Comments on pay

- It's more crucial when performance review is related to your pay.

- I know it isn't fair.

Observations

Staff were not so well disposed to performance management as their team leaders and managers. There were quite a few favourable comments on the advantages of one-to-one performance review meetings but less than half the overall comments were favourable. The negative reactions were, however, more focused on rating and pay issues and the feeling that ratings were likely to be unfair. If the rating and pay comments are excluded, the proportion of supportive comments goes up to 61 per cent. One of the factors that may have influenced the overall reactions may be that staff had received less training in performance processes than their superiors.

Focus groups: organization D (an oil exploration company)

Professional Staff

General comments on the performance review process

- There has been a general maturing of the performance contracting process here over the last three or four years. We're pretty good at getting some of the business issues 'contracted' so to speak, but the cascading of those into personal objectives is sometimes a wee bit hit-and-miss.

- From my point of view, as someone on the receiving end, I have yet to see it integrated into the real business.

- It makes you sit down and think: 'Why am I here? And how do I add value? Do I fit into the business objectives of the people I work for?'

- For me the real strength of the process lies in the continuing dialogue and negotiation as the year goes on. [general agreement]

- For me, it creates a sense of reality.

- The conversation assists the attainment of good performance. It's good for you, it's good for the company.

- It's tough giving negative feedback. But it is very important – a continuing dialogue with staff. It's a matter of finding the time to do it.

- I suppose one of the feelings I have is one of frustration. I am trying to be very careful here. It's not a personal thing. If you have one issue that you want discussed and it doesn't get resolved satisfactorily, then that becomes your negative perception of the way it worked.

- I find meetings a good opportunity to get your message across about where you want to go. It's a good time to get the feedback as to whether your aspirations are realistic and get agreement on levels of training and on where you want to be.

Comments on objective setting

- The performance contracts of senior managers flows downward and is directed as it goes down through different layers in the organization. There's nothing worse than when you're doing something that is of zero relevance to what the company's trying to do.

- It's the foundation of the company's success over the last few years, being able to articulate performance, particularly the hard edge side of it – financial and cost performance. The softer issues – the right-hand side of the performance contract – we're still learning about in my opinion.

- It is very clear that the team has to develop its objectives and get agreement with whoever sits above them that it's the right thing to do. It cannot be imposed.

- There are certain things where you know you'll be encouraged and challenged as part of the conversation. But fundamentally, they're a bottom-up process and I think that's absolutely vital.

- We're not a command-and-control organization. I hope we're a leadership organization – space, direction and support. So management creates the space and direction into which we fit our performance aspirations. If we were just told from the top what has to happen it would be dreadful.

- It [the performance contracting process] works reasonably well. It is not passed down from the top. It's a dialogue about one's performance, upwards as well as down.

Comments on development

- It's very much up to the individual to manage their own career.

- We have deconstructed where we were five or six years ago and are building something quite new. And it is a fledgling but I fully support it.

- The development plan is personal to you. It's my understanding that the content is almost like an agreement with the company and your boss about how you are going to develop over the next few years – what your career is going to look like.

Observations

The feedback was generally positive (73 per cent of the comments were favourable). The professional staff liked the way that the process made them focus on performance and created a sense of reality. One participant saw it as 'a necessary evil' and there were some doubts relating to the integration of objectives.

Team leaders

Comments on the overall process

- Performance contracts contribute quite well; they provide a framework to work within; they provide areas for measurement, quantitative or qualitative.

- One of the keys is to complete the loop. It's a case of 'go and deliver this, this is what I expect you to do'. Yet by the time you've gone a certain way down the road, things might be different. So somehow you have to complete the loop.

- People tend to regard quarterly meetings, reviews of your performance and the annual appraisal as second priorities. It's difficult to find the time and it's difficult to get the entire attention of your manager because he's working on something more important, which is business, and this isn't business.

- But circumstances don't count, that's the point. They say: 'Look, we appreciate that these things are not entirely within your control but it's up to you to manage that piece of business.'

Comments on objective setting

- A lot of it is about measuring quality and how well you did things, and this tends to be extremely difficult in a marketing or service type function.

- How does it work for me? – not very well.

- You can't move objectives down to the individual except in exceptional circumstances such as the sales force.

- You have to have sophisticated measures to avoid the danger of putting wrong signals and drivers on people to do things that end up being bad for the business.

- I always try to make it an individual thing such that if someone only wants to spend 15 minutes on it I didn't expect to spend 50 minutes. And if they wanted to spend two hours, we'd spend it.

- My performance appraisals with my line manager have been very good. They have been pretty honest.

Comments on development

- It's very much a personal responsibility, especially with line managers having such broad spans of control. You identify where you see gaps in your skills base, gaps in your competencies and where you see the need to learn.

- You can't expect managers to give you more than general guidance in these matters. They generally like to be guided by you on what you would like to do to develop your skills.

Observations

The team leaders were not so enthusiastic as the professional staff (55 per cent of the comments were favourable compared with 73 per cent of the comments made by the professionals). They liked some aspects of the process but were worried about the time it takes in relation to the benefits and about objective setting.

Focus groups: organization E (a local authority)

Senior managers

General comments about the review process

- I've found it very beneficial from my point of view – being able to focus more clearly on what our ultimate aims and goals should be in the medium-to-short term. And my relationship with my manager has benefited.

- For me and my people, it works – on the basis of all the feedback I am getting from the appraisal meetings so far. There was an element of scepticism initially, but after two appraisals, my staff are beginning to realize that it's not just a management tool to use as a whip but there is an opportunity for real communication; for targets and objectives to be agreed.

- One thing this has led to is better communication.

- Both my meetings have been difficult in the extreme in that they had to be deferred because they started to become a little heated. I felt I was being asked to do things that I couldn't achieve and therefore responded accordingly.

Comments on objectives setting

- Targets used to be set top down. There was a chance to discuss them but that wasn't formalized. The appraisal system bolted onto performance management and it formalized target setting and it allowed a measure of negotiation between the appraisee and the manager.

- The theory of cascading objectives is great in that you can see a task that the department has to do and then somehow break it down into project and individual objectives. And then you can cascade it down further and further until at the lowest level it's about an individual member of staff – that they've got to do this activity within a timescale. But we are not yet very good at it. We're still learning.

Comment on development

- I think performance management is helpful because it gives the individual a chance to speak to you in a semi-formal setting about what they perceive to be their training needs.

Observations

The comments by senior managers were very favourable (89 per cent). They liked every aspect of the process itself and their objections were relatively minor. They were, however, critical of their chief executive, who they felt was not taking part in performance management, leaving it entirely to his deputy. As one of them commented: 'I do resent the fact that it is very much middle-organization centred at the moment. I don't see any commitment from the top towards it. And my immediate subordinates are having a great deal of difficulty in generating enthusiasm to do the people below them because they can see what is happening above.' This is the classic situation of an HR process being prejudiced because of lack of support from the top.

Middle managers

General comments about the review process

- I came out of my meeting feeling as if I had met my boss for the first time. I knew more about him by the end than when I went in and we had a really good chat. And it changed our working relationship for the better.

- It's a good way to air things. It's a good forum to discuss things that could be improved and it's a relaxed interview. I think we've all tried to make it that way.

- I think it opens up discussion.

- Certainly I learnt more about individual members of my staff, and I've been with them for years.

- Appraisal must be the positive end of personnel management.

- It makes them [my staff] feel they are valued. You spend time talking to them and give them time to talk to you and that is a positive thing.

- I don't think anything new comes up at the appraisal. You're further away from the occasion and the discussion is more diluted. There shouldn't be that many surprises. You should be aware of what's happened. Appraisals are just a formality.

- I think it's sad that managers should need this kind of feedback from a meeting. They should be in touch with their staff already and be aware of the situation.

- Because it is a fairly informal, relaxed environment, people are prepared to raise issues themselves. If it's out in the open and you can then do something about it.

- If we have a problem at work, people come to me. So when we get into a performance appraisal situation there's nothing to be said.

Comments on objective setting

- You are not just setting targets, telling people – 'you've got to do it' – you do it by agreement.

Comment on development

- At the time all the talk about training and development goes well and people feel motivated. But when you come up against budgetary constraints then people think: 'What's the point, why did you do it?'

Observations

On the whole middle managers supported performance management (56 per cent of the comments were favourable). They liked the fact that it opened up discussion but some felt it was a bit of a waste of time and there were quite a few unfavourable comments to the effect that, because of budgetary constraints, relevant training did not happen.

Administrative and support staff

General comments on the review process

- I thought it was very helpful. We were relaxed over it. You could talk to him.

- You're one-to-one with your boss. You chatted, and it wasn't as if it was your boss. It was more relaxed. He would listen and then you'd chat about it. I enjoyed it.

- My manager handled the meeting very well. His manner was friendly and open and it was more like a chance to have a conversation than a formal meeting. I felt quite pleased at the end. Before that, I never got the opportunity to know him.

- I felt it was very positive.

- I think I dreaded my first meeting. But after the meeting I felt very positive about it.

- I think it gives you the opportunity to state how you feel you might be able to improve your job and make the job run smoother.

- You've just done your job ordinarily and you don't think twice about it. You don't need praise.

- I don't really get negative feedback. My boss tells me about areas where he feels I could improve. And this is constructive.

Comments on setting objectives

- I thought it was beneficial in that you see eye to eye with boss. But it was a bit like one-way traffic. It was about how they think your work should be done rather than taking up matters that are personal to you.

- It's very good. You can agree your targets, there and then, and you know where you are going.

Observations

The staff were remarkably positive about performance management – 84 per cent of their comments were favourable. They particularly liked the opportunity to talk to their managers and generally felt that the meetings went well.

Focus groups: organization F (a charity)

Managers

General comments about the process

- It tries to appraise and reward people at the same time. This is a fundamental mistake.

- It is quite useful, but it depends on how well it is connected with the operating plans of the department. Without a planning network in your own area, it is just words, without any substance.

- I find the best part of this appraisal is that it puts a clear focus on when you are going to talk to somebody.

- Your normal management skills involve interacting with employees – actively following up and discussing things. That is part of the process and the appraisal meeting is not a substitute for it.

Comment on objectives setting

- We sit down and think what, in the context of what we want to do, is best for that person to do. There is no opportunity for that person to contribute. It's top down.

Link with pay

- The appraisals are leading to PRP – the score on the door leads to money in your pocket.

- PRP is perceived by many as a possible problem because it will get back to what we had pre the grading system – favouritism.

Comment on rating

- I don't like the rating. You can't sum up someone in three numbers.

Observations

The feelings about performance management were mixed; only 55 per cent of the comments were favourable. Concern was expressed about the objective-setting process, rating and the link to pay, and some group members expressed doubts about the value of the performance review meetings.

Staff

General comments about the review process

- I definitely think it is worthwhile. It's useful to have a chat – you can discuss any issues on either side.

- The old reviews were just about someone giving you their opinions of what they thought of you rather than you giving feedback on what you think about it all.

- I have no problems with the process.

- Initially I thought it was a worthwhile exercise but I now think it's just total repetition. I know before I go in what conversation I'm going to have.

- If things do go wrong for reasons beyond your control you should raise them along the way. But I suspect that many people wait until the review process to tell their managers what's gone wrong. And that's not the way to do it.

Comment on setting objectives

- The targets you are asked to achieve can be very subjective and very difficult. We have this thing called 'stretch', which means that you think of a number and treble it. And that puts the fear of God into some people: 'How am I going to achieve those targets?'

Observations

There were quite a few negative comments – only 35 per cent were favourable. There was a fairly general feeling in the group that the meetings were not productive and staff disliked the target-setting process.

Overall comments on the focus group findings

Overall, and taking account of the caveats mentioned at the beginning of this chapter, there was a fairly high – sometimes very high – proportion of favourable comments from all the groups except those from Organization A (which were largely influenced by very negative feelings about performance-related pay) and the staff in Organization F. What appealed particularly to many people, managers and staff alike, was the opportunity performance management gave both parties to have a worthwhile discussion about work. There was no real evidence that either managers or staff disliked the process. Those who thought it a waste of time were in a tiny minority.

This finding is completely at variance with the assumptions made by many commentators about the inadequacies – iniquities according to some academics – of the process. If managements in these organizations were using performance management solely to get compliance with their commands, this fact had certainly escaped the people who attended the focus group meetings. And the sturdy way in which other criticisms were expressed about, for example, rating and performance-related pay (or in one case the lack of support at the top) indicated that the group members would not have hesitated to express their distrust of their managements' motives, if they had any.

In general the main messages that these groups delivered were that:

- They liked the performance review process itself.

- They disliked rating – often vehemently.

- They disliked the way in which performance-related pay was operated.

- They sometimes had problems with objective setting, especially if they were at the bottom of a cascade.

- They wholeheartedly approved of the developmental aspects of performance management as it affected them, although in some cases their enthusiasm was modified by a perceived inability or unwillingness to spend money on training.

Of course, the conclusion cannot be drawn from this small and unrepresentative sample that all is well with performance management elsewhere. But it does indicate that some organizations can get it right on the whole – and if they can, so can others. And getting it right is not about using 'best practice' systems but by a determination led from the top to explain why performance management is worthwhile and to make it work. This belief was shared with managers, team leaders and staff in these organizations by example, thorough communications, comprehensive training, and continuing support, encouragement and guidance to all concerned. And that is the secret of their success.

16

The Impact of
Performance Management

If performance management processes are intended to improve organizational performance, how well do they perform? This chapter aims to provide an answer to this question, so far as an answer can be provided. The chapter covers:

- how performance management is expected to improve performance;

- a review of the problems of establishing the impact of performance management on corporate performance – the causality issue;

- the evidence from research on the relationship between performance management and firm performance.

How performance management is expected to improve performance

Performance management is expected to improve organizational performance generally by creating a performance culture in which the achievement of high performance is a way of life. Specifically, the impact is supposed to be made by improving individual and, in the rare situations where this is catered for, team performance.

Individual performance development happens by defining what good performance looks like, agreeing performance goals, identifying where performance needs to improve and deciding on the steps required to achieve that improvement through performance improvement plans, personal development plans and coaching. A more detailed description of what performance management should contribute was defined by Jones *et al* (1995) as follows:

- Communicate a shared vision throughout the organization to help establish and support appropriate leadership and management styles.

- Define individual requirements and expectation of all employees in terms of the inputs and outputs expected from them, thus reducing confusion and ambiguity.

- Provide a framework and environment for teams to develop and succeed.

- Provide the climate and systems that support reward and communicate how people and the organization can achieve improved performance.

- Achieve improved performance.

- Help people manage ambiguity.

It is assumed that managers and their team members, working together on a continuing basis throughout the year to use performance management processes such as goal setting, feedback, performance analysis and coaching, will create a situation in which continuous improvement in results will be guaranteed. This could be regarded as an unrealistic aspiration – an optimistic belief – but it is the one that underpins the concept of performance management. The Holy Grail of performance management is to provide evidence that this belief is justified. But it isn't easy for the reasons given below.

Establishing the impact

Establishing the impact between human resource management (HRM) practices, including performance management, and firm performance is problematic. This is because causality – determining the link between independent and dependent variables (cause and effect) – is a major issue in research, especially in the HRM field. Correlation does not imply causation. It may be relatively easy to establish correlations in the shape of a demonstration that X is associated with Y; it is much more difficult and sometimes impossible to prove that X causes Y. There are two main reasons for this. The first one is the existence of multiple causation. There may be a number of factors contributing to a result. Researchers pursuing the Holy Grail of trying to establish what HRM as a whole or any aspect of HRM such as performance management contributes to firm performance are usually confronted with a number of reasons why a firm has done well in addition to adopting 'best practice' HRM, whatever that is. Statistical techniques can be used to 'control' some variables, that is to eliminate them from the analysis, but it is difficult if not impossible to ensure that HRM practices have been completely isolated and that their direct impact on firm performance has been measured. Boselie, Dietz and Boon (2005) referred to the causal distance between an HRM input and an output such as financial performance: 'Put simply, so many variables and events, both internal and external, affect organizations that this direct linkage strains credibility.'

> ## Multiple causation (London, Mone and Scott, 2004)
>
> HR practitioners might not be choosing the appropriate criteria to evaluate performance management programmes. Organizations may expect that these programmes will affect bottom line outcomes at the organization or company level, outcomes that are influenced by many factors, while the programmes were designed to affect individual learning and behaviours that have only indirect and long-term effects on bottom-line outcomes.

Second, there is the phenomenon of reverse causation when a cause is pre-dated by an effect – A might have caused B, but alternatively B may have come first and be responsible for A. For example, it is possible to demonstrate that firms with effective learning and development programmes do better than those without. But it might equally be the case that it is high-performing firms that introduce effective learning and development programmes. It can be hard to be certain. Purcell *et al* (2003) explained that while it is possible 'that more HR practices leads to higher economic return', it is just as possible 'that it is successful firms that can afford more extensive (and expensive) HRM practices'. Their conclusion was that HR practice feeds in as an 'ingredient' in the workplace and, through various mechanisms, feeds out through the other side as improved performance.

Any theory about the impact of an HRM practice such as performance management on organizational performance must be based on three propositions: 1) that the HR practice can make a direct impact on employee characteristics such as engagement, commitment, motivation and skill; 2) if employees have these characteristics it is probable that organizational performance in terms of productivity, quality and the delivery of high levels of customer service will improve; and 3) if such aspects of organizational performance improve, the financial results achieved by the organization will improve. Note, however, that there are two intermediate factors between the HRM practice and financial performance (employee characteristics affected by the practice and the impact of those characteristics on non-financial performance). According to these propositions, HRM or an HRM practice does not make a direct impact.

In the light of these problems it is hardly surprising that there is little if any convincing research evidence of a causal link between performance management and firm performance. As described below, there is indeed one research project that established a causal relationship between a performance management technique (goal setting) and individual performance (Latham and Locke, 1979) but this did not cover a complete performance management system. Research conducted by McDonald and Smith (1991) purported to demonstrate a causal relationship between performance management and firm performance but suffered from the problem of reversed causality. A few studies have found that high-performing firms had performance management (but did not establish a link between firm performance and the presence of performance management). There is evidence from a number of surveys that HR people believed that there was a link without offering supporting evidence. But the 1992 IPM research and rigorous analysis of later IPD research conducted by Guest and Conway (1998) failed to prove a connection.

Evidence from research

The following research projects and other analytical studies that deal with the impact of performance management on overall firm performance or as aspects of individual performance are summarized in this section:

- Latham and Locke (1976);
- McDonald and Smith (1991);
- IPM (1992);
- Rodgers and Hunter (1991);
- Bernardin *et al* (1995);
- Guest and Conway (1998);
- Gallup (2005);
- Sibson and WorldatWork (2007);
- Watson Wyatt (2008).

Latham and Locke

As reported by Latham and Locke (1979): 'In a 14-year programme of research, we have found that goal setting does not necessarily have to be part of a wider management system to motivate performance effectively. It can be used as a technique in its own right.'

Laboratory research established that 'individuals assigned hard goals persistently performed better than people assigned moderately difficult or easy goals'. Furthermore, individuals who had specific, challenging goals outperformed those who were given such vague goals as 'do your best'.

Field research in a logging company involving 292 supervisors established that those who set specific production goals achieved the highest productivity. A further study of 892 supervisors produced the same result.

Another study in a logging company involved setting a difficult but attainable target to drivers for the weight of wood they should load on their trucks. They were told that they would receive no reward for achieving the target but that no one would be criticized for failing to do so. After the third month performance exceeded 90 per cent of the trucks' capacity compared with 58–63 per cent previously. This level has been sustained for the seven years to date.

An experiment was conducted with typists to test whether participation in setting goals would yield better results than individually set goals. The only difference between these approaches was that the participative goals were set at a higher level than the non-participative goals. The impact on performance (typing speeds) was the same. The conclusion was that it did not matter how the goal was set. What mattered was that a goal was set. The results of this experiment were replicated later with engineers.

An analysis of 10 field studies conducted by various researchers for a range of jobs showed that the percentage change in performance after goal setting ranged from 11 per cent to 27 per cent (median 16 per cent).

This research had considerable influence on the management-by-objectives movement; it is still regarded as a fundamental motivation theory and the Latham and Locke advice on goal setting as given in Chapter 7 is still valid today.

McDonald and Smith

Research was conducted by McDonald and Smith (1991) covering 437 publicly quoted US companies. The findings were that the 205 respondents with performance management as opposed to the others without had:

- higher profits, better cash flows, stronger stock market performance and higher stock value;
- significant gains over three years in financial performance and productivity;
- higher sales growth per employee;
- lower real growth in number of employees.

The researchers commented that: 'In the successful companies the difference in managing employee performance seems to be that it is regarded as a mainstream business issue, not an isolated "personnel problem".'

This is a classic case of reversed causality. Performance management systems may have generated successful companies but it is just as likely that the successful companies were the ones with the inclination and money to introduce sophisticated practices such as performance management.

Institute of Personnel Management

It was reported by the IPM in 1992 that their extensive research found no evidence that improved performance in the private sector is associated with the pursuit of formal performance management programmes. Poor financial performers were as likely to introduce performance management as good performers. There were no readily available and comparable measures of performance in the public sector to test this link even though performance management is more likely to be adopted in the public sector.

However, one positive theme that was traced throughout the research was the extent to which performance management raised awareness of the pressures on the organization to perform.

Rodgers and Hunter

A meta-analysis by Rodgers and Hunter (1991) of 70 studies in goal setting, participation in decision making and objective feedback (as included in typical management by objectives programmes) found that 69 of them showed productivity gains and only two showed productivity losses. This led to the conclusion that management by objectives programmes, when properly implemented and when supported by top management, had an almost universally positive effect on productivity.

Bernardin, Hagan and Kane

Bernardin et al (1995) found improvements in subordinate and peer ratings following 360-degree feedback, but no changes in customer ratings or sales volume.

Guest and Conway

The analysis by Guest and Conway (1998) covered the 388 organizations with performance management surveyed by the IPD in 1997. The key criteria used for determining the effectiveness of performance management were the achievement of financial targets, development of skills, development of competence, improved customer care and improved quality. Against these criteria, over 90 per cent of respondents rated performance management as being moderately or highly effective. The personnel managers, who in the main responded to the survey, believed that others, and more particularly senior managers, are even more positive in their evaluation. Many also believe that the overall performance of their organization, judged by internal criteria such as quality, productivity and cost, and external criteria such as market share and profitability, are at least as good as and are often better than that of their main competitors.

The features of the performance management process that were likely to determine the degree to which performance management was rated as effective included the use of more innovative practices (eg 360-degree feedback), the presence of a formal evaluation system, a focus on employee contribution and achievement of individual objectives, and line management responsibility for keeping documentation.

But there were caveats. The analysis indicated that the views of respondents to the survey should all be viewed with extreme caution since they are often based on a very limited form of formal evaluation, or on an absence of any formal evaluation. This raises serious questions about the basis for the generally positive assessment of performance management.

Further more detailed statistical analysis of the replies to the questionnaire failed to demonstrate consistent evidence of any link between the practice of performance management and outcomes such as the achievement of financial targets, achievement of quality and customer service goals and employee development goals. The conclusion reached was that this survey has produced no convincing evidence that performance management has an impact on overall organizational performance.

Gallup

As reported by Risher (2005) Gallup has analysed its Q 12 survey and found that employers with a formal performance review process have more engaged employees – 33 per cent versus 21 per cent – and fewer disengaged employees – 12 per cent versus 29 per cent.

Sibson and WorldatWork

As reported by Kochanski (2007) a survey by Sibson and WorldatWork found that high-performing firms have strong leadership support for performance management. An analysis of total return to shareholders over a three-year period (2003–05) revealed that 64 per cent of the top performing companies had performance management systems that were rated as effective compared to only 36 per cent of the of bottom performing companies. The companies that excelled at performance management: 1) used their systems as the primary way to manage individual performance throughout the company; 2) have strong leadership support; and 3) have more line champions.

Watson Wyatt

As cited by Pulakos, Mueller-Hanson and O'Leary (2008) a recent Watson Wyatt survey found that only 30 per cent of workers felt that their performance management system helped to improve performance. Less than 40 per cent said that the system established clear performance goals or generated honest feedback.

Conclusions

The results of these studies are mixed. But it is still possible to believe in the benefits of performance management to organizations on the assumption that people are more likely to respond positively and are more likely to work to improve their performance and develop their capabilities if they share in the processes of defining expectations and reviewing performance and competency against those expectations, and are involved in creating and implementing plans for developing their skills and competences. If this happens generally (admittedly often a big if), and if the organization provides the managerial and systems support necessary, than the presumption that this will contribute to overall performance improvement is not unreasonable, even if it cannot be proved.

Part V

The Application of Performance Management

17

Managing
Organizational Performance

The management of organizational performance is the continuing responsibility of top management who plan, organize, monitor and control activities and provide leadership to achieve strategic objectives and satisfy the needs and requirements of stakeholders. Individual and team performance management systems as discussed elsewhere in this book play an important part. But they function within the context of what is done to manage organizational performance and to develop effective work systems.

Managing organizational performance is a complex business that is examined in this chapter under the following headings:

- the process of managing organizational performance;

- the strategic approach to managing organizational performance;

- business performance management systems;

- increasing organizational capability;

- performance management and human capital management;

- performance management and talent management;

- developing a high-performance culture;

- measuring performance.

The process of managing organizational performance

As Gheorghe and Hack (2007) observe: 'Actively managing performance is simply running a business – running the entire business as one entity. It's a continuous cycle of planning, executing, measuring results and planning the next actions. In the context of a larger strategic initiative, that means continuous improvement.'

> *Unified business performance management (Gheorghe and Hack, 2007)*
>
> The fundamental problem managers face as they make day-to-day decisions is an inability to link their actions to key performance measures. What managers need is more enterprise intelligence, actionable information that enables them to know where their problems are, in real time, know who their key performers are without combing through a stack of reports, know where their company is at risk, before the numbers turn bad, and, most of all, know which process could improve performance.

The management of organizational performance takes place on a number of dimensions. It is a strategic approach that has to take account of the needs of multiple stakeholders and makes use of business performance management systems.

The dimensions of managing organizational performance

Sink and Tuttle (1990) stated that managing organizational performance includes five dimensions:

- creating visions for the future;
- planning – determining the present organizational state, and developing strategies to improve that state;
- designing, developing and implementing improvement interventions;
- designing, redesigning, developing, and implementing measurement and evaluation systems;
- putting cultural support systems in place to reward and reinforce progress.

The overall approach to managing organizational performance

The overall approach to managing organizational performance as described in the rest of this chapter is based on processes of strategic performance management supported by the use of a business performance management system. In general it is concerned with developing organizational capability that involves creating a high-performance culture, human capital management and talent management. In particular it makes use of various approaches to measuring and monitoring performance.

The strategic approach to managing organizational performance

A strategic approach to managing organizational performance means taking a broad and long-term view of where the business is going and managing performance in ways that ensure that this strategic thrust is maintained. The objective is to provide a sense of direction in an often turbulent environment so that the business needs of the organization and the individual and collective needs of its employees can be met by the development and implementation of integrated systems for managing and developing performance.

Performance management strategy is based on the resource-based view that it is the strategic development of the organization's rare, hard to imitate and hard to substitute human resources that produces its unique character and creates competitive advantage. The strategic goal will be to 'create firms which are more intelligent and flexible than their competitors' (Boxall, 1996) by developing more talented staff and by extending their skills base, and this is exactly what performance management aims to do.

The strategic approach adopted by Johnson & Johnson was described by Wortzel-Hoffman and Boltizar (2007) as follows.

Performance management strategy at Johnson & Johnson

As we embarked on developing an integrated performance and development process into the organization, we knew that driving change and an enhanced process requires a cultural shift within an organization. The best performance management becomes a continuous process and is not a one time event; it takes time and effort and a dedication to developing people. We also knew that from a business standpoint it was critical to build and develop the talent pipeline of the organization to meet the aggressive business goals and dynamically changing marketplace.

Kathy Armstrong and Adrian Ward (2005) summed up the strategic role of performance management very well when they wrote:

There is also opportunity for performance management to help drive through organizational change. Instead of being a tactical initiative, perhaps performance management has a more strategic role to play. The challenge is for performance management to retain a strategic role rather than tending towards tactical activities, such as the process. Performance management can provide a new way of looking at performance and help to embed new behaviours and facilitate the move to a culture that is both more open and more focused on the achievement of new outputs.

Implementing strategic organizational performance management

Organizational performance management systems are strategic in the sense that they are aligned to the business strategy of the organization and support the achievement of its strategic goals. They will focus on developing work systems and the working environment as well as developing individuals. To develop the systems and make them function effectively it is necessary to ensure that the strategy is understood, including, as Kaplan and Norton (2000) put it, 'the crucial but perplexing processes by which intangible assets will be converted into tangible outcomes'. The notion of mapping strategy was originated by them as a development of their concept of the balanced scorecard (see later in this chapter). Strategy maps show the cause-and-effect links by which specific improvements create desired outcomes. They are means of describing the elements of the organization's systems and their interrelationships. They therefore provide a route map for systems improvement leading to performance improvement. In addition, they give employees a clear line of sight into how their jobs are linked to the overall objectives of the organization and provide a visual representation of a company's critical objectives and the relationships between them that drive organizational performance. Bourne, Franco and Wilkes (2003) call them 'success maps', which they describe as diagrams that show the logic of how the objectives of the organization interact to deliver overall performance. An example of a strategy map is given in Figure 17.1.

Figure 17.1 A strategy map

This map shows an overall objective to improve profitability as measured by return on capital employed. In the next line the map indicates that the main contributors to increased profitability are increases to the gross margin (the difference between the value of sales and the cost of sales), improvements to operational capability and better cost management. At the next level down the objective is to increase sales turnover in order to increase the gross margin. How this is to be achieved is set out in the next group of objectives and their interconnections, comprising increases in customer satisfaction and sales force effectiveness, innovations in product/market development and marketing, and improvements in customer service and quality levels. The key objective of improving operational capability is underpinned by developments in high-performance working and the contribution of the organization's human capital. The latter is supported by human resource management objectives in the fields of performance management, talent management, levels of employee engagement and learning and development.

The overall objective of increasing profitability in this example addresses the concerns of only one section of the stakeholders of an organization, namely the investors. This need would probably be given precedence by many quoted companies. But there are other objectives they could and should have that relate to their other stakeholders, for example those related to corporate social responsibility. These could be catered for in separate strategy maps. Better still, they could be linked to their commercial objectives. Public and voluntary sector organizations will certainly have objectives that relate to all their stakeholders as well as their overall purpose. A stakeholder approach to strategic performance management is required.

The stakeholder approach to strategic organizational performance management

Atkinson, Waterhouse and Wells (1997) argue that a company exists to serve the objectives of its multiple stakeholders – employees, customers, suppliers, regulators and the community at large as well as shareholders. Companies must provide for explicit or implicit contracts with their stakeholders. Their performance management systems should guide the design and implementation of processes that satisfy the requirements of each stakeholder group and monitor and evaluate the extent to which the organization is meeting these needs.

The performance prism

A multiple stakeholder framework for performance management – the performance prism – has been formulated by Neely, Adams and Kennerley (2002). This framework is based on the proposition that organizations exist to satisfy their stakeholders and their wants and needs should be considered first. Neely, Adams and Kennerley contend that companies in particular must assume a broader role than simply delivering value to their shareholders. To be successful over time, even for and on behalf of shareholders, businesses must address multiple stakeholders. If companies do not give each of their stakeholders the right level of focus, both their corporate reputation and their market capitalization – and therefore shareholder value – are likely to suffer in one way or another. They suggest that the performance prism can facilitate or structure the analysis of multiple stakeholders in preparation for applying performance measurement criteria.

They explain the term 'performance prism' as follows:

> *A prism refracts light. It illustrates the hidden complexity of something as apparently simple as white light. So it is with the Performance Prism. It illustrates the true complexity of performance measurement and management. It is a thinking aid that seeks to integrate five related perspectives and provide a structure that allows executives to think through the answers to five fundamental questions:*

- Stakeholder satisfaction: Who are our stakeholders and what do they want and need?

- Stakeholder contribution: What do we want and need from our stakeholders?

- Strategies: What strategies do we need to put in place to satisfy these wants and needs?

- Processes: What processes do we need to put in place to satisfy these wants and needs?

- Capabilities: What capabilities – people, practices, technology and infrastructure – do we need to put in place to allow us to operate our processes more effectively and efficiently?

Moullin (2002) described how the performance prism was applied in London Youth, a charity whose aim is to provide support and improve the range and quality of informal education and social activities available to young people in the Greater London area. The performance prism was used to develop a 'success map', which showed the main stakeholders and main needs of each, including youth workers, youth club management committees, London Youth staff and funders (statutory/trusts and individual/corporate). Performance measurements were then developed for each group of stakeholders followed by an integrative strategy.

Business performance management systems

A business performance management (BPM) system can be used to support the achievement of the performance management strategy. It is an information technology (IT) based approach to organizational performance management described by Frolick and Ariyachandra (2006) as a series of business processes and applications designed to optimize both the development and the execution of business strategy. It involves two primary tasks. First, it facilitates the creation of strategic goals. Second, it supports the subsequent management of the performance to those goals. Strategic goals are developed by stipulating specific objectives and key performance indicators that are meaningful to the organization. The objectives and indicators are then associated with operational metrics for planning, monitoring and control purposes that are linked to the business strategy. BPM is focused on the entire enterprise, in contrast to other IT applications focusing on specific operational areas such as customer relations.

The BPM framework is composed of four core processes. They are: 1) developing strategy; 2) planning; 3) monitoring and analysing; and 4) taking corrective action (as shown in Figure 17.2). The first two steps represent the formulation of business strategy while the last two define how to modify and execute strategy. This closed-loop process captures business strategy and then translates it into strategically aligned business operations.

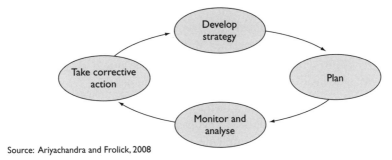

Source: Ariyachandra and Frolick, 2008

Figure 17.2   The business performance planning cycle

A BPM system as provided by suppliers such as Oracle is based on a common database and modular software design. The common database can allow every department of a business to store and retrieve information in real time. The information has to be reliable, accessible and easily shared. The modular software design means businesses can select the modules they need from the vendor and add new modules of their own to improve business performance.

Transactional systems such as enterprise resource planning (a company-wide information system designed to coordinate all the resources, information and activities needed to complete business processes such as order fulfilment or billing), customer relationship management (CRM), supply chain management (SCM), and human capital management (HCM) help to run day-to-day business operations. Business performance management systems integrate these systems and enable executives to manage the business strategically by providing information across all functions that is aligned to strategic imperatives by answering three basic questions: 1) Where have we been? 2) Where are we now? 3) Where are we going? and providing the basis for answering the fourth key question: 4) How do we get there?

Pritchard (2008) points out that any enterprise-wide business performance management improvement initiative must include managers and employees from across the organization. All functions have to operate in unison. And if the company doesn't integrate financial and non-financial data, there is only so much that a business performance management tool can do to help decision makers understand the results.

Organizational capability

Organizational capability is the capacity of an organization to function effectively. It is about its ability to guarantee high levels of performance, achieve its purpose (sustained competitive advantage in a commercial business), deliver results and, importantly, meet the needs of its stakeholders. It is concerned with the organization as a system and is in line with the belief expressed by Coens and Jenkins (2002) that to 'focus on the overall "system" of the organization yields better results than trying to get individual employees to improve their performance'.

The aim is to increase organizational effectiveness by obtaining better performance from people, getting them to work well together, improving organizational processes such as the formulation and implementation of strategy and the achievement of high quality and levels of customer service, and facilitating the management of change.

This has to take place in a context in which organizations are increasingly embracing a new management culture based on inclusion, involvement and participation, rather than on the traditional command, control and compliance paradigm that Flaherty (1999) claims 'cannot bring about the conditions and competence necessary to successfully meet the challenges of endless innovation; relentless downsizing, re-engineering, and multicultural working holistically'. This new management paradigm requires the development of a high-performance work environment through management practices that value and support achievement, growth and learning. It also calls for facilitative behaviours that focus on employee empowerment, learning and development. In other words, it needs performance management.

Organizational capability and organizational development

As described by Beer (1980), organizational development is 'a system wide process of data collection, diagnosis, action planning, intervention and evaluation'. Traditionally, organization development or OD was based on behavioural science concepts, but the focus has shifted to a number of other approaches such as human capital management, talent management, change management, high-performance work systems, total quality management and, importantly, performance management. These can be described as holistic processes that attempt to improve overall organizational effectiveness from a particular perspective. As noted by Cummins and Worley (2005), the practice of OD has gone 'far beyond its humanistic origins by incorporating concepts from organization strategy that complement the early emphasis on social processes'. Organizational capability could be regarded as an outcome of organizational development but with the focus more on performance management.

Performance management and human capital management

Human capital management (HCM) is concerned with obtaining, analysing and reporting on data that inform the direction of value-adding, people management, strategic, investment and operational decisions at corporate level and at the level of front-line management. Performance management data is an important source of information on human capital and its contribution to business. Lawler and McDermott (2003) made the point that: 'It is very difficult to effectively manage human capital without a system that measures performance and performance capability... An effective performance management system should be a key building block of every organization's human capital management system.'

Given the growing recognition of human capital as a source of organizational value (ie the resource-based view) and the pressure therefore on organizations to collect, analyse and report on their human capital, performance management data is likely to become a key source of information both on the value of human capital and on the management activity needed to manage and deploy this precious asset.

Performance management data can be used to:

- demonstrate an organization's ability to raise competence levels;
- assess how long it takes for a new employee to reach optimum performance;
- provide feedback on development programmes including induction, coaching and mentoring in terms of increased performance or capacity to take on new roles;
- demonstrate the success of internal recruitment programmes;
- indicate how successful an organization is at achieving its objectives at the individual, team and department levels;
- track skills levels and movement in any skills gap in the organization;
- match actual behaviour against desired behaviour;
- assess commitment to values and mission;
- assess understanding of strategy and contribution.

Most of this information is already captured during the performance management process. To turn this into measure of human capital evaluation, the data need to be processed in a systematic and widely accessible way.

Performance management and talent management

Talented people possess special gifts, abilities and aptitudes that enable them to perform effectively. Talent management is the process of identifying, developing, recruiting, retaining and deploying these people. The term may refer simply to management succession planning and management development activities, although this notion does not really add anything to these familiar processes except a new, although admittedly quite evocative, name. It is better to regard talent management as a more comprehensive and integrated bundle of activities, the aim of which is to secure the flow of talent in an organization, bearing in mind that talent is a major corporate resource.

Michaels, Handfield-Jones and Axelrod (2001), who coined the phrase 'the war on talent' and initiated the talent management movement, identified one of the five imperatives that companies need to act on if they are going to win this war as 'using job experience, coaching and mentoring to cultivate the potential in managers' – all aspects of performance management.

Talent management relies on performance management processes to provide a basis for identifying and rewarding (in the broadest sense) talented people. Performance management ensures that they develop their talent by learning from experience through constructive feedback, by coaching and by the formulation and implementation of personal development plans.

Developing a high-performance culture

Organizations achieve sustained high performance through the systems of work they adopt but these systems are managed and operated by people. Ultimately, therefore, high-performance working is about improving performance through people. This can be done through the development and implementation of a high-performance culture through high-performance work systems in which performance management plays an important part.

High-performance cultures

High-performance cultures are ones in which the achievement of high levels of performance is a way of life. The characteristics of such cultures are set out below.

Characteristics of a high-performance culture

- Management defines what it requires in the shape of performance improvements, sets goals for success and monitors performance to ensure that the goals are achieved.
- Alternative work practices are adopted such as job redesign, autonomous work teams, improvement groups, team briefing and flexible working.
- People know what's expected of them – they understand their goals and accountabilities.
- People feel that their job is worth doing, and there is a strong fit between the job and their capabilities.
- People are empowered to maximize their contribution.
- There is strong leadership from the top that engenders a shared belief in the importance of continuing improvement.
- There is a focus on promoting positive attitudes that result in an engaged, committed and motivated workforce.
- Performance management processes are aligned to business goals to ensure that people are engaged in achieving agreed objectives and standards.
- Capacities of people are developed through learning at all levels to support performance improvement and are provided with opportunities to make full use of their skills and abilities.
- A pool of talent ensures a continuous supply of high performers in key roles.
- People are valued and rewarded according to their contribution.
- People are involved in developing high-performance practices.
- There is a climate of trust and teamwork, aimed at delivering a distinctive service to the customer.
- A clear line of sight exists between the strategic aims of the organization and those of its departments and its staff at all levels.

High-performance work systems

High-performance cultures can be developed through a high-performance work system (HPWS), which as described by Becker and Huselid (1998) is 'an internally consistent and coherent HRM system that is focused on solving operational problems and implementing the firm's competitive strategy'. They suggest that such a system 'is the key to the acquisition, motivation and development of the underlying intellectual assets that can be a source of sustained competitive advantage'. This is because it has the following characteristics.

Characteristics of an HPWS

- It links the firm's selection and promotion decisions to validated competency models.

- It is the basis for developing strategies that provide timely and effective support for the skills demanded to implant the firm's strategies.

- It enacts compensation and performance management policies that attract, retain and motivate high-performance employees.

High-performance work systems provide the means for creating a performance culture. They embody ways of thinking about performance in organizations and how it can be improved. They are concerned with developing and implementing bundles of complementary practices that as an integrated whole will make a much more powerful impact on performance than if they were dealt with as separate entities.

The basic features of an HPWS were described by Shih, Chiang and Hsu (2005) as follows:

- Job infrastructure – workplace arrangements that equip workers with the proper abilities to do their jobs, provide them with the means to do their jobs, and give them the motivation to do their jobs. These practices must be combined to produce their proper effects.

- Training programmes to enhance employee skills – investment in increasing employee skills, knowledge and ability.

- Information sharing and worker involvement mechanisms – to understand the available alternatives and make correct decisions.

- Compensation and promotion opportunities that provide motivation – to encourage skilled employees to engage in effective discretionary decision making in a variety of environmental contingencies.

The contribution of performance management

Performance management contributes to the development of a high-performance culture through an HPWS by generally delivering the message in an organization that high performance is important. It defines what high performance is and how managers and their teams should achieve it. It explains how performance should be measured and the steps that should be taken to monitor results in comparison with expectations. The means of getting high performance are provided by motivating people, defining the performance expectations implicit in the psychological contract, creating high levels of engagement and enhancing skills and competencies through feedback, coaching and personal development planning.

Measuring performance

Managing organizational performance means measuring and monitoring performance by the use of measures or metrics. The significance of measurement and the principles governing its use are discussed below. As also covered in this section, there is a choice of measures and these can be expressed and categorized as key performance indicators (KPIs), scorecards or the balanced scorecard, and communicated by means of dashboards.

The significance of measurement

As was emphasized by the Association for Management Information in Financial Services (AMIF, 2005) 'Objectives, which may vary from organization to organization, are met by the choices management makes in deploying its resources. Management's ability to make informed decisions is tied to the quality of management information available to them.'

The approach to measurement

The approach to performance measurement (AMIFs Research Committee, 2005)

In order to determine 'good' performance versus 'bad' performance it is necessary to have a well-defined base against which to compare actual results. This includes defining in advance the expectation as to acceptable performance.

There are four principles as defined by Quinn (2003) governing the use of performance measures or metrics:

- Measure the right things – the system must measure activities that directly contribute to an organization's performance.

- Clearly communicate what will be measured – measures that are ill defined, and/or not communicated will not be used or understood.

- Consistently apply the measures – measures should be applied consistently to all units of the organization; failure to do so will result in loss of support for the system.

- Act on the measures – the measurement data must be used in a constructive way. Not using the data or misapplying the data will have the same results: a lack of support for the measurement system.

Neely, Adams and Kennerley (2002) counsel that it is necessary to question constantly what is measured by answering two fundamental questions: Do we need it? Why do we need it? They comment that: 'We need to evaluate constantly whether or not the measures we have are the right ones for the organization. And if not, we need to find a way to get rid of them so that we do not waste time and effort capturing data that no one is using. In short, we need to practise "metricide" (ie do not let any metric or measure persist beyond its natural and useful life).'

At BP Lubricants as reported by Elliott and Coley-Smith (2005) the principles followed in developing their performance measurement system were:

- To focus the business on areas of strategic importance.

- To make sure employees have the right information at the right time to make the right decisions in support of strategy.

- To clearly understand the value-to-cost relationship of communication activities.

- To develop a measurement mindset that focuses people on improving performance.

But a word of caution is necessary about the concept of managing by metrics. Figures can conceal more than they reveal and it is possible for people to hide behind them. Data can be misleading. It is not enough just to tick boxes. Metrics may be a start but they cannot be relied on by themselves. If there is a problem the story behind the figures needs to be investigated, especially when the failure is systemic.

Types of measures

Traditionally, performance management systems were uni-dimensional – focused entirely on financial measures related to shareholder value such as return on capital employed, economic value added, earnings per share and price/earnings ratio and added value. But such traditional accounting-based performance measurement systems are insufficient in modern organizations where it is recognized that relationships with employees, customers, suppliers and other stakeholders are crucial aspects of how the organization is performing. Financial measures cannot evaluate important factors such as innovation, employee engagement, employee relations and levels of customer and employee satisfaction. These factors are sometimes called leading indicators (Gjerde and Hughes, 2007) because they inform management of the progress made on initiatives undertaken to improve performance. Measures of financial performance are lagging indicators because they reflect past results. Achieving an objective related to a lead measure indicates that performance is on track, and achieving an objective related to a lag measure shows that the goal has been accomplished. To identify lead measures it is necessary to establish what are the key factors that drive performance – the key performance indicators (KPIs) that form the basis of the performance monitoring and measurement system.

Jack Welch, former CEO of the General Electric Company, was quoted by Krames (2004) as saying that the three most important things you need to measure in a business are customer satisfaction, employee satisfaction and cash flow. Sink and Tuttle (1990) went further when they listed seven measurement categories of organizational performance: 1) effectiveness;

2) efficiency; 3) quality; 4) quality of working life; 5) innovation; 6) cost and prices; and 7) productivity.

The European Foundation for Quality Management (EFQM) model has the following elements:

- Leadership – how the behaviour and actions of the executive team and all other leaders inspire, support and promote a culture of total quality management.

- Policy and strategy – how the organization formulates, deploys and reviews its policy and strategy and turns it into plans and actions.

- People management – how the organization realizes the full potential of its people.

- Resources – how the organization manages resources effectively and efficiently.

- Processes – how the organization identifies, manages, reviews and improves its processes.

- Customer satisfaction – what the organization is achieving in relation to the satisfaction of its external customers.

- People satisfaction – what the organization is achieving in relation to the satisfaction of its people.

- Impact on society – What the organization is achieving in satisfying the needs and the expectations of the local, national and international community at large.

- Business results – what the organization is achieving in relation to its planned business objectives and in satisfying the needs and expectations of everyone with a financial interest or stake in the organization.

Key performance indicators

Key performance indicators (KPIs) are the results or outcomes that are identified as being crucial to the achievement of high performance and provide the basis for setting objectives and measuring performance. They must take account of the requirements of all stakeholders and should add social responsibility to the list of business objectives by including discretionary environmental initiatives, diversity and employee well-being in the set of KPIs.

A KPI is a special kind of metric. It measures something that is strategically important to the organization such as sales per square metre, added value per employee, rate of stock turnover, cost per unit of output, time to market and levels of employee engagement. In other words, as Schiff (2008) put it: 'A KPI is a metric that matters. You can have many metrics, but an organization needs only a handful of KPIs. Everything can't be considered "key," or nothing will stand out from the pack and get the attention it deserves.' The range of KPIs in different organizations is typically between six and 12, with potentially dozens of supporting metrics. However, the number depends on the type of organization and can be as low as three or as high as 24.

KPIs provide the basis for defining the crucial goals for which individuals are accountable. The measurement system has to ensure that performance in relation to the KPIs is recorded and analysed and that this information is passed on to accountable managers for action.

Scorecards

Scorecards record performance related to a set of KPIs. In effect, they are report cards on the organization's performance. For example, they can show sales per square metre in a store, comparing actuals with targets and analysing trends. As Dagan (2007) emphasizes: 'You should also not get carried away with trying to jam too many KPIs into your scorecard displays. Although the optimal number depends on your organization, a rule of thumb is that 6 to 10 KPIs are sufficient in most cases.' It should be possible to drill down into supporting tabular and graphical data to investigate any issues raised by the scorecard.

The balanced scorecard

Traditionally, scorecards tended to concentrate on financial measures. The aim of the balanced scorecard as originally formulated by Kaplan and Norton (1992, 1996) was to counter the tendency of companies to concentrate on short-term financial reporting. They emphasized that 'no single measure can provide a clear performance target or focus attention on the critical areas of the business. Managers want a balanced presentation of both financial and operational measures.' Their original concept of the scorecard required managers to answer four basic questions, which means looking at the business from four related perspectives as shown in Figure 17.3.

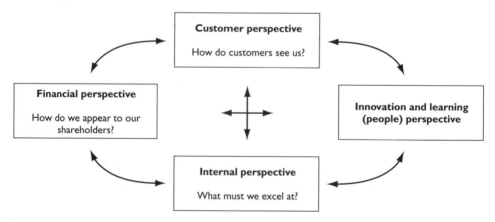

Figure 17.3   The balanced scorecard

Some organizations have replaced the innovation and learning perspective with a broader people or human capital element.

Kaplan and Norton believe that the balanced scorecard approach 'puts strategy and vision, not control at the centre'. They suggest that while it defines goals, it assumes that people will adopt whatever behaviours and take whatever actions are required to achieve those goals: 'Senior managers may know what the end result should be, but they cannot tell employees exactly how to achieve that result, if only because the conditions in which employees operate are constantly changing.'

They claim that the balanced scorecard can help to align employees' individual performance with the overall strategy: 'Scorecard users generally engage in three activities: communicating and educating, setting goals and linking rewards to performance measures.' They comment that:

Many people think of measurement as a tool to control behaviour and to evaluate past performance. The measures on a balanced scorecard, however, should be used as the cornerstone of a management system that communicates strategy, aligns individuals and teams to the strategy, establishes long-term strategic targets, aligns initiatives, allocates long and short-term resources and, finally, provides feedback and learning · about the strategy.

Research by Deloitte & Touche and *Personnel Today* (2002) found that 32 per cent of large UK companies were using balanced scorecards, although the methods varied. At Lloyds TSB the balanced scorecard blends a mix of financial metrics and non-financial indicators to provide a single integrated measure of performance that focuses on key indicators, from which a true reflection of organization performance could be gained. The scorecard thus enables the organization to focus on a small number of critical measures that create value for the organization.

Norwich Union Insurance described its balanced scorecard as a 'mechanism for implementing our strategy and measuring performance against our objectives and critical success factors to achieve the strategy'. The scorecard is cascaded throughout the organization to measure the operational activities that are contributing to the overall company strategy. The balanced scorecard changes from year to year. Most recently, it set out to achieve three goals: positive benefit, staff impacts and financial performance – in short, service, morale and profits. Previously, the emphasis was predominantly on profit, in order to deliver the promises made to the City and shareholders, but the company feels that more focus is now needed on service and morale.

A balanced scorecard was designed by Moullin (2002) specifically for the public and voluntary sectors, rather than being an adaptation from the private or other sectors. It has five perspectives:

- Strategic refers to the key performance outcomes, reflecting why the service exists and what it hopes to achieve.

- Service is concerned with how the organization looks to service users and other key stakeholders.

- Operational excellence refers to the effectiveness of process and of staff, and includes measures such as staff satisfaction.

- Financial refers to how well an organization manages its funds and keeps costs down.

- Innovation and learning looks at whether it is continuing to improve, learning from others and creating additional value for service users and other stakeholders.

But according to Schneiderman (1999): 'the vast majority of so-called balanced scorecards fail over time to meet the expectations of their creators.' He attributed this failure to three causes and suggests solutions. The first problem is a lack of clearly defined improvement objectives so that 'doing what you did gets you what you got'. It is necessary to set specific goals that take account of the means available to achieve them. The second is the absence of good metrics. To overcome this problem metrics should be clearly defined and easy to understand, accessible when needed to those who can best use them and linked to an underlying data system that enables the root causes of poor scorecard results to be identified and dealt with. The third is a failure to involve people in developing the balanced scorecard. It is necessary to get as many interested parties as possible to take part in selecting the right KPIs and deciding on what metrics should be associated with them.

Dashboards

A dashboard is a graphical display, designed to convey key performance measures on an organization's intranet system to a wide audience so that they can be assimilated and acted upon easily and swiftly. As Dover (2004) remarked: 'Dashboards are predominantly a data-delivery vehicle.' Dashboards use dials, 'traffic light' displays and graphs to make performance information available as and when required. An example of a basic dashboard with just three dials is illustrated in Figure 17.4.

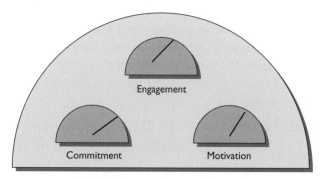

Figure 17.4   Example of a dashboard

As described by Dagan (2007), dashboards provide a rapid and convenient way for people to assess how they are doing by reference to the business metrics critical to their place in the organization. They can thus initiate prompt corrective action as needed. Dashboards can be constructed using real-time or near real-time feeds from a data warehouse frontline system. Dashboard displays can be enhanced with charts, graphs or even tabular data. However, it is important not to make the entry screen too busy because this might divert attention away from the important metrics. An alternative is to provide facilities for obtaining supporting information. For example, if a traffic light system shows a KPI that is red or yellow, then a click of the mouse should enable the user to drill down to pinpoint some of the underlying causes. Drill-down could be available to several layers with each layer providing even more details. Examples of a more elaborate dashboard that incorporates a traffic light system and one based entirely on traffic lights are given in Figures 17.5 and 17.6 respectively.

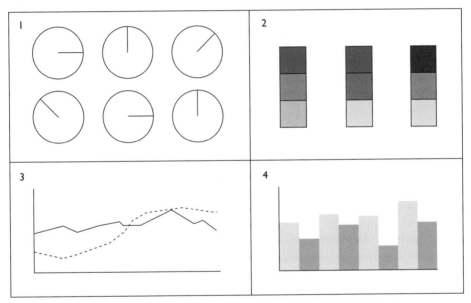

Figure 17.5   Example of dashboard with: (1) dials, (2) traffic lights, (3 and 4) graphs

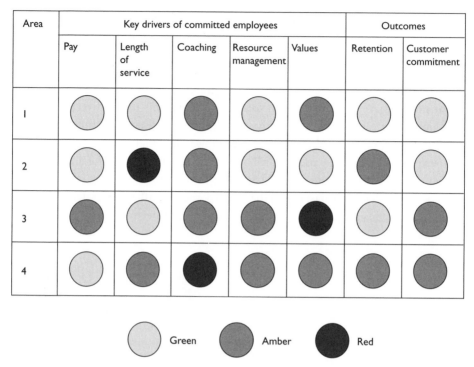

Figure 17.6   Human capital reporting dashboard for area managers: Nationwide

Developing measures

Each of the approaches to performance management based on measurement described above – scorecards, balanced scorecards and dashboards – depends on the quality of the measures used. The following steps should be taken when developing them:

- Involve as many as possible of those concerned in the development programme.

- Identify the key factors that drive performance.

- Define the key performance indicators (KPIs).

- Define what metrics are required, ie what should be measured and why, in order to provide information on performance related to each KPI.

- Decide how to measure – how information related to the measures and performance with regard to each KPI should be collected and presented.

- Set up a system for communicating information on performance through such media as scorecards or dashboards.

18

Managing
Team Performance

It is remarkable how little has been researched or written about performance management for teams. One of the most recently published books in the UK on performance management (Houldsworth and Jirasinghe, 2006) does not deal with it at all. This is in spite of the emphasis on good teamwork and high-performance teams, which, as described by Katzenbach and Smith (1993): 'invest much time and effort explaining, shaping and agreeing on a purpose that belongs to them, both collectively and individually. They are characterized by a deep sense of commitment to their growth and success.'

One of the frequently voiced criticisms of individual performance management is that it inhibits good teamwork. But the possibility of extending it to teams does not seem to have occurred to those critics.

Teams and performance

As Purcell, Hutchinson and Kinnie (1998) point out, teams can provide the 'elusive bridge between the aims of the individual employee and the objectives of the organization... teams can provide the medium for linking employee performance targets to the factors critical to the success of the business.' This is an important aspect of performance management and provides further justification for the payment of more attention to applying it to teams. How it is applied will be related to the following factors that affect team performance:

- the clarity of the team's goals in terms of expectations and priorities;

- how work is allocated to the team;

- how the team is working (its processes) in terms of cohesion, ability to handle internal conflict and pressure, relationships with other teams;

- the extent to which the team is capable of managing itself – setting goals and priorities, monitoring performance;

- the quality of leadership – even self-managed teams need a sense of direction that they cannot necessarily generate by themselves;

- the level of skill possessed by individual team members (including multi-skilling);
- the systems and resources support available to the team.

Overall, as suggested by Jones (1995):

> Teams need to have a shared purpose. They also need to have the necessary mix of skills and abilities and to be mutually accountable for the outcome.

The performance of individual team members

Individual team members can influence team performance in three ways: 1) the actual job they are doing and the skills, competences and behaviour they apply to the work; 2) the job they perform as team members; and 3) the team performance as a whole.

Although it is important to consider the performance management of teams as a whole (which is what the rest of this chapter is about), it is also important to consider the levels of performance and competence achieved by individual team members. Obviously, a prime criterion will be the contribution they make to the team in terms of both results and process.

Team competencies

The following is a selection of some of the key competencies for team members as developed by Hay/McBer (Gross, 1995):

> ## Competencies for team members: Hay/McBer
> - Interpersonal understanding – accurate interpretation of others' concerns, motives and feelings and recognition of their strengths and weaknesses.
> - Influence – using appropriate interpersonal styles and logical arguments to convince others to accept ideas or pleas.
> - Customer service orientation – demonstrating concern for meeting the needs of internal and external customers.
> - Adaptability – adapting easily to change.
> - Teamwork and cooperation – developing collaborative work that generates acceptable solutions.
> - Oral communication – expressing ideas in group situations.
> - Achievement orientation – setting and meeting challenging objectives.
> - Organizational commitment – performing work with broader organizational goals in mind.

Definition of a team

Before embarking on the development of team performance management processes it is necessary to define which teams will be involved. There are four basic types of teams:

- Organizational teams consist of people broadly linked together as in a top management team, or departmental heads in an organization. The team members can be associated with each other by the requirement to achieve an overall objective.

- Work teams consist of self-contained and permanent members who work closely together and interdependently to achieve specified results.

- Project teams consist of people brought together from different functions to complete a task over a period of months or even years.

- Ad hoc teams consist of people brought together from within a department or from a number of functions to tackle an immediate problem.

Performance management processes are most appropriate in tightly knit workteams and long-standing project teams. In a general sense, they can play a part in the management of performance in organizational teams. They will be inappropriate on a formal and continuing basis in an ad hoc team.

Performance measures for teams

Performance measures for teams will be related to the purpose of the team and its particular objectives and standards of performance. The following are some examples of how performance measures are established and used by various organizations.

- Automobile Association Finance Division – in the processing department, where high volume and routine tasks have to be performed, the measures are productivity and quality.

- The Benefits Agency – measures are agreed between managers and team members based on task definition, performance standards and timescales.

- Dartford Borough Council – measures are related to targets that are set for tasks that are suitable for all or most of the team to undertake together and are distinct from the tasks set for individual team members.

- IBM – 'bid teams' (project teams responsible for developing solutions for customers) have their performance measured by reference to their success in winning contracts.

- Lloyds Bank – the performance of branch teams below junior management level is related to two challenges: the 'sales challenge', which is linked to branch sales against target, and the 'service challenge', which is based on data obtained from customer questionnaires and mystery shopping.

- Norwich Union – performance measures for the financial planning consultant teams is based on 'net issued business', and on criteria for activity levels, appointments attended, questionnaires completed and cases issued.

- Pearl Assurance – the performance measures for policy processing and claims teams consist of 'hard' measures for speed and accuracy of processing, and 'soft' measures for levels of service to internal and external customers.

- Rank Xerox – the performance measures or 'metrics' for sales teams are based on customer satisfaction, sales revenue and market share.

Type of measures

Team performance measures in this sample are therefore mainly concerned with output, activity levels (eg speed of servicing), customer service and satisfaction, and financial results). Most measures for teams, as for individuals (see Chapter 4), are likely to fall into one or more of these categories.

A distinction is made by Harrington-Mackin (1994) between output/result measures of team performance and input/process measures. The output/results comprise:

- the achievement of team goals;

- customer satisfaction;

- quantity of work;

- quality of work;

- process knowledge;

- maintenance of technical systems.

The input/process measures comprise:

- support of team process;

- participation;

- collaboration and collective effort;

- participative decision making;

- interpersonal relations;

- acceptance of change;

- adaptability and flexibility.

Project team measures

Project team measures will refer to the project's goals, which may be staged over a number of intermediate milestones. The measure will primarily be the extent to which the goals, as defined in the terms of reference or brief to the project team, have been achieved, the time taken, the costs incurred, the effectiveness with which team members have worked together, the degree to which internal and external customers or clients are satisfied and, ultimately, the impact the project has made on organizational performance.

Team performance management processes

Team performance management activities follow the same sequence as for individual performance management:

- agree objectives;
- formulate plans to achieve objectives
- implement plans;
- monitor progress;
- review and assess achievement;
- redefine objectives and plans in the light of the review.

The aim should be to give teams with their team leaders the maximum amount of responsibility to carry out all activities. The focus should be on self-management and self-direction.

The key activities of setting work and process objectives and conducting team reviews and individual reviews are described below.

Setting work objectives

Work objectives for teams are set in much the same way as individual objectives (see Chapter 7). They will be based on an analysis of the purpose of the team and its accountabilities for achieving results. Targets and standards of performance should be discussed and agreed by the team as a whole. These may specify what individual members are expected to contribute. Project teams will agree project plans that define what has to be done, who does it, the standards expected and the timescale.

Setting process objectives

Process objectives are also best defined by the team getting together and agreeing how they should conduct themselves as a team under headings related to the list of team competencies and performance measures referred to earlier in this chapter, including:

- interpersonal relationships;
- the quality of participation and collaborative effort and decision making;
- the team's relationships with internal and external customers;
- the capacity of the team to plan and control its activities;
- the ability of the team and its members to adapt to new demands and situations;
- the flexibility with which the team operates;
- the effectiveness with which individual skills are used;
- the quality of communications within the team and between the team and other teams or individuals.

Team performance reviews

Team performance review meetings analyse and assess feedback and control information on their joint achievements against objectives and project plans. The agenda for such meetings could be as follows:

1. General feedback review:

    –   progress of the team as a whole;

    –   problems encountered by the team that have caused difficulties or hampered progress;

    –   helps and hindrances to the operation of the team.

2. Work reviews:

    –   how well the team has functioned;

    –   review of the individual contribution made by each team member – ie peer review (see below);

    –   discussion of any new problems encountered by individual team members.

3. Group problem solving:

    –   analysis of reasons for any shortfalls or other problems;

    –   agreement of what needs to be done to solve them and prevent their recurrence.

4. Update objectives:

    –   review of new requirements, opportunities or threats;

    –   amendment and updating of objectives and project plans.

Reviewing the performance of individual team members

Processes for managing team performance should not neglect the needs of team members. As Mohrman and Mohrman (1995) point out: 'Performance among individuals, teams and organizations [needs] to fit, but individual needs must be met at the same time.' They ask how individual needs can be met while still encouraging the sharing required at the group level. Their answer is:

Meeting individual as well as team needs (Mohrman and Mohrman, 1995)

First, teams have to be managed in a way that enables individuals to feel they can influence group performance. They must provide opportunities for involvement and for team self-management. Second, the team must be managed so that the individual's needs to have excellent performance recognized are met.

Individuals should receive feedback on their contribution to the team and recognition by their team leader and fellow team members for their accomplishments. Special attention should be given to their personal development, not only as members of their existing team but also for any future roles they may assume in other teams, as individual contributors or as team leaders.

Individuals should agree their objectives as team members with their team leader but these can also be discussed at team meetings. Personal objectives and personal development plans can also be formulated for agreement with the team leader. Performance and development reviews between team leaders and individuals can concentrate on the latter's contribution to the team, the level of performance in terms of teamwork competencies, and progress in implementing personal development plans.

Peer review processes can also be used in which team members assess each other under headings such as:

- overall contribution to team performance;
- contribution to planning, monitoring and team review activities;
- maintaining relationships with other team members and internal/external customers;
- communicating;
- working flexibly (taking on different roles in the team as necessary);
- cooperation with other team members.

Peer reviews can form part of a 360-degree feedback process as described in Chapter 9, in which the requirements for its successful application are discussed.

19

Performance Management and Learning

The primary purpose of performance management is to develop performance. This is the all-important learning and developmental aspect of performance management. It takes place at every point in the cycle: planning, managing performance throughout the year, and monitoring and reviewing outcomes. It could therefore be regarded as a natural process but the likelihood of its happening is increased if: 1) there is a framework for personal development that is provided by personal development plans as part of the overall planning and implementation activities; and 2) the opportunity to coach is seized upon whenever possible. This chapter starts with a discussion of how people learn through performance management and this leads to an analysis of the learning opportunities. It concludes with a description of personal development planning. Coaching was dealt with in Chapter 12.

Helping people to learn through performance management

Reynolds (2004) makes the point that: 'Improvement and learning are causally related; obtain the will to improve and the process of learning will follow.' He also believes that: 'The experience of work always will provide the richest learning laboratory.' This is where performance management has a key role to play; first by specifically helping people to appreciate the need for developing their performance and where and how it should take place, and second by ensuring that they learn from experience. Performance management can also help to identify specific learning needs that can be satisfied by formal courses on or off the job or by e-learning. But the most important contribution of performance management is the help it provides to the development of a climate for learning – a 'growth culture'. This offers scope for guiding people through their work challenges, ensuring that they have the time and resources required to learn and, crucially, giving them the feedback and support they need to learn.

Learning opportunities

Performance management provides learning opportunities during its three main stages: performance agreement and planning, managing performance throughout the year and performance review.

The performance agreement as a framework for learning

The learning opportunities offered by performance management are based on the initial activities in the performance agreement and planning part of the cycle. This includes a joint analysis of the individual's role so that a new or updated role profile can be produced that sets out what results are to be achieved and what competences are needed to deliver those results. Discussions take place on ways in which the individual's role could be developed so that it becomes more challenging from the viewpoint not only of new tasks to be accomplished but also the need to acquire or extend knowledge and skills in order to carry out those tasks. The aim is to provide what Reynolds (2004) calls 'supported autonomy'; freedom for employees to manage their work within certain boundaries (policies and expected behaviours) but with support available as required. Career opportunities and the learning required to realize them are also discussed. Areas where performance needs to be improved are identified and the learning required to achieve these improvements is agreed. The outcome is a personal development plan as described later in this chapter.

Learning throughout the year

Learning is inseparable from activity, and like performance management it is a continuous process. Every task carried out by someone presents a learning opportunity and it is the duty of managers to help people become aware of this and to support the day-to-day learning that takes place. They should enable people to understand how they should tackle a new task and what additional knowledge or skills they will need. Guidance can be provided by asking questions on what individuals need to know and be able to do to undertake a task, leaving them as far as possible to think for themselves but helping them when necessary.

Feedback throughout the year rather than during an annual performance review is also an important means of helping people to learn. They can be asked to analyse their performance and, where it can be improved, come up with ideas about any additional coaching, training or experience they need.

Performance reviews as learning events

Performance reviews, whether conducted formally or informally, can be regarded as learning events. Learning opportunities are provided before, during and after formal meetings. Prior to a review individuals can be encouraged to think about what they feel they want to learn, new skills they would like to acquire and the direction in which they want to develop. During the review individuals can present to the reviewer their views about what they have learned and what they need to learn. A dialogue can take place in which learning needs can be analysed and a diagnosis agreed on priority areas. Individuals should be encouraged to take responsibility for their own learning and for implementing the outcomes of the learning process. The outcome of the review could be a personal development plan as described below. Following the review learners and their managers can monitor progress against agreed targets.

Personal development planning

Personal development planning aims to promote learning and to provide people with the knowledge and portfolio of transferable skills that will help to advance their careers. A personal development plan sets out what people need to learn to develop their capabilities, improve their performance and further their career. It provides a self-organized learning framework, indicating the actions required by individuals, their managers and the organization. It serves as a point of reference for monitoring and reviewing the implementation of the plan. Personal development planning is carried out by individuals with guidance, encouragement and help from their managers as necessary. Individuals take responsibility for formulating and implementing the plan but they receive support as required from the organization and their managers in doing so.

The planning process

Personal development plans are based on an understanding of what people do, what they have achieved, what knowledge and skills they have, and what knowledge and skills they need. The aims of the planning process are to be specific about what is to be achieved and how it is to be achieved, to ensure that the learning needs and actions are relevant, to indicate the timescale, to identify responsibility and, within reason, to ensure that the learning activities will stretch those concerned.

Plans are always related to work and the capacity to carry it out effectively. They are not just about identifying training needs and suitable courses to satisfy them. Training courses may form part of the development plan, but a minor part; other learning activities such as those listed below are more important.

- coaching;
- adopting a role model (mentor);
- observing and analysing what others do (good practice);
- extending the role (job enrichment);

- project work (special assignments);
- involvement in other work areas;
- involvement in communities of practice (learning from others carrying out similar work);
- action learning;
- e-learning;
- guided reading.

Action planning

The action plan sets out what needs to be done and how it will be done under headings such as:

- learning needs;
- outcomes expected (learning objectives);
- learning activities to meet the needs;
- responsibility for learning – what individuals will do and what support they will require from their manager, the HR department or other people;
- timing – when the learning activity is expected to start and be completed.

The plans can be recorded on simple forms with four columns covering: 1) development objectives and outcome expected; 2) action to be taken and when; 3) support required; and 4) evidence required to show that the planned learning activity has been undertaken successfully.

Introducing personal development planning

The introduction of personal development planning should not be undertaken lightly. It is not just a matter of designing a new back page to the performance review form and telling people to fill it up. Neither is it sufficient just to issue guidance notes and expect people to get on with it.

Managers, team leaders and individuals all need to learn about personal development planning. They should be involved in deciding how the planning process will work and what their roles will be. The benefits to them should be understood and accepted. It has to be recognized that everyone will need time and support to adjust to a culture in which they have to take much more responsibility for their own learning. Importantly, all concerned should be given guidance on how to identify learning needs, on the means of satisfying those needs, and how they should make use of the facilities and opportunities that can be made available to them.

20

Performance Management and Reward

Performance management can play an important part in a total reward system in which all reward elements are linked together and treated as an integrated and coherent whole. These elements comprise base pay, contingent pay, employee benefits and non-financial rewards, which include intrinsic rewards from the work itself.

It is sometimes assumed that the main purpose of performance management is to generate ratings to inform contribution or performance-related pay decisions. Nothing could be further from the truth. Performance management can provide for a whole range of rewards in order to encourage job engagement and promote commitment. These rewards can take the form of recognition through feedback, opportunities to achieve, the scope to develop skills, and guidance on career paths. All these are non-financial rewards that can make a longer-lasting and more powerful impact than financial rewards.

Performance management is, or should be, about developing people and rewarding them in the broadest sense. Approaches to using performance management to provide non-financial rewards are discussed below. The rest of this chapter deals with performance management and pay.

Performance management and non-financial rewards

Non-financial rewards are provided by performance management through recognition, the provision of opportunities to succeed, skills development and career planning, and enhancing job engagement and commitment.

Performance management and recognition

Performance management involves recognizing people's achievements and strengths. They can be informed through feedback about how well they are performing by reference to achievements and behaviours. They can be thanked, formally and informally, for what they have done. They can be helped to understand how they can do even better by taking action to make the best use of the opportunities the feedback has revealed.

Performance management and the provision of opportunities to achieve

Performance management processes are founded on joint agreements between managers and their people on what the roles of the latter are and how they can be developed (enriched). It is therefore an essential part of job or role design and development activities.

Performance management and skills development

Performance management can provide a basis for motivating people by enabling them to develop their skills. It provides an agreed framework for coaching and support to enhance and focus learning.

Performance management and career planning

Performance management reviews provide opportunities to discuss the direction in which the careers of individuals are going and what they can do – with the help of the organization – to ensure that they follow the best career path for themselves and the organization.

Performance management and job engagement

People are engaged with their jobs when they are interested in what they do and have a sense of excitement in their work. This can be created by performance management when it concentrates on intrinsic motivating factors such as taking responsibility for job outcomes (autonomy), job satisfaction, achievement and fulfilment of personal goals and objectives.

Performance management and commitment

One of the prime aims of performance management is to promote commitment to the organization and its goals by integrating individual and organizational objectives.

Performance management and pay

Performance management is not inevitably associated with pay, although this is often assumed to be the case. Only 42 per cent of respondents to the CIPD 2003/04 survey (Armstrong and Baron, 2004) with performance management had contingent pay.

However, those who do have contingent pay must have a means of deciding on increases and this has to be based on some form of assessment. The most typical approach is the generation of ratings following performance reviews as described in Chapter 11 – 73 per cent of respondents to the 2004 e-reward survey adopted this approach. Ratings can be used to inform contingent pay decisions.

But quite a few organizations do not use ratings at all (27 per cent of the e-reward respondents). Instead they adopt what might be called 'holistic' assessment. This involves assessing the level of contribution and therefore possible awards in the shape of base pay increases or bonuses. Consideration is given both to what individuals have contributed to the success of their team and to the level of competence they have achieved and deployed. Team members who are contributing at the expected level will be paid at or around what is often called 'the reference point' for the grade (a reference point represents the rate of pay appropriate for someone who is fully competent in the role and will be aligned to market rates in accordance with the organization's market pay policies). If, in the judgement of the line manager, individuals are achieving this level of contribution but are paid below their peers at the reference point, the pay of such individuals would be brought up to the level of their peers, or towards that level if it is felt that the increase should be phased. Individuals may be paid above the reference point if they are making a particularly strong contribution or if their market worth is higher.

The policy guideline would be that the average pay of those in the grade should broadly be in line with the reference point unless there are special market rate considerations that justify a higher rate. Those at or above the reference point who are contributing well could be eligible for a cash bonus. A 'pay pot' would be made available for distribution with guidelines on how it should be used.

This approach depends largely on the judgement of line managers, although they would be guided and helped in the exercise of that judgement by HR. Its acceptability to staff as a fair process depends on precise communications generally on how it operates and equally precise communications individually on why decisions have been made. The assessment of contribution should be a joint one as part of performance management, and the link between that assessment and the pay decision should be clear.

Making pay decisions in a finance sector company

We look at a number of things when making a decision on an individual's pay. One will be the size of the role as determined by job evaluation, and we also consider market data and location to determine the average salary that you would expect to pay for that role. We then look at how the individual has performed over the last 12 months: Have they contributed what was expected of them? Have they contributed above and beyond their peers? Have they under-performed in respect of what was required of them? These are not ratings, they are just guidelines given to managers as to whether the individual should be given an average, above-average or below-average increase. We have a devolved budget and managers have to make decisions as to what percentage they should give to different people. We suggest that if, for example, a manager has six people carrying out the same roles then, from an equal pay point of view, if they are delivering at the same level and are all competent, they should be getting similar salaries. Individuals paid below the market rate who are performing effectively may get a bigger pay rise to bring them nearer the market rate for the role.

Reconciling performance management and pay

Focusing on performance management as a means of deciding on pay awards may conflict with the developmental purposes of performance management. This is likely to be the case if ratings are used – the performance review meeting will concentrate on the ratings that emerge from it and how much money will be forthcoming. Issues concerning development and the non-financial reward approaches discussed earlier will be subordinated to this preoccupation with pay. Many organizations attempt to get over this problem by holding development and pay review meetings on separate dates, often several months apart (decoupling). Some, such as the finance company described earlier, do without formulaic approaches (ratings) altogether, although it is impossible to dissociate contingent pay completely from some form of assessment.

The problem of reconciling the developmental aspects of performance management or appraisal and pay has been with us for decades. Armstrong commented as long ago as 1976 that: 'It is undesirable to have a direct link between the performance review and the reward review. The former must aim primarily at improving performance and, possibly, assessing potential. If this is confused with a salary review, everyone becomes over-concerned about the impact of the assessment on the increment... It is better to separate the two.'

Many people since then have accepted this view in principle but have found it difficult to apply in practice. As Kessler and Purcell (1993) argue: 'How distinct these processes (performance review and performance-related pay) can ever be or, in managerial terms, should ever be, is perhaps debatable. It is unrealistic to assume that a manager can separate these two processes easily and it could be argued that the evaluations in a broad sense should be congruent.'

And Armstrong and Murlis (1998) comment that: 'Some organizations separate entirely performance pay ratings from the performance management review. But there will, of course, inevitably be a read-across from the performance management review to the pay-for-performance review.'

The issue is that if you want to pay for performance or competence you have to measure performance or competence. And if you want, as you should do, the process of measurement to be fair, equitable, consistent and transparent, then you cannot make pay decisions, on whatever evidence, behind closed doors. You must convey to people how the assessment has been made and how it has been converted into a pay increase. This is a matter of procedural justice, which demands that where there is a system for assessing performance and competence: 1) the assessment should be based on 'good information and informed opinion'; 2) the person affected should be able to contribute to the process of obtaining evidence to support the assessment; 3) the person should know how and why the assessment has been made; and 4) the person should be able to appeal against the assessment.

Part VI

Developing and Maintaining Performance Management

21
Developing Performance Management

It is not too difficult to conceptualize how performance management should function. It is much harder to ensure that it works in practice. It takes time, energy and determination to launch performance management successfully and to ensure that it continues to operate effectively. As described in this chapter it is necessary to start by understanding the development framework, the development stages and the contextual factors affecting performance management. Against this background, the next steps are to:

- conduct a diagnostic review;
- set objectives for performance management;
- decide on the approach to development;
- prepare and carry out the development and implementation programme.

The toolkit in Appendix A covers the actions required in more detail.

The development framework

Performance management can be regarded as a framework, as illustrated in Figure 21.1, within which a number of factors operate that will affect how it should be developed, introduced and evaluated.

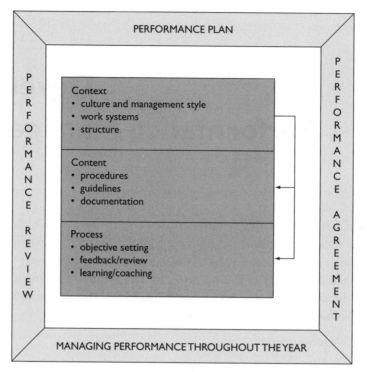

Figure 21.1 The performance management development framework

The framework or essence of performance management is provided by the arrangements for agreeing performance requirements or expectations, preparing performance plans, managing performance throughout the year and analysing, assessing and reviewing performance.

Stages of development

The stages of development leading into operation and evaluation are shown in Figure 21.2.

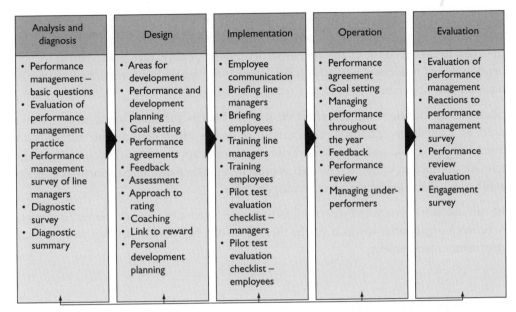

Figure 21.2   Development, implementation, operation and evaluation of performance management

Contextual factors

The contextual or environmental factors of culture, management style, work systems and structure will strongly influence the content of performance management procedures, guidelines and documentation and the all-important processes that make it work (role analysis, goal setting, providing feedback, analysing and assessing performance, and coaching).

Cultural considerations will affect performance management because it works best when it fits the existing values of the organization. Ideally, these should support high performance, quality, involvement, openness, freedom of communication and mutual trust. These may not have been put into practice in full, however vigorously they have been espoused. But top management must genuinely want to move in these directions and need to make it clear that everyone else should go along with them, using performance management as a lever for change. In performance management, there is too often a gap between the rhetoric and the reality. The process of developing and introducing performance management must concentrate on ensuring that worthy ambitions are translated into effective action by all concerned.

It has been argued by commentators such as Deming (1986) and Coens and Jenkins (2002) that it is the system of work that fundamentally determines the level of individual performance. It can be claimed equally strongly that systems are designed by people. Alternatively, they evolve through the actions and interactions of people without being consciously designed.

They are certainly managed and operated by people. It can therefore be argued that people are part of the system and that some of them will work more effectively within it than others. It is important to take account of the system in developing performance management but this attention should be focused not only on the nature of the system but also on the impact it has on people and vice versa.

Structural considerations will also affect the way in which performance management is introduced. In a highly decentralized organization, or one in which considerable authority and power is devolved to some functions or divisions, it may be appropriate to encourage or permit each unit or function to develop its own approach to performance management as long as it conforms to central guidelines on the basic principles.

The cultural, work system and structural factors to be taken into account will vary considerably between organizations, which is why there is no one best way to develop and introduce performance management.

Approach to development

The approach adopted to developing performance management has to recognize the reality of these contextual factors and the problems involved in meeting possibly demanding objectives and overcoming the practical and political difficulties that will get in the way of achieving sustained success. Following their research Strebler, Bevan and Robertson (2001) wrote about this as follows:

Rationality meets reality (Strebler, Bevan and Robertson, 2001)

Personnel management textbooks are full of touching accounts of how to design and implement performance appraisal and management schemes in organizations. The models they propose are based on a rational and linear logic which assumes that an organization's goals can be translated into individual goals which, in turn, can be delivered through feedback, training, development and reward. The reality of organizational life is, as we have seen, somewhat different.

The following excellent practical advice on the dos and don'ts of introducing performance management or making substantial changes to an existing scheme was given by the respondents to the e-Reward 2005 survey.

Dos

- Get buy-in from senior management from the start.

- Keep it simple. Keep it transparent. Train, train, train!

- You can never do enough training/coaching of both staff and line managers. You can never do too much communication on the new changes.

- Ensure the process is seen as a business one, not an HR process.

- Keep it simple and concentrate on the quality going into the process rather than the design of the process itself (although the design must be appropriate to the organization).

- Ensure that there is an understanding in the line of how the process can help the business – so it's not seen as an 'HR add-on' process. Get buy-in from senior management from the start. Involve staff in development. Keep it simple. Train, train, train managers. Review effectiveness.

- Engage all managers in why it is important and ensure that they have the necessary understanding and skills to carry out the process. Get buy-in and tailor it to the specific needs of the organization. Get the support of key stakeholders such as the union from the start, and get them to work with you to sell the scheme. Agree the overall objectives and guiding principles with all concerned. Keep employees informed and ensure the message is consistent throughout

- Aim to maintain clarity throughout the process and construct transparent support documentation for the users. Use a group of people to run your ideas through and give feedback to make sure you are achieving what you set out to achieve

- Consider the desired output in terms of results and behaviours you want the system to achieve. Consider the training requirements for the managers and staff expected to use the system. Spend sufficient time on communication and change management. Bear in mind that the more complex the scheme, the less transparent it may become and the more time it may take to administer!

- Do involve managers and staff in the development of the process through focus groups and take on board their input. Develop a comprehensive communications programme adjusted in style for different populations. Ensure appropriate training has taken place before launching. Track the implementation to analyse success.

- Include completing effective performance management reviews in the objectives of managers and team leaders so that part of their performance review is based on this criterion.

- Understand clearly why you are doing it and the desired objectives. Engage others in design of scheme. Communicate purpose etc clearly. Get line managers and supervisors on board. Train all. Consider how you will evaluate success.

Don'ts

- Don't expect that staff will leap for joy at the prospect of what they would see as another way of criticizing them in their jobs. Start your change management process where you think the staff are, not where you've assumed they are.

- Don't assume that what seems obvious and logical to you, as an HR manager, will also seem logical to other managers and staff. Don't get caught up in HR-speak and become precious about the differences between 'performance management' and 'appraisals' or between a 'personal development/learning plan' and a 'training plan'. As HR professionals we may be able to eloquently argue the subtle differences and merits of each – for most people the distinction is absolutely meaningless!

- Don't just make it a form-filling exercise – you need managers to believe that the system is beneficial, otherwise it won't work.

- Don't put in a lengthy complicated process – it will become a chore to do rather than a meaningful exercise.

- Don't make HR own the initiative – it is a business improvement model and one that the business needs to manage.

- Don't implement without investigating main needs and requirements, or without sufficient training for managers. Don't try to aim too high at the start.

- Don't assume that supervisors have the requisite skills to manage performance fairly and equitably.

- Don't embark upon such an initiative without clear goals and without the support of respected key players in the organization, or set the wheels in motion until extensive briefings/training have been completed.

- Don't underestimate the amount of work involved!

- Don't underestimate the time it takes to embed, underestimate how managers wriggle to avoid making judgements, or meet with unions until you are sure of where you intend to head, and the costs are approved.

- Don't expect it to work quickly. It takes a few years to embed performance management in the organization's ethos.

Performance management development programme

The development of performance management can be carried out in the 10 stages shown in Figure 21.3 and described below. At each stage arrangements should be made to consult and involve staff. It is particularly important to make every effort to gain the commitment of line managers through involvement (in order to promote ownership) and communications. It is desirable to set up a project team to develop performance management composed of managers, staff, trade union representatives and HR specialists. A project manager should be appointed who, together with the project team, should report to a steering committee of senior managers.

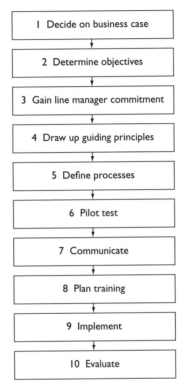

Figure 21.3   Performance management development stages

Stage 1. Decide on the business case for introducing performance management

The business case for introducing performance management should be agreed by top management. Essentially, this could be to develop a high-performance culture in order to achieve business goals by improving the performance of individuals and teams and ensuring that individual objectives are integrated with corporate objectives.

Stage 2. Determine objectives for performance management

Performance management must be designed to meet business as well as individual needs. Specific objectives could include:

- to improve organizational, team and individual performance;
- to provide for the closer integration of organizational, team and individual objectives and thus focus people on doing the right things;
- to clarify expectations on what individuals and teams have to achieve;
- to support the realization of the organization's core values;
- to develop individuals' skills and capabilities;
- to foster a closer relationship between individuals and their managers based on the agreement of objectives, feedback and coaching;
- to provide for a more objective and fairer method of assessing performance;
- to empower individuals to manage their own performance and learning.

Stage 3. Get the commitment and active participation of top management and line managers

The power of the words and behaviour of top managers should never be underestimated. They can set the example and build commitment at all levels. They need to be convinced that there is a powerful business case for performance management. Once they are on-side, get them actively engaged as champions for performance management.

It is equally important to develop the engagement of line managers. It is they who will implement performance management and if they are not on board the system will probably fail.

Stage 4. Draw up guiding principles on how performance management should work

The guiding principles should emphasize that performance management is regarded as a normal and continuous process of management that is owned by the managers and staff who are involved. It should be made clear that it operates as a partnership between managers and their staff, who are equally involved in planning and reviewing performance and in implementing personal development and performance improvement plans

The following is an example of guiding principles developed by a working party in a local authority:

- clearly stated work objectives/tasks subject to regular review and updating;
- clearly stated standards of performance;
- feedback on job behaviour;
- comments rather than performance ratings;

- identification of development needs;

- agreed training plan;

- reach agreement through a two-way process;

- incorporate appeal procedure;

- used as a day-to-day management tool;

- no link to pay;

- if no commitment from the head of department, don't do it.

Stage 5. Define performance management processes

Each stage of the performance management cycle needs to be defined. The performance agreement and planning process is first. It is necessary to define how role profiles should be agreed and used as the basis for performance management, how goals should be set, how performance measures should be agreed, and how performance improvement and personal development plans should be drawn up. Secondly, the basis upon which performance management works as a continuous process (performance management throughout the year) through informal reviews of progress and feedback should be explained. Finally, the approach to conducting performance reviews should be made clear. Rating methods, if required, have to be decided and thought given to how to ensure that they are consistent and fair. The link, if any between performance management and performance or contribution pay also needs to be determined.

Consideration should be given at this stage on the extent to which the process should be web-enabled. This will probably mean obtaining the software from a supplier but it will have to be customized, which will include designing the forms and displays to be used, and briefing and training managers and individuals in operating the system. If the system is not to be computerized, paper documents will need to be designed with guidelines on how they should be used. The watchwords are 'keep it simple'. Complex and lengthy forms whether on a computer or on paper are a major cause of performance management failure. It should be emphasized that the forms should simply act as an aide memoire. They should not be allowed to dominate the procedure.

Stage 6. Pilot test

It is essential to pilot test performance management in two or three different types of departments. The procedures as set out on paper or as computerized must be exposed to real-life conditions so that problems and issues in applying them can be identified. The tests will indicate what changes need to be made but they will also reveal what managers and staff have to learn about performance management. This will feed into the implementation programme, during which steps are taken to ensure that everyone learns what they need to know. If the departments are selected carefully with a committed management team and staff who are likely to be cooperative, the pilot test can identify champions of performance management who can act as coaches and mentors and provide practical guidance.

The test should cover the main performance management processes: developing role profiles, setting goals, deciding on performance measures, formulating performance improvement and development plans, conducting performance review, giving feedback and coaching and completing the documentation on the screen or on paper. Ideally, it should cover the whole 12-month cycle. This may be too long but at least three months and preferably six should be allowed. Superficial tests are worse than useless. Performance management takes time to establish. It should never be rushed.

Stage 7. Communicate

Considerable care needs to be taken to communicate to all concerned – managers, team leaders, staff and trade union representatives – the aims of performance management, how it will work and how people will be affected by it. The communication strategy should have been a constant preoccupation of the developers of the scheme. They should consider for each feature of the process as it is being developed how it can be explained and presented to the people concerned.

Communication can be through documentation (an explanatory brochure), the intranet and face-to-face briefings (the more of the latter the better). Below is an example of a guide to performance management prepared by a not-for-profit organization.

A GUIDE TO PERFORMANCE MANAGEMENT

Introduction

The purpose of performance management is to help and encourage everyone to raise their performance, develop their abilities, increase job satisfaction and achieve their full potential to the benefit of the individual and the organization as a whole.

What is performance management?

Performance management is a means of getting better results from the organization, teams and individuals by understanding and managing performance within an agreed framework of planned goals and standards.

It is based on the simple proposition that when people know and understand what is expected of them, and have been able to take part in forming those expectations, they can and will meet them.

Why do we need performance management?

There are two main reasons for introducing performance management:

- We want to focus everyone's attention on what they are expected to achieve in their jobs and how best to achieve it.
- We would like to help everyone to identify and satisfy their development needs – to improve performance and realize their potential.

How does performance management work?

Performance management works like this:

- You and your manager will discuss and agree your objectives, action plans and development and training needs – this is called the performance agreement.
- During the review period (normally 12 months) you and your manager will keep under review your progress in meeting your objectives – as necessary you will agree revisions to those objectives and your priorities.
- Towards the end of the review period you and your manager will separately prepare for the performance and development review meeting – deciding in advance on any points you wish to raise and noting these down on a preparation form.
- A review meeting will then be held at which you can discuss with your manager how you got on during the review period and any other points you want to raise. You will then together draw up a new performance agreement.
- Your manager's manager will see the form and will add any comments he or she feels may be appropriate. You will also see these comments.
- You and your manager will then retain your own copies of the review form – no other copies will be held by anyone else.
- Performance management will:
  - focus on developing strengths as well as considering any performance problems;
  - be based on open and constructive discussion;
  - be an everyday and natural management process – not an annual form-filling exercise;
  - be a positive process – looking to the future rather than dwelling on the past.

The part you will play

We hope that you will contribute to the success of this scheme in the following ways:

- by preparing carefully for the review – noting any points you want to raise with your manager;

- by entering into the spirit of the review meeting, which is intended to provide an opportunity for you to have 'quality time' with your manager during which an open and friendly exchange of views will take place about your job and your prospects;

- by thinking carefully about how you are going to achieve the objectives and plans agreed at the meeting;

- by reviewing how you are getting on during the year and agreeing any actions required.

The part managers will play

All managers will be expected to play their part with you in preparing for the meeting, reviewing your performance and drawing up your performance agreement. They are being specially trained in how to do this. Managers are also expected to work with you in preparing and implementing your personal development plan.

Benefits to you

We hope performance management will benefit you by ensuring that:

- You know what is expected of you.

- You know how you stand.

- You know what you need to do to reach your objectives.

- You can discuss with your manager your present job, your development and training needs and your future.

Benefits to your manager

Managers will gain the opportunity to:

- clarify expectations with the individual members of their teams;

- have 'quality time' with their staff to discuss matters affecting work, performance and development away from the hurly-burly of everyday working life;

- provide better feedback to individuals about their performance and progress based on a mutual understanding of needs;

- identify areas of individual concern and provide guidance to enable individuals to make the best use of their abilities;

- build closer working relationships based on mutual trust and respect;

- identify individual training and development needs.

Benefits to the organization

The organization gains the opportunity to:

- integrate individual, team and corporate objectives;
- guide individual and team effort to meet overall business needs;
- recognize individual contribution;
- plan individual careers;
- introduce relevant and effective learning and development programmes to meet identified needs.

Examples of communications from HRG and the Royal College of Nursing are given in Appendix B.

Stage 8. Plan arrangements for training in performance management

It is essential to provide training for both line managers and staff generally in performance management. It is particularly important that line managers have the skills required. These are demanding and the programme should provide for coaching, mentoring and ongoing guidance as well as formal training courses. A half or one-day course, which is the typical time the e-reward research established was devoted to training, is not enough. Training arrangements are described in Chapter 23.

Stage 9. Implement

The implementation programme should cover communications, training and the provision of guidance and help.

Stage 10. Evaluate

It is important to carry out a thorough evaluation as described in Chapter 24 of how performance management works after its first year of operation.

22

The Performance Management Role of Line Managers

Line managers play a crucial role in performance management. The 'black box' research conducted by John Purcell and his colleagues (2003) led to the conclusion that: 'front line management or leadership played a pivotal role in terms of implementing and enacting HR policies and practices since it is the front line managers that bring policies to life.' Ellinger, Ellinger and Keller (2003) stated that short-term demands on line managers, time pressures, lack of rewards or recognition for assuming developmental roles, confusion about their roles, lack of an organizational climate conducive to employee development, and inadequate skills and competence may serve as barriers that impede performance management.

An important consideration in designing and operating performance management is how to gain the commitment of line managers and ensure that they have the skills required. The need is to fill the gap between rhetoric and reality, between what top management and HR want line managers to do and what line managers actually do. This chapter deals with the performance management role of line managers under the following headings:

- what the performance management role of line management is;
- issues with the performance management role of line managers;
- how the issues can be addressed.

The performance management role of line managers

Performance management is what line managers do. They are there to achieve results through people and therefore have to manage the performance of their people. The aim of performance management systems is to help them to do this. Line managers play a crucial role in each stage of the performance management cycle.

At the planning and performance agreement stage they agree with team members their roles, goals and performance improvement and personal development plans. They manage performance throughout the year by monitoring achievements against the plan, providing feedback and coaching as necessary. At the review stage they conduct formal review meetings and provide formal feedback as the basis for forward planning.

To do all this they need the following skills:

- preparing role profiles – defining key result areas and competency requirements;
- defining goals;
- identifying and using performance measures;
- giving and receiving feedback;
- taking part in review meetings – ensuring that there is a proper dialogue that enables the manager and the individual jointly, frankly and freely to discuss performance requirements and learning needs;
- identifying learning needs and preparing and implementing personal development plans;
- diagnosing and solving performance problems (managing poor performance);
- coaching.

Issues with the performance management role of line managers

Performance management may be what line managers do but they don't seem to do it very well. Respondents to the e-reward (2005) survey listed the following problems with line managers as the four biggest ones they had to face in their performance management systems:

- 88 per cent believed that line managers did not have the skills required.
- 84 per cent believed that line managers did not discriminate sufficiently when assessing performance.
- 75 per cent believed that line managers were not committed to performance management.
- 74 per cent believed that line managers were reluctant to conduct performance management reviews.

On the basis of the Bath University research, Hutchinson and Purcell (2003) discussed 'performance appraisal' as an HR activity (they did not refer to performance management as a management activity). They noted that: 'Performance appraisal is an area in which front line managers have traditionally had direct involvement with their staff, and provides a good example of the key role these managers have to play in their delivery of HR policies.' They also found that:

Findings about the effectiveness of performance appraisal (Hutchinson and Purcell, 2003)

Looking at the sample of employees interviewed over the two years (n = 608) we found that performance appraisal was rated as the least effective HR policy (in terms of levels of satisfaction) after pay, and in a fair number of organizations it was the least favourite HR activity. The reasons given were numerous, and included the views that the measurements and targets were felt to be unclear and/or not relevant, and that the system was too complicated and time consuming. Many of the problems could be directly linked to the behaviour of managers, as the interviews with employees revealed.

The research conducted by Kathy Armstrong and Adrian Ward (2005) for the Work Foundation identified the following problems with line managers and performance management:

Line managers and performance management (Kathy Armstrong and Adrian Ward, 2005)

Our case study organizations were all finding it difficult to improve their managers' capacity to manage performance effectively. A particular issue for all of the organizations was the lack of consistency in capability. Some managers were managing performance well, delivering fair and accurate feedback and setting goals that motivate. Others were doing much less well. A key skill gap was the ability to deliver feedback in a constructive way and having those 'difficult' conversations with under-performers.

Addressing the issues

These issues can also arise in up-to-date performance management systems that, even if they emphasize dialogue and agreement rather than control from above, still depend on the commitment and ability of line managers to carry out the process in a way that will meet the needs of all the stakeholders – the organization, the manager and, importantly, the individual. They are even more likely to occur in an old-fashioned performance appraisal system that involves ratings and, often, a direct and formulaic link to performance-related pay.

It is relatively easy to design a performance management 'system'; it is much more difficult to make it work. There are no quick fixes. But it is important to ensure that all the stakeholders are involved in the development of the system (see Chapter 21) and that all concerned are given as much opportunity as possible to learn about performance management, through communications, formal training and, especially for line managers, less formal ways of helping people to learn the demanding skills involved such as coaching and mentoring. It is necessary to gain the commitment of line managers and to ensure that they are capable of carrying out their performance management responsibilities.

Gaining the commitment of line managers

Too often, line managers regard performance management in the shape of the formal review as a bureaucratic chore. They believe, rightly or wrongly, that they are doing it anyway so, they say: 'Why should we conform to a system imposed on us by the HR department?' Even if they don't believe that formal reviews are a waste of time, some managers are reluctant to conduct them because they find it difficult to criticize people and imagine that they will be faced by unpleasant confrontations. Others are nervous about reviews because they feel that they lack the skills required to provide feedback, analyse performance and agree objectives.

Gaining the commitment of line managers takes a lot of time, effort and persistence but it has to be done. Below are some of the approaches that can be used.

Provide leadership from the top

Top management has a crucial role to play in implementing performance management. Senior staff have to communicate and act on the belief that performance management is an integral part of the fabric of the managerial practices of the organization. They should demonstrate their conviction that this is what good management is about and this is how managers are expected to play their part.

Communicate

Simply telling line managers that performance management is a good thing will not get you very far. But somehow the message has to reach them that managing performance is what they are expected to do. The message should come from the top and be cascaded down through the organization. It should not come from HR except, incidentally, as part of a training or induction programme. The message should be built into management development programmes, especially for potential managers. It should be understood by them from the outset that performance management is an important part of their responsibilities and that these are the skills they must acquire and use. The significance of performance management can also be conveyed by including the effectiveness with which managers carry out their performance management responsibilities as one of the criteria used when assessing their performance.

Keep it simple

Willing participation in performance management activities is more likely to be achieved if managers do not see it as a bureaucratic chore. If forms are used – and they don't have to be – they should be as simple as possible, no more than two sides of one piece of paper. It should be emphasized that performance management is not a form-filling exercise and that the important thing is the dialogue between managers and individuals that continues throughout the year and is not just an annual event. Web-enabled performance management will eliminate paper work and speed up the process.

Reduce the pressure

Line managers can feel pressurized and exposed if they perceive that performance management is just about carrying out an annual appraisal meeting in which they have to tell employees where they have gone wrong, rate their performance and decide on the pay increase they should be given. This pressure can be reduced if the emphasis is on 'performance management throughout the year'. This should be regarded as part of normal good management practice that involves providing informal feedback whenever appropriate – recognizing good work as it happens and dealing with performance problems as they arise, and revising roles and objectives as required. The annual review meeting takes the form of a stocktaking exercise – no surprises – but more importantly, becomes a forward looking exercise – where do we go from here?

Pressure can also be reduced if managers do not have to make and defend ratings, although they still have to reach agreement on areas for development and improvement and what needs to be done about them. A further reduction of pressure can be achieved if pay reviews are 'decoupled' from performance reviews, ie they take place several months later.

Involve

Involve line managers in the design and development of performance management processes as members of project teams or by taking part in pilot studies. This could be extended by the use of focus groups and general surveys of opinions and reactions. Line managers can also be involved in reviewing the effectiveness of performance management. Commitment can be enhanced by getting them to act as coaches in developing performance management skills and as mentors to managers unfamiliar with the process. The more performance management is owned by line managers the better.

Encourage

Line managers can be encouraged to believe in performance management through communities of practice – gatherings of managers during which information is exchanged on good practice. They are more likely to take notice of their peers than someone from HR. But HR can still play a useful role in encouraging managers.

Developing skills

Systematic formal training as described in Chapter 23 is necessary for the performance management skills managers need to use. This should take place when launching a new scheme but, importantly, also during management development programmes for potential managers and induction programmes for new managers. Coaching and guidance to individual managers should be provided to supplement formal training. This can be provided by HR specialists although, better still, experienced, committed and competent line managers can be used as coaches and mentors.

It is also necessary to monitor the performance of managers as performance managers. This is not just a matter of checking on completed performance management forms, as practised in some organizations. HR specialists or line manager mentors can usefully follow up newly appointed or promoted managers to discuss how they are getting on and provide advice on dealing with any problems. 360-degree feedback or upward assessment can be used to review the performance management abilities of line managers when dealing with their staff and to indicate on an individual basis where improvements are required. Regular surveys can be conducted of the reactions of employees to performance management; these can lead to the identification of any common weaknesses and the remedial action required.

An HR business partner had this to say about the situation faced by her organization and how it was dealt with:

Performance management works very well with managers who are competent. Those who are less competent with the behavioural requirements of their role find it difficult, as this approach requires them to make some business judgements and discuss the rationale for them. Previously, they relied on the tick box approach where there was sometimes a perception that they did not need to discuss performance in detail. We have had to do quite a lot of coaching with managers to get them to feel comfortable with the new model as some feel the safety net of the tick box system has been removed. We have introduced role profiles that describe the 'how' and the 'what' and provide something against which managers and colleagues can be measured/assessed.

The Standard Chartered Bank model of their approach to developing performance management skills is shown in Figure 22.1

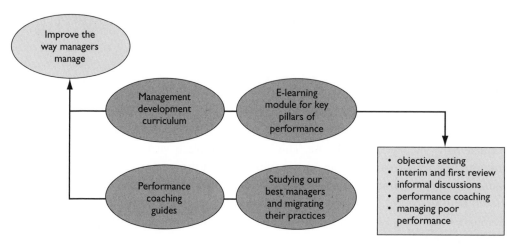

Figure 22.1 Developing performance management skills at Standard Chartered Bank

23

Learning About Performance Management

To introduce and sustain performance management successfully it is essential to ensure that all concerned – individuals as well as managers – learn about how performance management works and why it is important, and develop the skills they need. The objectives of a performance management learning programme are to:

- let people know about the rationale for the processes with which they will be involved – these will include the business drivers that have led the organization to introduce performance management as well as a description of the processes themselves;

- spell out their contribution – why it is important, how they make it and the benefits that will accrue to them and the organization;

- develop the skills people have to use.

The rationale for performance management

Performance management may be regarded with indifference – 'it doesn't concern me' – suspicion – 'a waste of time' – cynicism – 'we've seen it all before' – or outright hostility – 'it won't work'. These negative reactions must be overcome by leadership from the top, communications (oral briefings as well as the intranet and brochures), training, coaching and mentoring.

It is vital to get the message across that top management regards the process as a vital part of the drive to improve performance. A business case for performance management must be made by demonstrating how it will contribute to improving organizational effectiveness and overall performance. It should be treated as a crucial component in the drive to develop a high-performance culture. The message should be delivered as strongly as possible that performance management is about how performance is managed in the organization – a core value. It should be treated as a normal process of management that is owned by line managers, not the HR department.

Contribution

It is important to reinforce the messages about the business case for performance management with more precise information on the parts played by managers and individuals. The emphasis should be on the need for partnership and dialogue, the open and honest exchange of information (feedback) and sharing the process to the mutual benefit of both parties.

When spelling out the contribution of managers and team leaders the message should be that they are there to help and to coach, not to judge. For individuals, the message will be how they can benefit from self-assessment and the part they can play in developing themselves.

Skills

Performance management is not easy. It requires high levels of skill by everyone involved and the skills are likely to be ones that have not yet been developed or put into practice. For example, providing feedback that will motivate and help to develop people is not easy for those who have not done it before. Receiving, responding to and acting on feedback are similarly unfamiliar skills for many people. The agreement of role profiles, objectives and competency requirements, the application of performance measures and methods of analysing and using the outcomes of reviews may also be strange. The concepts of personal development planning and self-managed learning will be new to many people. Managers need to develop their coaching skills. Both managers and individuals need to know how to prepare for and conduct review meetings.

Formal learning

All these skills should be covered in a performance management learning programme, which can take the form of modules dealing with the overall processes and skills. An example of a programme on reviewing performance is given below.

Workshop aims

On completing this workshop participants will:

- understand the purpose of performance reviews
- know how to prepare for a constructive review
- know how to conduct an effective performance review
- be able to provide good feedback
- have gained some initial understanding of the processes of coaching and counselling.

Programme

09.00   **Objectives of the workshop**
The purpose of the performance review
Preparing for the review
Coffee
Giving feedback
Conducting the review
Lunch

13.30   **Practice in conducting reviews (1)**
Tea
Practice in conducting reviews (2)

16.30   **Putting the review to good use**
Close

One course such as this is probably insufficient. A whole suite of courses may be required as described below.

Performance management learning events in a large pharmaceutical company

I. Performance management workshop

Objectives

A two-day workshop providing the knowledge and skills necessary to operate the whole performance management process effectively. The workshop also offers an opportunity for refresher training where required.

By the end of the workshop participants will:

- be able to describe the four-stage performance management process and the key skills required;
- be able to apply a structured approach to help them establish team objectives, personal targets and development plans and conduct effective performance reviews;
- be able to explain the difference between performance review and career review;
- have practised the key skills required to operate each stage of the performance management process;
- be able, supported by coaching from their manager, to operate the performance management process back in the workplace.

Format

A two-day non-residential workshop.

Designed for

Those requiring an understanding of and a chance to practise the concepts and skills of performance management.

2. Coaching skills

Objectives

Coaching is the ability to take the opportunities presented by the job itself and use them in a conscious manner to improve the knowledge, skills, competencies, and therefore performance, of the learner. It is fundamental to performance management and generally to good management practice.

By the end of the workshop participants will:

- be able to describe and apply factors that help others to learn;
- be able to apply a systematic approach towards achieving learning through the conscious use of on-the-job opportunities;
- have practised skills/behaviours associated with effective coaching.

Format

A one-day workshop.

Designed for

People who have some existing experience of operating the performance management system.

3. Individual development workshop

The aim of this workshop is to enable participants to gain a clear understanding of what development planning is and how they can implement it effectively.

Objectives

By the end of the workshop participants will be able to:

- derive an agreed individual development plan;
- implement the skills associated with improving performance.

Format

A one-day workshop. In order to make the most practical use of the one-day event, participants will be invited to work on real issues and situations and tutors will demonstrate real examples. Case studies and role plays will not be used.

Designed for

Those who have some experience of performance management and who want to improve their understanding and skill in individual development planning.

4. Performance review workshop

Performance management is a continuous process aiming to increase business effectiveness by improving the performance of individuals. The planning, development and evaluation of performance throughout the year require frequent review between the people involved to monitor targets, discuss achievements, and progress development plans. This workshop will enable people to conduct effective discussions throughout the year and at the annual performance summary review session. It explores how reward in its widest sense can be used to reinforce performance.

Objectives

By the end of the workshop participants will be able to:

- describe good practice for reviewing performance;
- apply a structured approach to preparing for and conducting review meetings;
- create conditions that encourage good performance;
- apply a variety of methods to reward performance.

Format

A one-day workshop designed for people at all levels who have a good understanding of performance management and who want to enhance their ability to conduct effective performance review discussions and reinforce good performance.

Methods

Learning, especially skills development, should mainly be achieved by participative methods – guided discussions, role plays and other exercises – although it can be supplemented by e-learning covering the areas of knowledge needed.

Guided discussion

The aim of guided discussions would be to get participants to think through for themselves the learning points. When covering review meetings the trainer asks questions such as:

- What do you think makes for a good review meeting? Can you provide any examples from your previous experience?
- What do you think can go wrong with a meeting? Have you any examples?
- Why is it important to create the right environment?
- How do you set about doing so?
- What sort of things should be discussed in a review meeting?
- Why is it important for managers to let the individual do most of the talking?
- Why could self-assessment be useful?

Role plays

Role plays are usually based on a written brief that defines the same situation from each participant's point of view so that they can understand what it feels like to be in either position.

Course members are then asked to play out the roles and fellow members assess their performance (this in itself provides some practice in performance assessment). Each person playing the role will also describe his or her feelings about the review, and assess the other person's performance or behaviour.

Exercises

An approach that can be more realistic is to get participants to perform a task on which they are appraised by fellow course members. This could be a group exercise. If there is sufficient time available each member could take it in turn to lead the group and be appraised on his or her performance by the rest of the group. Such exercises can also be used to practise formulating team objectives and reviewing team performance.

A further variation is to get one course member to give a short presentation on a topic, have a second one assess the presenter and get a third person to assess the quality of the assessment. This gives the opportunity to practise assessment skills.

Less formal learning

Formal training programmes are useful but not enough. Performance management skills are best developed through coaching and mentoring, which can be supplemented by e-learning programmes. The HR department can play an important role in organizing these learning activities but it is best to use experienced line managers as coaches and mentors.

24

Evaluating
Performance Management

It is hard to ensure that performance management systems function effectively, however carefully they have been developed and introduced. Their operation must be monitored continuously and evaluated regularly to ensure that they are working well and identify any remedial actions required, such as focused training. The criteria and methods that can be used and a typical approach are outlined in this chapter. Further guidance on evaluation is provided in the toolkit in Appendix A.

Criteria

The criteria for evaluating performance management should have been defined when the system was introduced or amended. They will be based on its objectives and how well they have been achieved. If, for example, performance development is a major objective, how the impact of the system on performance can be measured should be described. The system design should specify how it is intended to operate, and the evaluation will aim to determine the extent to which these operational requirements are being met.

Success criteria such as those set out below should be defined in advance and used as the basis for evaluation:

- measures of improved performance by reference to key performance indicators in such terms as output, productivity, sales, quality, customer satisfaction, return on investment;
- achievement of defined and agreed goals;
- measures of employee engagement before and after the introduction of performance management, and then at regular intervals;
- assessments of reactions of managers and employees to performance management;
- personal development plans agreed and implemented;
- performance improvement plans agreed and implemented;

- assessment of the extent to which managers and employees have reached agreement on goals and performance improvement plans.

There are two perspectives as identified by Lawler, Mohrman and Resnick (1984) in evaluating a performance management system: 1) the effectiveness of the system as judged by management; and 2) the effectiveness of the system as judged by employees. Performance management should meet both these criteria. If it is to meet the needs of management it must help the organization to use the skills of employees and motivate and develop them to perform effectively. To meet the needs of employees it must help them to know what is expected of them, how well they are doing and how they can improve their performance to meet their own and the organization's goals

Additionally, as pointed out by Lee (2005): 'All performance management systems should be judged by one standard – how well they create the climate necessary for performance conversations to occur so that the employee and supervisor can diagnose problems and work together to overcome them.'

Method

The best method of monitoring and evaluation is to ask those involved – managers and individuals – how it worked. As many as possible should be seen, individually and in groups, by members of a project team and/or the HR function. Detailed check lists are provided in Appendix A but the main things to examine are set out below.

Performance management evaluation areas

For managers:

- How well the goal setting process worked.
- How well the process of giving informal and formal feedback worked.
- How well the formal performance review worked.
- Any evidence of performance improvement (individual and departmental) as a result of performance management.

For individuals:

- How well the goal setting process worked.
- The quality and helpfulness of any feedback received from their manager.
- How well the formal performance review was conducted.
- The extent to which the process provided justified indications of where improvement was necessary.

- The clarity of the process.
- The usefulness or otherwise of documentation or a web-based system.
- The quality of the guidance, training and support received.
- The extent to which the whole process was worthwhile from their viewpoint as managers.

- Any examples of performance improvement as a result of performance management.
- The extent to which the process provided guidance on learning and development needs.
- Any examples of useful coaching or training received as a result of the performance management system.
- The extent to which they were motivated by the process.

Individual interviews and focus group discussions can be supplemented by a special survey of reactions to performance management that could be completed anonymously by all managers and staff. The results should be fed back to all concerned and analysed to assess the need for any amendments to the process or further training requirements. Examples of a performance review evaluation form and typical attitude survey questions are given in the performance management toolkit in Appendix A.

The ultimate test, of course, is analysing organizational performance to establish the extent to which improvements can be attributed to performance management. It may be impossible to prove a direct connection, but more detailed assessments with managers and staff on the impact of the process may reveal specific areas in which performance has been improved that could be assumed to impact on overall performance.

A typical approach

When performance management was introduced in a NHS Trust it was decided that monitoring could be carried out by:

- recording and analysing performance assessments, which helps establish how managers are using performance management;
- one-to-one interviews with managers, identifying how they are finding the experience of performance management and where they need more support;
- employee attitude surveys and focused discussion groups;
- reviewing improvements in the performance of the organization.

To maintain high standards it was deemed necessary to:

- maintain training in performance management for all new staff (including individuals who are promoted to management posts);
- top up training to keep the principles and practices fresh;
- use one-to-one coaching where necessary;
- conduct workshops for managers to share their experiences.

These guidelines are valid for any organization that wants to develop and maintain effective performance management processes.

Appendix A
Performance
Management Toolkit

The toolkit is concerned with the design, implementation, operation and evaluation of new or substantially amended performance management systems on the basis of an analytical and diagnostic survey.

Contents

Introduction to the toolkit

The purpose of the toolkit is to provide practical guidance to those who want to review exist-ing performance management systems and processes or develop and implement new ones. The toolkit can be used by line managers as a guide to their performance management prac-tices. It can also be the basis for developing understanding and skills through coaching, men-toring, formal training and e-learning.

Definition of a performance management system

A performance management system is defined as a set of interrelated activities and processes that are treated holistically as an integrated and key component of an organization's approach to managing performance through people and to developing the skills and capabilities of its human capital.

Structure of the toolkit

The toolkit is divided into the five sections described below and illustrated in Figure A1.

1. The analytical and diagnostic toolkit covers the analysis of present arrangements and the diagnosis of the causes of any problems. It provides the basis for the design or modifica-tion of a performance management system.

2. The design toolkit covers the development of the constituents of a performance manage-ment system – performance planning and agreements, goal setting, feedback, perform-ance analysis and assessment, rating, coaching, and the link to reward and personal development.

3. The implementation toolkit covers the processes of communicating, briefing, training and pilot testing that must be carried out to ensure the successful operation of perform-ance management.

4. The operational toolkit covers the main performance management activities of complet-ing performance agreements, goal setting, performance review, managing managerial performance and dealing with under-performers.

5. The evaluation toolkit covers methods of evaluating the effectiveness of performance management through checklists and surveys.

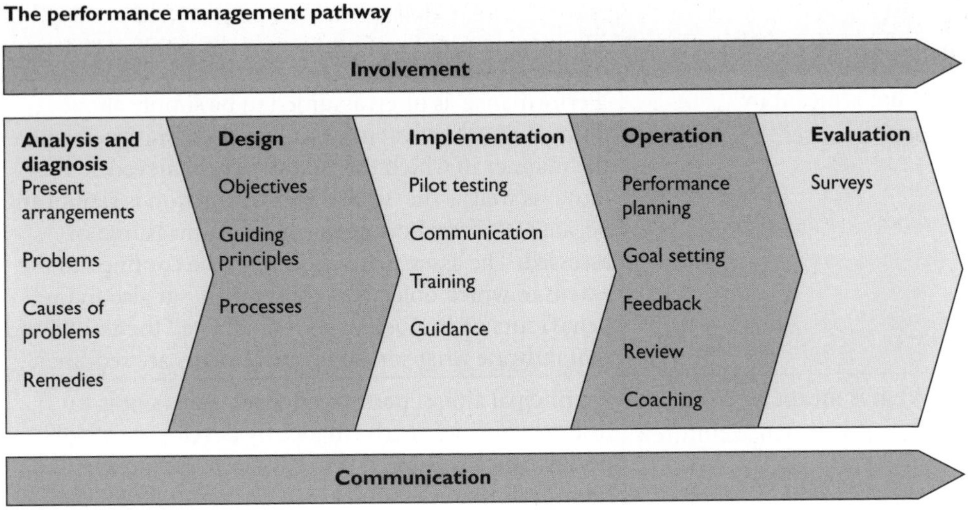

The performance management pathway

Figure A1 The performance management design, development, implementation and maintenance pathway

Analysis and diagnosis toolkit

It is necessary to analyse and understand the strengths and weaknesses of the present arrangements. As far as possible the analysis and diagnosis should involve line managers and employees through surveys, workshops and focus groups.

Initial discussions with stakeholders

The following questionnaires or a selection of them can be used to initiate discussions with stakeholders on performance management requirements:

● an overall analysis of performance management practices;

● performance management goals;

● evaluation of performance management practices;

● gap analysis of performance review practices;

● analysis of performance management practice.

Question	Significance of question
1. What is meant by performance?	'Performance' is often assumed to be simply about outputs or achievements. But it is also concerned with the manner in which the results were achieved, ie the 'how' as well as the 'what'. This distinction is significant because it affects how performance is measured or assessed. The assessment should not be confined to the extent to which objectives are reached but also to the behaviours or competencies that affected the results and that indicate what sort of improvements are required.
2. What is meant by 'a high-performance culture'?	A principal aim of performance management is to improve business performance by developing a high-performance culture. It is necessary to define what a high-performance culture is to understand how performance management can help to create one.
3. Can good or poor performance be identified?	This is at the heart of performance management. The processes used must establish how well people are doing in order to identify how they can build on their success. They must also indicate any aspects of less effective performance in order to plan improvements.
4. Can the causes of good or poor performance be established?	This follows question 3. Performance management processes need to ensure that performance is analysed in order to determine what has affected it and decide on any actions required.
5. How can people be encouraged to engage with their work?	Performance management is fundamentally about encouraging and helping people to be engaged with their jobs by becoming more aware of what they are expected to do, by receiving feedback on how well they have done it and by being given the opportunity to exercise and develop their skills.
6. What can be done about under-performers?	Performance management should always be positive and forward looking. But it is necessary to differentiate between people who are performing at different levels and agree on action to help the under-performers to improve.
7. Can all this be done fairly?	Performance management has to be seen to be fair by ensuring that it is based on a dialogue and agreed conclusions based on evidence rather than opinion. It is not 'appraisal' in the sense of a top-down judgement on people.

Questionnaire 1   Overall performance management analysis questionnaire

Performance management goals

Possible goals for performance management are set out below. A useful analytical exercise is to rate the importance of each of these goals and assess the effectiveness with which any relevant goals are reached. This can be done by individuals or in focus groups or workshops and the outcomes of the assessment analysed to indicate where changes or developments are required.

Possible goals	Importance	Effectiveness
• Align individual and organizational objectives		
• Improve organizational performance		
• Develop a high-performance culture		
• Improve individual performance		
• Provide basis for personal development		
• Increase motivation and engagement		
• Inform contribution/performance pay decisions		
• Measure performance against quantified objectives		
• Encourage appropriate behaviours – 'living the values'		
• Clarify performance expectations in the role		
• Identify potential		
• Identify poor performers		

Scale: 10 = high, 1 = low

Questionnaire 2   Performance management goals

Performance management gap analysis

The gap analysis shown below assesses the extent to which desirable characteristics of performance management exist in the organization. It provides the basis for the design and development of performance management systems and processes. Start gap analysis with senior management, line managers and staff by getting them to complete the grid individually or in groups by marking with an X the position they think the organization is in at present and an O where they believe the organization should be placed. A gap between X and O – between what is and what should be – reveals areas for development. The next step is to get those involved to discuss and agree priorities.

Desirable characteristics	X = current O = desired	Undesirable characteristics
Performance management is perceived by top management as a key process for managing the business.	⊢—⊢—⊢—⊢	Top management pays lip service to performance management.
Line managers are committed to performance management.	⊢—⊢—⊢—⊢	Line managers see performance management as a chore.
Line managers have the skills to manage performance effectively	⊢—⊢—⊢—⊢	There are serious deficiencies in the skill levels displayed by line managers.
Performance management is owned and driven by line managers.	⊢—⊢—⊢—⊢	Performance management is seen as the preserve of HR.
Employees believe that performance management operates fairly.	⊢—⊢—⊢—⊢	Employees do not trust line managers to review their performance fairly.
There is hard evidence that performance management improves business performance in our organization.	⊢—⊢—⊢—⊢	There is no evidence that performance management improves business performance in our organization.
Performance management is based on agreed definitions of roles, key result areas and competency requirements.	⊢—⊢—⊢—⊢	Performance management is not related to the reality of what people are expected to do and in terms of how they are expected to behave.
Clear objectives and performance standards are agreed at the performance planning stage.	⊢—⊢—⊢—⊢	Objectives and standards, if agreed at all, are vague or undemanding.
Methods of measuring performance (key performance indicators) and assessing levels of competence are agreed at the performance planning stage.	⊢—⊢—⊢—⊢	No attempt is made to agree performance or competency indicators.
Performance development plans are agreed at the planning stage.	⊢—⊢—⊢—⊢	Performance development planning is generally neglected.
Performance management in the form of review and feedback is practised throughout the year.	⊢—⊢—⊢—⊢	Performance appraisal takes place, if at all, as a dishonest annual ritual.
Line managers provide helpful feedback and support during formal reviews.	⊢—⊢—⊢—⊢	The quality of feedback and support is generally inadequate.
Line managers recognize their responsibility for coaching people and act accordingly.	⊢—⊢—⊢—⊢	Coaching by line management is sparse and often inadequate.

Questionnaire 3   Gap analysis of performance management practice

Review practice	Fully in place	Partly in place	Not in place	Action
1. The content of the performance review is based on a role profile.				
2. Performance expectations are agreed with employees.				
3. Performance objectives are aligned with business goals.				
4. The review is based on evidence in the form of observable job behaviours.				
5. The review process is clearly defined for everyone involved.				
6. Employees participate fully in the review process.				
7. Reviewers are capable of making fair and consistent assessments.				
8. The review focuses on development and improvement needs.				
9. A higher authority checks and comments on reviews.				
10. Reviewers are trained in feedback and assessment techniques.				

Questionnaire 4   Analysis of performance review practices

Views on performance management

Besides the use of questionnaires as the basis for discussions with stakeholders, surveys covering all or large proportions of staff can be used to obtain views on present arrangements and a special survey can be made of the opinions of the line managers upon whom the success of performance management largely depends.

Rate the following statements on a scale of 1–5 where: 1 = fully agree, 2 = agree, 3 = not sure, 4 = disagree, 5 = strongly disagree	
Our performance management system:	
Translates corporate goals into divisional, departmental, team and individual goals	1 2 3 4 5
Helps to clarify corporate goals	1 2 3 4 5
Is a continuous and evolutionary process in which performance improves over time	1 2 3 4 5
Relies on consensus and cooperation rather than control and coercion	1 2 3 4 5
Creates a shared understanding of what is required to improve performance and how it will be achieved	1 2 3 4 5
Encourages self-management of individual performance	1 2 3 4 5
Encourages a management style that is open and honest and encourages two-way communication between managers and staff at all levels	1 2 3 4 5
Delivers continuous feedback on organizational, team and individual performance to all staff	1 2 3 4 5
Analyses and assesses performance against jointly agreed goals	1 2 3 4 5
Enables individual staff members to modify their objectives	1 2 3 4 5
Demonstrates respect for the individual	1 2 3 4 5
Has fair procedures	1 2 3 4 5

Questionnaire 5   General survey of views on performance management

Rate the following statements on a scale of 1–5 where: 1 = fully agree, 2 = agree, 3 = not sure, 4 = disagree, 5 = strongly disagree	
1.	I believe that an effective system of performance management will help me to improve the performance of my team.	1 2 3 4 5
2.	I am quite satisfied that I can manage performance well without the help of a formal performance management system.	1 2 3 4 5
3.	I think that performance management could usefully ensure that the individual goals of my team members are aligned to departmental and organizational goals.	1 2 3 4 5
4.	I recognize the need to be systematic about agreeing performance goals, providing feedback and reviewing performance.	1 2 3 4 5
5.	I think my team members will benefit from a more deliberate planned approach to performance management.	1 2 3 4 5
6.	I regularly provide good feedback to my team members, which in most cases they are prepared to accept.	1 2 3 4 5
7.	I am quite confident that I will be able to define and agree goals with my team members.	1 2 3 4 5
8.	I think I have the skills required to coach my team members.	1 2 3 4 5
9.	I consider that it is possible to ensure that performance ratings are meaningful and fair.	1 2 3 4 5
10.	I am confident that I can run a performance review meeting which has positive results and motivates my team members.	1 2 3 4 5

Questionnaire 6   Questionnaire for line managers

Diagnosis

Following the analysis any problems, their causes and possible remedies should be identified.

List any significant problems identified by the analysis and indicate the likely causes of the problems and their likely remedies.		
Problem	**Likely cause**	**Possible remedy**

Questionnaire 7   Diagnostic summary

Design toolkit

The design should be based on the initial analysis and diagnosis and should involve stakeholders: that is, senior management, line managers, employees and their representatives. It is advisable to build on existing practices in order to promote acceptance and assimilation.

There is always a choice in the design of the elements of a performance management system. The factors governing the choice will be the objectives of the system, the culture of the organization (including norms on the extent to which it is believed that a formal system is required and the amount of flexibility allowed in operating the system), the system of work, the structure of the organization and the views of management, line managers, employees and their representatives, and HR. The steps in the design programme are illustrated in Figure A2.

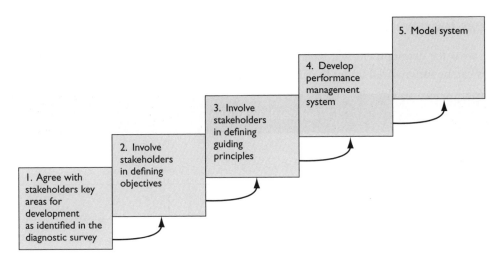

Figure A2 Steps in the design programme

The instruments and guidelines set out below can be used to inform the design programme:

- areas for choice;

- analysis of possible objectives and success criteria;

- checklist of possible success criteria;

- guiding principles questionnaire;

- analysis of the components of the performance management system;

- arguments for and against rating;

- arguments for and against forced distribution;

- model of a performance management system.

Areas for development

The areas for development will have been identified if a diagnostic survey has taken place. They can be summarized under the headings given below.

Area	What needs to be done	How it can be done
Performance planning and agreement		
Goal setting		
Providing feedback		
Conducting performance reviews		
Assessment and rating		
Coaching		
Documentation		
Use of computers		
Increasing commitment of line managers to performance management		
Developing performance management skills of line managers		
Educating employees generally on the purpose of performance management, how it works, how it affects them and what part they play		

Questionnaire 8   Areas for development

Areas for choice

There is plenty of room for choice in the design of a performance management system, and much of the design programme will be taken up with an analysis of the pros and cons of the various alternatives as set out below within the context of the organization and its people.

Areas for choice	Examples of possible alternatives
Objectives of performance management	• To improve organizational performance • To improve individual performance • To provide the basis for employee development • To inform performance or contribution pay decisions • Others, including a combination of two or more of the above
Control and flexibility	• Processes based on guiding principles • Flexibility in operation in line with principles • Tightly controlled system • Common system throughout organization – no variations allowed
Role profiles	• Provide clear basis for planning and review, cover both key result areas (accountabilities) and competency requirements and are reviewed annually • Focus on required role outputs and inputs • Rely on existing job descriptions
Individual goals	• Aligned to organizational goals • Focus only on job requirements • Must be SMART • Include qualitative performance standards • Cascaded from above • Refer only to specific and time constrained tasks and projects • Refer to ongoing work goals as specified in the role profile
Personal development planning	• Regarded as a key part of the performance agreement • Treated as an incidental activity
Performance review	• Treated as a once-a-year event • Emphasis on continuous review and feedback • Top down • Dialogue • Ratings • No ratings (overall assessment or use of performance matrix)

Areas for choice	Examples of possible alternatives
Documentation	• Detailed forms to be completed by manager • Documentation minimized
Relationship to performance or contribution pay	• Ratings inform position on pay matrix and therefore pay increase • Pay reviews take place at the same time as performance reviews • Pay reviews are 'decoupled' from performance reviews, ie take place some time later

Questionnaire 9   Areas for choice

Analysis of possible objectives and success criteria

It is essential that everyone involved is clear about the objectives of performance management and the criteria that will be used to evaluate the extent to which the objectives have been successfully achieved. Managers and employees should be involved in setting objectives and success criteria. They should consider not only what performance management will do for the organization but also what they hope it will do for them. It is advisable, however, not to try to attempt too much, especially when this is a new development. Some prioritization of objectives may therefore be required.

Possible objectives	For the organization	For line managers	For employees	Possible success criteria (see checklist)
Rate the possible objective on a scale of 1–5 where: 1 = crucial, 2 = important, 3 = not sure, 4 = not very important, 5 = irrelevant				
Improve performance	1 2 3 4 5	1 2 3 4 5	1 2 3 4 5	
Develop a performance culture	1 2 3 4 5	1 2 3 4 5	1 2 3 4 5	
Identify people with high potential	1 2 3 4 5	1 2 3 4 5	1 2 3 4 5	
Identify under-performers	1 2 3 4 5	1 2 3 4 5	1 2 3 4 5	

Possible objectives	For the organization	For line managers	For employees	Possible success criteria (see checklist)
Rate the possible objective on a scale of 1–5 where: 1 = crucial, 2 = important, 3 = not sure, 4 = not very important, 5 = irrelevant				
Align individual and organizational objectives	1 2 3 4 5	1 2 3 4 5	1 2 3 4 5	
Provide the basis for personal development	1 2 3 4 5	1 2 3 4 5	1 2 3 4 5	
Enable people to know where they stand	1 2 3 4 5	1 2 3 4 5	1 2 3 4 5	
Provide the basis for performance pay decisions	1 2 3 4 5	1 2 3 4 5	1 2 3 4 5	
Other	1 2 3 4 5	1 2 3 4 5	1 2 3 4 5	

Questionnaire 10   Analysis of possible objectives

Checklist 1. Checklist of possible success criteria

- Measures of improved performance by reference to key performance indicators in such terms as output, productivity, sales, quality, customer satisfaction, return on investment.

- Achievement of defined and agreed objectives.

- Measures of employee engagement before and after the introduction of performance management and then at regular intervals.

- Assessments of reactions of managers and employees to performance management.

- Assessment of the extent to which managers and employees have reached agreement on goals and performance improvement plans.

- Personal development plans agreed and implemented.

- Performance improvement plans agreed and implemented.

Definition of guiding principles

It is important to involve stakeholders in agreeing a set of guiding principles that can be used as a basis for performance management design, operation and evaluation and can be communicated to employees. A questionnaire is shown below.

Possible guiding principle	Assessment of importance/ relevance 1 Vital 2 Very important 3 Fairly important 4 Not very relevant
Clearly stated work goals/tasks subject to regular review and updating	1 2 3 4
Clearly stated standards of performance	1 2 3 4
Feedback on job behaviour	1 2 3 4
Comments rather than performance ratings	1 2 3 4
Identification of development needs	1 2 3 4
Agreed training plan	1 2 3 4
Reach agreement through a two-way process	1 2 3 4
Incorporate appeal procedure	1 2 3 4
Used as a day-to-day management tool	1 2 3 4
No direct link to pay	1 2 3 4
Requires commitment from all concerned	1 2 3 4
Other	1 2 3 4

Questionnaire 11   Guiding principles

Development of performance management system

The development of a performance management system involves first selecting and describing the components of the system (Table A1) and then modelling the system (Figure A3).

Table A1   Analysis of the components of the performance management system

Component	Contents	Considerations
Performance planning and agreement	• Agreeing role profiles • Agreeing objectives (see also goal setting) • Agreeing performance measures • Agreeing development needs (see also personal development planning) • Agreeing areas for performance improvement • Recording decisions in an agreement	• Format of role profiles • Methods of preparing and updating role profiles • Choice of measures • Format of agreement
Goal setting	• Identifying key result areas • Identifying key performance indicators • Agreeing targets and standards of performance	• Methods of goal setting • Ensuring 'SMART' goals are agreed • Selecting appropriate measures
Personal development planning	• Deciding areas for development • Planning methods of development	• Format of development plan • Approaches to development • Emphasis on self-directed development
Feedback	• Provision during year • Provision during formal review	• Developing feedback skills • Use of informal and formal feedback
Performance reviews	• Purpose • Content • Timing	• Use of informal reviews throughout year • Preparation for formal reviews • Conduct of formal reviews
Performance analysis	• Methodology • Use of metrics	• Performance analysis skills • Data collection and analysis

Component	Contents	Considerations
Performance assessment and rating	• Use of overall assessment • Use of rating • Use of forced distribution rating	• Provision of guidelines for overall assessments • Arguments for and against rating (see Table A2 below) • Decisions on type of rating to be used, if at all • Developing assessment/rating skills • Providing rating guidelines, if appropriate • Arguments for and against forced distribution (see Table A3 below)
Link to performance pay	• How assessment/ratings will inform performance pay decisions • The timing of pay reviews and performance reviews	• Arguments for and against performance pay
Coaching	• Methods • Responsibility of line managers for	• Developing coaching skills
Administration	• Documentation • Use of computers	• Design of documentation • Design of computer system • Decision on extent to which a standard approach to performance management should be used

Table A2   Arguments for and against rating

Arguments for rating	Arguments against rating
• Ratings let people know where they stand • It is necessary to sum up judgements about people. • Ratings give people something to strive for. • They provide a basis for assessing potential. • They are needed to inform performance or contribute to pay decisions.	• Ratings are likely to be subjective and inconsistent. • To sum the overall performance of a person with a single rating is a gross oversimplification of what may be a complex set of factors affecting that person's performance. • It is hard to rate qualitative aspects of performance. • To label people as 'average' or 'below average', or whatever equivalent terms are used, is both demeaning and demotivating. • Line managers tend not to differentiate between ratings. • The use of ratings to inform decisions on performance pay or inclusion in a talent management programme will dominate performance reviews and prejudice the real purpose of such reviews, which is to provide the basis for developing skills and improving performance.

Table A3   Arguments for and against forced distribution

Arguments for forced distribution	Arguments against forced distribution
• Identifies 'best' and 'worst' performance so that action can be taken. • Achieves a more appropriate (ie 'normal') distribution of ratings. • Overcomes the 'centralizing' tendency of raters, ie a preference for rating in the middle 'boxes' and avoiding extremes. • Helps to achieve consistency in rating between different raters.	• Based on some form of rating or ranking system which suffers from all the disadvantages inherent in any rating approach (see Table A2). • No evidence that ability is distributed normally. • Assumes that the same distribution of ability/performance occurs in all departments, which is unlikely to be the case. • Managers do not like to be forced into a straight-jacket. • Employees resent the fact that their future is determined by some form of artificial quota or ranking system or that their ratings may be 'moderated' downwards to fit a forced distribution. • A 'rank and yank' system can produce a climate of fear in an organization and will at least inhibit and at worst destroy any possibility that performance management is perceived and used as a developmental process.

Modelling the performance management system

A model of a performance management system is a useful way of summing up how it operates. It can be used in communication and training programmes to provide an easily absorbed picture of what performance management is about. Typical models illustrate the cyclical nature of a performance management system, as shown in Figure A3.

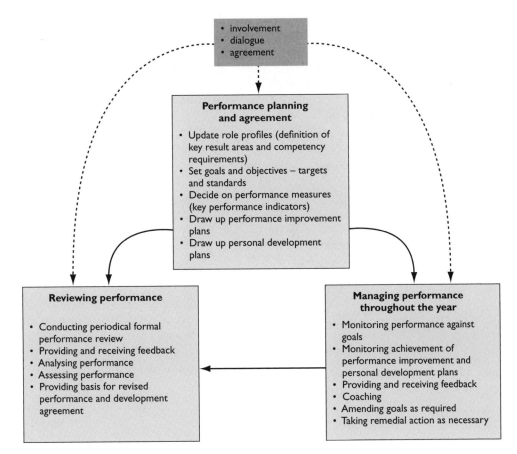

Figure A3   Model of a performance management system

Implementation toolkit

The implementation programme as illustrated in Figure A4 should start with a pilot test of performance management process and approaches to communication and training that can inform full communication and training programmes and, subject to any modifications required, the launch of the system.

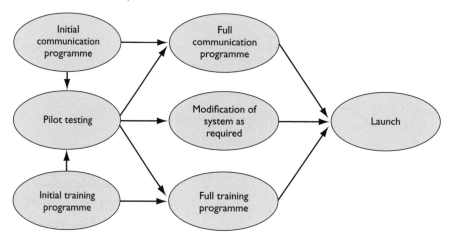

Figure A4 Implementation programme

Pilot testing

Before embarking on full implementation it is essential to pilot test the process. This should be done in two or three departments where the managers are sympathetic to performance management and will therefore give it their backing. The test should be preceded by a briefing and training for participants in the processes and skills they should use. Ideally, it should extend over the whole of the performance management cycle, ie 12 months, but a period of between 6 and 12 months will provide an adequate test. The purpose of the test, which should be explained to those taking part, is to ensure that an appropriate and acceptable form of performance management is introduced. Another way of testing is to do it top down – get senior managers to try it out first so that they know all the wrinkles before cascading it throughout the organization.

The following questionnaires can be used to evaluate the test.

Rate the following statements on a scale of 1-5 where: 1 = fully agree, 2 = agree, 3 = not sure, 4 = disagree, 5 = strongly disagree					
1. The objectives and processes of performance management were described clearly to me.	1	2	3	4	5
2. I received good training in performance management skills.	1	2	3	4	5
3. I had no difficulty in agreeing role profiles.	1	2	3	4	5
4. I had no difficulty in agreeing objectives.	1	2	3	4	5
5. I had no difficulty in agreeing performance and development plans.	1	2	3	4	5
6. I was able to monitor performance well, providing feedback and coaching as required.	1	2	3	4	5
7. The performance review meeting went very well.	1	2	3	4	5
8. I was able to assess performance accurately and fairly.	1	2	3	4	5
9. I believe that performance management will enable me to do my job as a manager better.	1	2	3	4	5
10. I believe that performance management is a waste of time.	1	2	3	4	5

Questionnaire 12 Pilot test questionnaire for managers

Rate the following statements on a scale of 1-5 where: 1 = fully agree, 2 = agree, 3 = not sure, 4 = disagree, 5 = strongly disagree					
1. The objectives and processes of performance management were described clearly to me.	1	2	3	4	5
2. I received good training in performance management skills.	1	2	3	4	5
3. I had no difficulty in agreeing my role profile.	1	2	3	4	5
4. I had no difficulty in agreeing my objectives.	1	2	3	4	5
5. I had no difficulty in agreeing my performance and development plans.	1	2	3	4	5
6. I was able to monitor my own performance well and was provided with feedback and with coaching as required.	1	2	3	4	5
7. The performance review meeting went very well.	1	2	3	4	5
8. I was able to assess performance accurately and fairly.	1	2	3	4	5
9. I believe that performance management will enable me to do my job better.	1	2	3	4	5
10. I believe that performance management is a waste of time.	1	2	3	4	5

Questionnaire 13 Pilot test questionnaire for employees

Communications

It is vital to have a communications strategy that informs all concerned, from the very beginning of the exercise, what is being planned, what it will look like and how it will affect them. A checklist is set out below.

---

1. Has the best use been made of different methods of communication, eg team briefing, DVDs and brochures?

2. Have the objectives of performance management been explained?

3. Have the various processes involved been explained?

4. Have the benefits of performance management to the organization, line managers and individual employees been explained?

5. Have the links, if any, to performance management been explained?

6. Has every attempt been made to convince employees that performance management will be operated fairly?

Checklist 2 Communications checklist

Training

Training for both managers and employees in performance management skills is essential. A checklist is set out below.

---

1. Have all managers received training in the operation of performance management generally and in basic performance management skills, ie defining role profiles, goal setting, drawing up performance and development agreements, providing feedback, analysing and assessing performance, conducting performance reviews and coaching?

2. Have employees received training in their role in agreeing and implementing performance and development plans, goal setting, monitoring their own performance, generating their own feedback and preparing for and participating in performance reviews?

3. Have arrangements been made to provide coaching and mentoring for line managers in performance management skills?

Checklist 3 Performance management training

Performance management operations toolkit

The operations toolkit is concerned with the major performance management process of agreeing performance and development plans, goal setting, providing feedback, preparing for and conducting performance reviews, coaching, and dealing with under-performers. A summary of performance management activities over the year is given in Table A4, followed by checklists for each of the above activities together with a checklist on assessing managerial performance.

Table A4   Performance management activities over the year

Start of year	Performance and development agreement	• Define role profiles, updating as necessary. • Ensure that role profiles set out updated key result areas and competency requirements. • Define goals and standards of performance. • Identify and define key performance indicators. • Draw up performance development plans. • Draw up personal development plans.
Continuing dialogue	Managing performance throughout the year	• Monitor progress and review evidence of achievement. • Provide informal feedback as required. • Provide coaching as required. • Update role profiles and objectives as necessary.
End of year	Performance review	• Prepare for performance review by analysing achievements (work and learning) against objectives. • Identify specific strengths and weaknesses on the basis of evidence. • Assess overall performance. • Provide feedback. • Use conclusions of performance review as the basis for next year's performance and development agreement.

1. Is there an up-to-date role profile that sets out key result areas and competency requirements?

2. Have 'SMART' objectives been set for each of the key result areas?

3. Have individuals been encouraged to formulate for themselves performance and personal development plans.

4. Has a realistic performance development plan to enhance strengths and overcome any weaknesses been agreed?

5. Has an attainable personal development plan been agreed?

6. Are plans based on an analysis of past performance and an assessment of future demands (new skills to be acquired, new tasks for the role holder, changes in the role or scope of the function)?

7. Do the plans indicate success criteria – how the individual and the manager will know that the desired results have been achieved?

8. Has the agreement been reached through constructive dialogue, with the full involvement of the individual and without any sort of coercion from the manager?

9. Have individuals been empowered to implement the plans?

10. Has provision been made for monitoring and reviewing progress without being oppressive?

Checklist 4 Performance and development agreement checklist

1. Has the goal setting process been based on an agreed and up-to-date role profile that sets out key result areas?

2. Are goals clearly related to key result areas in the role profile?

3. Are individual goals integrated with corporate goals?

4. If goals have been cascaded downwards, is there some scope for individuals to discuss and modify their own goals?

5. Has goal setting been carried out jointly by the manager and the individual?

6. Do goals clearly and specifically support the achievement of team and department goals?

7. Are goals specific and time related?

8. Are goals challenging?

9. Are goals realistic and attainable?

10. Have success criteria for each goal been determined?

Checklist 5 Goal setting checklist

1. Is feedback provided on actual events or observed behaviour?

2. Is feedback presented as a description of what has happened and not expressed as a judgement?

3. Is feedback related to specific items of behaviour rather than transmitting general feelings or impressions?

4. Is feedback based on questions rather than statements?

5. Has feedback been restricted to key issues?

6   Does the feedback focus on aspects of performance the individual can improve?

7. Is feedback positive?

8. Is feedback constructive?

9. Has feedback been built into the job so that it can be generated by individuals?

10. Does feedback provide a sound basis for action?

Checklist 6 Feedback checklist

1. How well do you think the individual has done in achieving his/her goals during the review period?

2. To what extent have the actions and behaviour of the individual been in line with competency requirements?

3   How well have any improvement, development or training plans as agreed at the last review meeting been put into effect?

4. What goals relating to the individual's key tasks would you like to agree with him/her for the next review period?

5. Has the individual had any problems in carrying out his/her work? If so, what sort of problems and what can be done about them?

6. Are you satisfied that you have given the individual sufficient guidance or help on what he/she is expected to do? If not, what extra help/guidance could you provide?

7. Is the best use being made of the individual's skills and abilities? If not, what should be done?

8. Is the individual ready to take on additional responsibilities in his/her present job? If so, what?

9. Do you think the individual and the organization would benefit if he/she were provided with further experience in other areas of work?

10. What direction do you think the individual's career could take within the organization?

11. What development or training does the individual need to help in his/her work and/or to further his/her career with the organization?

12. Are there any special projects the individual could take part in which would help with his/her development?

Checklist 7 Review meeting preparation manager's checklist

1. How well do you think you have done in achieving your objectives during the review period?

2. How well have any improvement, development or training plans as agreed at your last review meeting been put into effect?

3. What goals relating to the key tasks in your present job would you like to agree with your manager for the next review period?

4. Have you met any problems in carrying out your work? If so, what sort of problems and what can be done about them?

5. Do you think your manager could provide you with more guidance or help in what he or she expects you to do? If so, what guidance or help do you need?

6. Do you think the best use is being made of your skills and abilities? If not, what needs to be done about it?

7. Do you feel you are ready to take on additional responsibilities in your present job? If so, what would you like to do?

8. Would you like to gain further experience in other related areas of work? If so, what?

9. What direction would you like your future career to take with the organization?

10. What development or training would you like to help you in your job and/or further your career with the organization?

Checklist 8 Review meeting preparation – individual's checklist

1. Have achievements been discussed in relation to goals and performance/personal development plans?

2. Has self-assessment by the individual been encouraged, including any comments about the manager's support, resource availability or objectives?

3. Has the level of competency achieved against the headings and descriptors in the individual's role definition been discussed?

4. Has there been a discussion on the extent to which the individual's behaviour is in accord with the organization's core values?

5. Have any problems in achieving agreed goals or standards of performance been identified?

6. Have the reasons for such problems been agreed, including any factors beyond the individual's control as well as those that can be attributed to the individual's behaviour?

7. Have any other problems relating to work and the individual's relationships with his/her manager, colleagues and, if appropriate, subordinates been discussed?

8. Have any actions required to overcome problems been agreed?

9. Have any necessary changes to the role profile in terms of key result areas or competency requirements been agreed?

10. Have performance measures been reviewed and revised if necessary?

Checklist 9 Performance review meeting contents

1. Has the manager prepared for the meeting by reference to a list of agreed objectives and notes on performance throughout the year?

2. Has the meeting been conducted in accordance with a clear structure covering all the points identified during preparation?

3. Has an informal environment in which a full, frank but friendly exchange of views can take place been maintained?

4. Has good feedback been provided?

5. To what extent has the meeting taken the form of a dialogue between two interested and involved parties, both of whom are seeking a positive conclusion?

6. Has praise been used effectively?

7. Have individuals been encouraged to do most of the talking?

8. Has self-assessment been encouraged?

9. Has the focus been on performance not personality?

11. Has the analysis of performance been encouraged?

12. Have unexpected criticisms been avoided?

13. Has the review meeting ended on a positive note with an agreed action plan?

Checklist 10 Approach used in performance review meeting

Checklists for managing under-performers

The following checklists set out the questions that can usefully be answered when dealing with different aspects of sub-standard performance. However, it is important to remember that poor performance may be caused by faults in the system rather than in the people who work within it.

---

1. To what extent have goals not been achieved?

2. What specific instances have there been of sub-standard performance?

3. Did the individual fully understand what he/she was expected to achieve?

4. Were these expectations reasonable in the light of the individual's experience and qualifications to do the job?

5. Did the individual get sufficient leadership, guidance and support from his/her manager or team leader?

6. Did the individual get sufficient support from his/her colleagues?

7. Did the individual have the resources required?

8. Were there any other factors outside the individual's control such as an inadequate system of work or unforeseeable external events and pressures that affected his or her performance?

9. Was the problem caused by inadequate knowledge or lack of skill in any respect?

10. To what extent, if any, was the failure to achieve targets or meet performance standards simply due to a lack of effort or interest on the part of the individual?

Checklist 11 Failure to achieve goals – possible remedial actions

1. Clarify goals and as necessary reformulate them to make them attainable (but not too easily).

2. Re-design the job (adjusting tasks and responsibilities) to provide a sounder basis for obtaining better results.

3. Improve the system of work.

4. Improve leadership, guidance and support from the manager or team leader.

5. Re-examine the composition of the team and its methods of working, followed if necessary by a team-building programme.

6. Improve the feedback on results to the individual, and monitor performance following the feedback to ensure that action is taken as necessary.

7. Encourage individuals to develop the additional knowledge or skills themselves while providing guidance and coaching as required. If a self-development approach is inappropriate or insufficient, arrange for specific training or coaching in areas where deficiencies in knowledge or skill have been identified.

8. Help individuals to learn from their mistakes so they know how to minimize the risk of repeating them.

9. Encourage individuals to recognize that certain aspects of their behaviour have contributed to the sub-standard results and get them to agree to the achievement of specified modifications in behaviour.

10. Agree an overall performance improvement plan.

Checklist 12 Failure to achieve goals – possible actions

1. Why do you believe that there is a problem over the employee's attitude or behaviour?

2. What evidence do you have that the attitude/behaviour is creating a performance problem? (Quote actual examples.)

3. Have you discussed with the individual at the time any instance of poor performance that you believe could be attributed to negative attitudes or behaviour?

4. How did the individual react when asked to comment on any such instances?

5. What steps have you taken to enable the employee to recognize his/her own problem or situation and discuss it with you?

6. Have you taken into account the fact that in general it is easier to change behaviour than deep-seated attitudes?

7. Have you been successful in obtaining agreement on the cause of the problem and what should be done about it?

8. If so, have you agreed how the problem should be managed by the individual with whatever help you and, possibly, other people could provide?

9. Will additional coaching or mentoring help?

10. Is this a problem that you would refer to another counselling source (eg a member of the human resource department) for resolution?

Checklist 13 Handling attitude and behavioural problems

1. How certain am I that this is an attainable goal or standard?

2. Have I any 'benchmarking' evidence that targets or standards of this nature have been achieved by other people in similar circumstances?

3   Is it reasonable for me to ask this particular individual to achieve this goal or standard in the light of his/her experience or qualifications or the circumstances in which the job is carried out?

4. Does the individual have any reasonable grounds for rejecting the goal or standard?

5. If not, why is he/she adopting this attitude?

6. Do I insist on this goal or standard in spite of the individual's objections? If not, to what extent am I prepared to modify the goal?

Checklist 14 Unwillingness to accept goals

Factors affecting managerial performance

Managing performance is what line managers do. But it is necessary to be aware of the factors that affect their own performance and therefore their ability to manage that of others. The following checklists and schedule of management standards can be used for this purpose.

1. Unforeseeable changes in the circumstances in which the job is carried out – either internal or imposed by external events.

2. Poorly defined responsibilities.

3. Inappropriate or unachievable goals or targets.

4. Insufficient guidance or support from the manager or other individuals at higher levels in the organization.

5. Inadequate cooperation or support from colleagues.

6. A faulty system of work.

7. Inadequate resources – money, staff, equipment or time.

8. Insufficient training.

9. The job demands levels of skill or knowledge that the individual does not have – and could not reasonably be expected to possess.

10. Insufficient support or guidance.

Checklist 15 Factors outside the manager's control

1. Poor leadership.

2. Insufficient attention to people responsibilities.

3. Poor judgement.

4. Indecisiveness.

5. Uncooperativeness.

6. Poor team member.

7. Lack of planning and organizing skills.

8. Unwillingness to learn from experience.

9. Unwillingness to learn from training or coaching programmes.

10. Laziness.

Checklist 16 Performance or behavioural characteristics within the manager's control

The manager's standards listed in the following Table A5 can be used as the basis for a competency framework as illustrated in Table A6.

Table A5 Managerial standards

1. Leadership:
    - develops cohesive groups and teamwork;
    - guides others to the accomplishment of objectives;
    - resolves conflicts;
    - provides direction under uncertain conditions.

2. Managing skills:
    - delegates work responsibility among employees for maximum efficiency;
    - monitors employees' performance to achieve organizational goals and maintain control;
    - sets clear, understandable objectives and priorities for department, self and with each employee;
    - schedules and develops contingency plans;
    - motivates people toward effective, cooperative group and individual efforts.

3. Learning and development:
    - conducts performance reviews according to established guidelines;
    - provides good feedback to employees at the time of the event and in

performance review meetings;

- praises and recognizes positive performance of employees; builds confidence in employees by supporting their appropriate decisions and actions;
- provides support to employees in preparing and implementing personal development plans;
- takes prompt corrective measures when employees' performance needs improvement;
- encourages and assists individuals through coaching, training and other methods to acquire knowledge, skills and expertise necessary for effective job performance and promotion.

4. Decision making and problem solving:
    - identifies and anticipates potential problems;
    - recognizes critical situations and takes appropriate action;
    - investigates and analyses problems and situations adequately and appropriately for the circumstances;
    - solicits and encourages ideas and input from others, involving them in the decision making process;
    - considers the whole organization when making decisions;
    - looks for, evaluates and considers alternatives and options in solving problems prior to making decisions and recommendations;
    - willing to accept responsibility for decisions whatever the outcome.

5. Innovation/creativity:
    - recommends new methods and ideas;
    - accepts ideas and builds on them; adds value to given efforts;
    - questions constructively why things are done in a particular way.

6. Flexibility/adaptability:
    - willing to accept new assignments and complete them according to set standards;
    - can handle a wide variety of assignments;
    - willing to consider new ideas and methods;
    - open to constructive criticism and suggestions.

7. Teamwork:
    - collaborates effectively with colleagues and other internal customers;
    - obtains cooperation from others.

8. Responsiveness:
   - understands and responds to needs and requests quickly and willingly;
   - makes his/her expertise available to others;
   - represents the department's services in a precise and acceptable manner.

9. Communication:
   - communicates all matters of importance up and down the organization in an accurate, timely manner;
   - provides complete and reliable information;
   - participates easily and influentially in meetings;
   - listens carefully to others;
   - writes and speaks clearly, concisely, accurately and persuasively.

10. Technical/professional expertise:
    - has the knowledge required in specified areas to achieve objectives;
    - has the skills required in specified areas to achieve objectives.

The following is an example of a competency framework which can be used as the basis for assessing competency levels.

Table A6 Competency frameworks

Leadership
- Develops cohesive groups and teamwork.
- Guides others to the accomplishment of objectives.
- Resolves conflicts.
- Provides direction under uncertain conditions.

Managing skills
- Delegates work responsibility among employees for maximum efficiency.
- Monitors employees' performance to achieve organizational goals and maintain control.
- Sets clear, understandable objectives and priorities for department, self and with each employee.
- Schedules and develops contingency plans.
- Motivates people toward effective, co-operative group and individual efforts.

Learning and development

- Conducts performance reviews according to established guidelines.
- Provides good feedback to employees at the time of the event and in performance review meetings.
- Praises and recognizes positive performance of employees; builds confidence in employees by supporting their appropriate decisions and actions.
- Provides support to employees in preparing and implementing personal development plans.
- Takes prompt corrective measures when employees' performance needs improvement.
- Encourages and assists individuals through coaching, training and other methods to acquire knowledge, skills and expertise necessary for effective job performance and promotion.

Decision making and problem solving

- Identifies and anticipates potential problems.
- Recognizes critical situations and takes appropriate action.
- Investigates and analyses problems and situations adequately and appropriately for the circumstances
- Solicits and encourages ideas and input from others, involving them in the decision making process.
- Considers the whole organization when making decisions.
- Looks for, evaluates and considers alternatives and options in solving problems prior to making decisions and recommendations.
- Willing to accept responsibility for decisions whatever the outcome.

Innovation/creativity

- Recommends new methods and ideas.
- Accepts ideas and builds on them; adds value to given efforts.
- Questions constructively why things are done in a particular way.

Flexibility/adaptability

- Willing to accept new assignments and complete them according to set standards.
- Can handle a wide variety of assignments.
- Willing to consider new ideas and methods.
- Open to constructive criticism and suggestions.

Teamwork

- Collaborates effectively with colleagues and other internal customers.
- Obtains co-operation from others.

Responsiveness

- Understands and responds to needs and requests quickly and willingly.
- Makes his/her expertise available to others.
- Represents the department's services in a precise and acceptable manner.

Communication

- Communicates all matters of importance up and down the organization in an accurate, timely manner.
- Provides complete and reliable information.
- Participates easily and influentially in meetings.
- Listens carefully to others.
- Writes and speaks clearly, concisely, accurately and persuasively.

Technical/professional expertise

- Has the knowledge required in specified areas to achieve objectives.
- Has the skills required in specified areas to achieve objectives.

Evaluation toolkit

It is essential to evaluate the success of performance management in meeting its objectives and in each of the main processes involved. Evaluation can take place against success criteria (Questionnaire 14) and by means of the overall checklist (Checklist 17). It can also be conducted through an assessment of reactions to performance management (Questionnaire 15) and an engagement survey (Questionnaire 16).

Evaluation against success criteria

Reference needs to be made to the effectiveness of performance management with regard to established success criteria. Unless such evaluation takes place regularly and leads to any remedial action required, the system is likely to decline.

Evaluate effectiveness as follows: 1 = high level of achievement, 2 = acceptable level of achievement, 3 = poor level of achievement	
Measures of improved performance by reference to key performance indicators in such terms as output, productivity, sales, quality, customer satisfaction, return on investment.	1 2 3
Achievement of defined and agreed objectives for performance management.	1 2 3
Measures of employee engagement before and after the introduction of performance management and then at regular intervals.	1 2 3
Assessments of reactions of managers and employees to performance management.	1 2 3
Assessment of the extent to which managers and employees have reached agreement on goals and performance development plans.	1 2 3
Performance development plans agreed and implemented.	1 2 3
Personal development plans agreed and implemented.	1 2 3

Questionnaire 14   Evaluation of performance management against success criteria

1. Are performance agreements being completed properly?

2. Do they generally spell out realistic goals, attribute and competence requirements, work plans and performance improvement and development plans?

3. Are goals being agreed properly?

4. Are they related clearly to key result areas?

5. Do they generally meet agreed criteria for good objectives, ie are they demanding but attainable, relevant, measurable, agreed and time based?

6. Are they integrated with organizational and departmental goals?

7. Are individuals and teams given scope to contribute to the formulation of higher-level goals?

8. Are appropriate performance measures being agreed?

9. Are managers providing good feedback throughout the year as well as during formal review meetings?

10. Are both managers and individuals preparing properly for performance review meetings?

11. How well are managers conducting such meetings?

12. How effective has performance management been in motivating employees?

13. Is performance management providing a good basis for recognizing high performance and valuing those who achieve it?

14. How effective has performance management been in developing skills and capabilities?

15. How well have managers and team leaders carried out their roles as coaches or mentors?

16. Have ratings been fair and consistently applied?

17. How well is poor performance recognized and dealt with?

18. How well have the performance management forms been completed?

19. How effective have the briefing and training programmes been?

20. What impact has performance management had on individual, team and organizational performance?

Checklist 17   Performance management overall evaluation

Rate the following statements on a scale of 1–5 where: 1 = fully agree, 2 = agree, 3 = not sure, 4 = disagree, 5 = strongly disagree					
1. I am quite satisfied that the objectives I agreed were fair.	1	2	3	4	5
2. I felt that the meeting to agree objectives and standards of performance helped me to focus on what I should be aiming to achieve.	1	2	3	4	5
3. I received good feedback from my manager on how I was doing.	1	2	3	4	5
4. My manager was always prepared to provide guidance when I ran into problems at work.	1	2	3	4	5
5. The performance review meeting was conducted by my manager in a friendly and helpful manner.	1	2	3	4	5
6. My manager fully recognized my achievements during the year.	1	2	3	4	5
7. If any criticisms were made during the review meeting, they were acceptable because they were based on fact, not opinion.	1	2	3	4	5
8. I was given plenty of opportunity by my manager to discuss the reasons for any of my work problems.	1	2	3	4	5
9. I felt generally that the comments made by my manager at the meeting were fair.	1	2	3	4	5
10. The meeting ended with a clear plan of action for the future with which I agreed.	1	2	3	4	5
11. I felt motivated after the meeting.	1	2	3	4	5
12. I felt that the time spent in the meeting was well worth while.	1	2	3	4	5

Questionnaire 15   Reactions to performance management

Engagement survey

Data on levels of engagement obtained from an employee opinion survey as set out below (Questionnaire 16) provide one of the most important means of measuring the effectiveness of performance management in terms of its impact on people. Such surveys should be conducted before the introduction of performance management and thereafter every year or other year to establish trends.

Rate the following statements on a scale of 1–5 where: 1 = fully agree, 2 = agree, 3 = not sure, 4 = disagree, 5 = strongly disagree					
1. I am very satisfied with the work I do.	1	2	3	4	5
2. My job is interesting.	1	2	3	4	5
3. I know exactly what I am expected to do.	1	2	3	4	5
4. I am prepared to put myself out to do my work.	1	2	3	4	5
5. My job is challenging.	1	2	3	4	5
6. I am given plenty of freedom to decide how to do my work.	1	2	3	4	5
7. I get plenty of opportunities to learn in this job.	1	2	3	4	5
8. The facilities/equipment/tools provided are excellent.	1	2	3	4	5
9. I get excellent support from my boss.	1	2	3	4	5
10. My contribution is fully recognized.	1	2	3	4	5
11. The experience I am getting now will be a great help in advancing my future career.	1	2	3	4	5
12. I find it easy to keep up with the demands of my job.	1	2	3	4	5
13. I have no problems in achieving a balance between my work and my private life.	1	2	3	4	5
14. I like working for my boss.	1	2	3	4	5
15. I get on well with my work colleagues.	1	2	3	4	5
16. I think this organization is a great place in which to work.	1	2	3	4	5
17. I believe I have a good future in this organization.	1	2	3	4	5
18. I intend to go on working for this organization.	1	2	3	4	5
19. I am happy about the values of this organization – how it conducts its business.	1	2	3	4	5
20. I believe that the products/services provided by this organization are excellent.	1	2	3	4	5

Questionnaire 16   Engagement survey

Appendix B
Performance Management Case Studies

This appendix contains case studies for CEMEX UK, DHL, Hitachi Europe, and The Royal College of Nursing.

CEMEX UK

CEMEX UK is a supplier of cement, ready-mixed concrete and aggregates with 4,000 employees. It is a subsidiary of the Mexican company CEMEX.

Aims of performance management

The aims of the Performance and Potential Assessment (P&PA) scheme at CEMEX UK are to:

- promote strategic alignment and respond to business needs;
- facilitate clear communication and understanding of standards;
- ensure objective grading and differentiation of potential levels;
- promote continuous feedback and development;
- reinforce high-performance attitudes.

The annual cycle

CEMEX's performance management scheme runs over the calendar year as follows:

- The company's overall budget is set in January and from this the most senior managers' objectives are established that are then cascaded down the organization.
- Around July, there is a mid-year review of initial objectives set and discussions on how the individual has been progressing over the first part of the year.
- Lastly, between November and January a final meeting takes place where line managers and individuals meet and staff are rated between 1 and 5 by their line managers.

Objective setting

CEMEX states that the purpose of objectives is to communicate clearly the kind of work to be performed. The company says that there are three types of objectives that can be set:

- Operative/functional: activities designed to strengthen the quality of service and to make the existing processes or procedures more efficient by innovation.

- Continuous improvement: responsibilities that are inherent to the position and functional area of the employee.

- Development and training: activities that will help the employee improve their performance.

Setting objectives is a two-way process and all objectives must align with the common acronym 'SMART'. Two more conditions are laid down – first, that objectives should be relevant, and second, that they should be limited in number (no more than 10 on the grounds that research has shown that any more than this limits impact and causes dilution).

Objectives are cascaded down through the organization, which promotes their alignment of objectives with the corporate strategy and ensures the level of challenge among the overall team is calibrated. In practice, direct supervisors can cascade objectives down by up to two levels, while indirect supervisors can do so by one level.

In addition, the various objectives are weighted and each has a specific unit of measure. For example, a salesperson might have a specific amount of a product to sell, which means that there is no ambiguity and it is easy to determine whether this sort of target has been achieved or not. By using clear evaluation criteria with a description of what it means to accomplish them, CEMEX believes that there can be no disagreement when it comes to determining a score for the year.

Mid-year and final review

CEMEX recognizes that the individual's and company's situation can change over the course of the year so a further mid-year review is held in July. This ensures that managers can amend objectives as a consequence of any work or other changes that have taken place. The end-of-year meeting takes place between November and January, when there is a one-to-one discussion between the employee and his or her immediate supervisor. At the meeting, a final rating is agreed, which helps determine the bonus to be received the following March.

360-degree appraisal

CEMEX's performance management scheme also incorporates a 360-degree appraisal process whereby managers, staff and clients provide additional feedback. Although the results of this are considered when determining bonus levels, this process is designed mainly to gauge the future potential of the individual, with the main rating more important in the bonus decision.

The 360-degree appraisal does consider outcomes, but perhaps more important is an emphasis on 'how' people accomplish their objectives, drawing on the company's nine key competencies:

- Team work: genuine willingness to work with others in a cooperative, assertive and transparent manner to achieve a common goal, placing group interests above those of the individual.

- Creativity: generation and development of ideas, considering both internal and external context to create and take advantage of business opportunities in CEMEX.

- Focus on stakeholders: adaptation of personal behaviour to the values, priorities and objectives of CEMEX, looking for the benefit of the different stakeholders.

- Entrepreneurial spirit: development of opportunities to improve the business, within and outside one's own working environment, undertaking risks and overcoming obstacles.

- Strategic thinking: understanding the circumstances that prevail in the external environment and those within the company, to make decisions that lead to the achievement of CEMEX's strategies.

- Customer service orientation: willingness to serve and anticipate the needs of the clients, both internal and external, and to take the necessary actions to satisfy them.

- Development of others: continuous commitment to stimulate learning and development of others, in order to further their professional success.

- Information management: ability to search, generate, manage and share relevant information for decision making in the organization.

- Development of alliances: identify and maintain long-term relationships among individuals, groups and institutions, both within and outside the organization, that contribute to the achievement of CEMEX's strategies.

The 360-degree process allows up to six people to appraise each staff member. These include any individuals that have observed their behaviours in relationship to the competencies, and should include at least one internal client, at least one internal supplier and at least one peer. Once the individual has selected their evaluators, the immediate manager either approves or rejects those chosen. This may even involve the rejection of the entire proposal, in which case the employee will need to come up with a new set of evaluators. When examining a proposal, line managers are advised to avoid approving the same evaluators over a number of years in order to promote greater diversity.

Guidance on feedback

The following guidance is provided to both those giving and receiving feedback.

Managers

- Criticisms or praise should be communicated continually throughout the year and should be followed up at the end-of-year meeting.

- The purpose of feedback should be explained, pointing out that reviews can make the employee a more valuable member of staff and provide greater opportunities for job satisfaction, usefulness and promotion.

- Start with positive performance and do not overload – choose one or two critical issues or behaviours to concentrate on.

- Focus on the specific behaviours that the person can change.

- Offer suggestions, support and include clear action plans with follow-up dates.

Staff

- Approach feedback as a partnership process not a debate.

- Take notes if possible.

- Select a convenient time so you are not rushed.

- Ask for clarification if what is being said is not clear.

- Seek a balance between positive and negative feedback; if you only get one, ask for the other.

Online tool

CEMEX's online tool, known as CEMEX Plaza, enables managers and staff to enter and store all of the information and results produced from the 360-degree appraisals.

Bonus scheme

Bonuses are determined by individuals' ratings in their end-of-year appraisal meetings as long as threshold financial performance has been achieved by their own unit, the UK. In some cases, for more senior staff, the performance of CEMEX Worldwide can also be a factor. Objectives are graded on a five-point scale, with a corresponding numerical value:

Significantly above target = 5.

Above target = 4.

On target = 3.

Below target = 2.

Unsatisfactory = 1.

The final rating is the weighted average of the different objectives.

Non-performers

Anyone who receives a score of '2' or below at their end-of-year meeting is considered to be performing below the level that CEMEX expects and in such cases action is taken. The initial step in the process is to set up a specific programme to help the employee improve. If this is not successful a 'safety track' is put in place with 'mini-objectives' that are shorter term than the annual ones. Where necessary the line manager, along with the HR department, engages in training and development and coaching to help the employees improve their performance.

DHL

DHL is a global market leader in the international express and logistics industry with 45,000 staff in Europe.

The performance management process

DHL's annual performance management process begins in August when the bonus framework and core elements of the scheme are designed at the top level. Following this, in mid-November, based on the aims decided upon in August, targets are set for the year by a panel of senior staff. Once devised, these targets are cascaded down the organization into individual personal objectives following discussions between line managers and HR.

The cascading process is designed to ensure that targets are refined and altered to align with each individual's actual job. Further discussions then take place to decide what each target means for employees in practice and their implications for competencies. Around the same time, attainment levels and scoring based on the previous year's performance take place to determine bonus levels and salary rises. Following this, with targets already set, around the middle of January an outline for recording performance targets for personal and financial performance for the coming year is designed, and in mid-February the company's financial results become known. This makes it possible to determine the pot available for bonus payments and salary increases relating to the previous year. Bonuses are paid in either March or April while salary reviews take place in April.

Setting the tone for the year

The initial stage of establishing overall objectives and the target-setting framework sets the tone for the year. From year to year, conditions change, with the priorities of senior management reflecting the current state of affairs. As a result, each year there are a number of overarching themes such as serving customers, or health and safety. These core individual key objectives (IKOs) are strictly adhered to, although local managers can determine themselves how to manage their attainment. In contrast, more flexibility exists for other objectives with managers at lower levels able to alter them to align with their particular needs. There is further flexibility in the system with regard to its timing.

Performance management tools

To ensure the smooth running of the system, managers and staff alike are provided with a number of tools to help them during the performance management process. These include:

- A performance evaluation template: This template enables the appropriate competency model to be reviewed and evaluated.

- An objective agreement template: This is located within the performance evaluation template and is used to capture both performance and personal objectives.

- Competency models: These are available as support tools for personal development planning.

- Technical competencies: These represent a support framework for identifying core technical competencies for key operational roles.

- Development guides: Guidelines for use in developing a personal development plan.

- Personal development plan (PDP): A template for assessing individuals against management competencies and developing actions for them to progress their career.

- Career ladder: A guide to support the development of a personal development plan.

- Passport of success: A small booklet retained by the individual (non-management) that identifies completed training.

- Site succession plan: A plan developed utilizing information from the performance review and PDP process.

The annual face-to-face meeting

A key element of the performance management cycle is the face-to-face meeting between line managers and each member of their teams. For operational employees (non-management) the company recommends, as a minimum, this should be a discussion of around 30 minutes, while for managers a one-hour meeting is suggested. During the meeting, the managers and their direct reports examine performance over the last 12 months with reference to the previous year's objectives. Discussions cover what was achieved, whether support provided was sufficient and, if relevant, what could have been done differently for a more effective result.

Following this they agree performance objectives for the coming year, along with any support in the form of training and development that can be offered. Objectives are documented in a 'target agreement form', information on levels of attainment captured on the 'performance evaluation tool', while training and support needs are recorded in the 'performance development plan'. In addition, as mentioned, further support tools include competency models, development guides, technical competencies and career ladders. Where tools, guides or advice are provided, the company states that any suggestions are minimum standards and if managers wish to invest more time and effort in any procedures they can. For example, while there are guidelines for the number of meetings to discuss progress throughout the year, the company informs managers that they can arrange more if they feel it is appropriate.

Nevertheless, the company adds the proviso that where managers diverge from policy to a significant degree they must gain agreement and support from their own management and HR. DHL says that the key aim of the meeting is to discuss and agree objectives for the forthcoming year, adding that 'setting and agreeing objectives focuses an individual on their performance areas and defines clear outcomes and results'. In total, no more than five individual objectives are established: up to three relating to individual performance and two to personal development. The company also says that both types of objective need to adhere to the SMART acronym.

Development objectives

Unlike performance objectives, development objectives are primarily the individual's responsibility to identify, with support provided by managers via the supply of appropriate resources and by contributing objectivity in discussions on staff potential. In some circumstances, DHL guidance says that it may be appropriate to develop a full performance development action plan, while in others this may not be necessary. In either case though, the tools mentioned above are available to assist. DHL says it is committed to personal development planning because it supports the growth of individuals across the organization, stating that 'growing its people develops talent to meet the organization's future management and leadership requirements'. Further, it is a 'motivator for the individual and allows development priorities to be clearly identified creating opportunities to fully achieve their potential.'

Competencies

Closely linked to objectives, competencies play an important part throughout DHL's performance management process. In addition to the management of performance, they are used for recruitment, selection, induction and job sizing, and feed into decisions on pay increases. There are different competencies for different roles.

Progress meetings

In addition to the main performance management meetings, managers are advised to arrange progress meetings throughout the year. The number will depend on the individual in question, but the company suggests that there should be at least one every 12 months. In this meeting, discussions cover how attainment against objectives and competencies is progressing, whether training and development support aligns with expectations and whether additional support can be provided. Moreover, in some cases, certain senior employees are consulted on their own aspirations, and questions, such as whether they want to move upwards or into a different role or perhaps to change location, are asked.

Performance measurement/scoring

At the end of the year in the subsequent annual meeting the process begins again while, at the same time, ratings for the last 12 months are given on the basis of performance against objectives and the individual's competencies. To aid in the evaluation process, the 'performance evaluation tool' is used, which includes a competency and development needs assessment. Using this, progress against last year's performance evaluation is discussed, particularly drawing on successes during the year. Individual achievement is based on a combination of two ratings. First, there is a measure of achievement against personal objectives – also known as personal targets or individual key objectives (IKOs). This concentrates on what is achieved, as distinct from a second rating that examines how things are achieved, drawing on competencies. While there is no particular formula, both ratings are taken into account when making decisions on pay, bonuses and career progression. Under the first measure, target achievement level is linked to IKOs and scores are on a scale of zero to 133.33 per cent. On-target performance gives a score of 100 per cent. Competency ratings are on a scale of one to five where five is exceptional and one unsatisfactory, as follows:

- Far exceeds: Consistently demonstrating the competency behaviours effectively, role model.

- Exceeds: Demonstrates the competency behaviours beyond what is expected.

- Fully meets: Behaviours fully correspond with what is expected in the current role.

- Partially meets: Demonstrates minor deficiencies (coachable) in the behaviour.

- Does not meet: Does not demonstrate behaviours expected in the current role.

When it comes to decisions on salary increases, ratings are moderated by employees' positions in their pay bands, local budget constraints and the market. Ratings are used to determine bonus levels and they also tie in to decisions on promotion and succession planning.

Succession planning

Following the evaluation and rating stage, the line manager's immediate superior reviews the results and, in the light of them, considers succession and career planning, among other things. By using the overall results, senior managers can determine where there are skills gaps or other deficiencies. In addition, it enables them to take a closer look at individual employees to consider whether they might be more suited to be employed elsewhere in the organization. Similarly, managers can examine strengths and weaknesses that might flag up a shortage of certain abilities, such as commercial acumen for example. Such issues can then be addressed and recruitment can be directed appropriately. Moreover, the review also helps when employees leave the organization, making it simple to determine the corresponding skills and behaviours that leave the organization with that individual. To aid with this task, managers are also able to draw on an additional rating for certain senior staff, termed 'potential for job'. This gauges potential for the future and helps by feeding into future decisions on promotion and succession planning.

Hitachi Europe

Hitachi Europe has a well-established performance management system that has been in place for a number of years. It is designed primarily to enhance staff development in order to add value to the organization and all of the company's 450 staff are covered by the system.

The process involves an open, two-way discussion between employees and their managers, with meetings taking place at least twice a year. During meetings, staff and managers focus on current and past performance and future development, and although there is no direct link to pay the system does help inform pay decisions. In contrast, appraisal results for two-thirds of staff are directly linked to one of the company's five bonus plans with performance ratings determining payout levels.

The process is as much about building relationships with employees in order to agree what is reasonably attainable in the year as it is about setting objectives. It is effective because it focuses people's intentions and produces new thinking on the way they work rather than simply continuing to perform at the same level day-in-day-out.

The performance management cycle

Hitachi Europe's year begins in April, and prior to this managers and staff are advised to consider performance over the previous year and expectations for the coming 12 months. Around March, managers meet with employees to devise a performance development plan that, in practice, involves two discussions:

- performance planning discussion;
- development planning discussion.

The performance planning discussion is focused primarily on whether past objectives have been achieved and what future targets should be. In contrast, the Development Planning Discussion helps the manager and employee consider the individual's development needs and ties in with training and other requirements necessary to help them achieve future objectives.

Hitachi Europe's performance management guidance says that the purpose of these meetings is:

> To ensure that an open, two-way discussion takes place between an employee and their manager. The discussion should review both past performance and development and identify whether past objectives have been met and to agree future objectives. The objectives set should align to both group and team objectives.

Performance planning discussion

During the performance planning meeting, managers are encouraged to use examples to illustrate to employees where they have performed adequately, exceptionally and below expectations. In addition, they also refer to information acquired via consultation with other managers and colleagues of the employee.

This rounded approach ensures they have a good understanding of how the employee is performing and, while the focus of the discussion is on the employee's performance, managers must also be prepared to discuss the role they themselves played in helping or hindering the employee in achieving their objectives. Throughout the meeting, Hitachi Europe says that there should be mutual understanding and agreement, especially regarding decisions on past objectives and key actions for the future.

Objectives

Objectives emerging from discussions should be SMART – specific, measurable, achievable, realistic and time bound. From a time perspective, while the process is an annual event some objectives are likely to have differing timescales. In some cases, these may cover periods of less than six months, so managers and staff are given the option to meet more frequently than the usual two times a year if they wish.

While the company's guidance says that objectives need to be business related, in practice this is not always strictly the case for all staff. Those in more senior roles, for example, have objectives linked to overall business objectives such as market share and profit targets, while lower down the hierarchy aims are often more closely aligned to specific jobs and sales-specific targets. In practice, the company says that objectives are really intended to encourage individuals to perform beyond the level normally associated with their job roles.

In addition to setting objectives, performance planning meetings provide time for managers to outline key dates and deadlines and while the documentation associated with the process is paper-based, all forms and related information are also available on the firm's intranet.

Development planning discussion

Unlike the performance planning meeting the development planning discussion is employee-led. This is because Hitachi believes it is the employees' responsibility to consider their own development requirements for the coming year. To help them do this, there are a number of development tools available, while managers also guide and coach where necessary. The range of development tools available is explained in a dedicated section available in the company's guidance and includes information on a learning log, a development record and a career plan.

In addition, in the past the company used a competency framework as part of a previous version of its performance management system and while this is no longer formally in use, employees can refer to its 'success factors', as the company says they are a useful reference point when exploring and diagnosing development needs.

Using these tools, and prior to the development planning discussion, employees are encouraged to consider their development needs, looking back over the past 12 months and looking forward over the coming year. Moreover, they need to review their previous development objectives, thinking about what they wish to achieve in the future. To aid in the process employees are advised to collate evidence in order to clarify their strengths and areas for improvement. Using this information, they can prepare a plan of recommended solutions to aid in their development for discussion with their manager.

While these meetings are employee-led, in some cases, Hitachi employees may be unclear or need guidance on their development needs so managers can help them reach a decision. Similarly, and where appropriate, managers can challenge the proposed development options, but in both cases only after the employee has voiced his or her own opinions.

Hitachi is aware of the dangers of the managers leading the process, and provides clear guidance outlining certain boundaries to which they should adhere. While the guidance says that is acceptable for managers to question employees' proposed development strategies, for example, it adds that they should avoid trying to make career choices for the employees. Similarly, they are told not to try to push people to develop if they are not ready to, letting the employees make up their own minds.

Training not always the best option

The company finds that in many cases employees conclude that they require a training course as this is an obvious option. Despite this, Hitachi advises employees to avoid jumping to this conclusion as there are a number of other less obvious but more appropriate options that are often also available. The company guidance, for example, highlights on-the-job training and learning because it believes that these are the most effective ways of developing and acquiring new skills, knowledge and experience. This is not to say that training is discouraged, however, as the company states that training courses are a very good way of supporting development needs, providing a foundation for future skills and knowledge.

Interim reviews

In the autumn, six months on from the initial meetings, managers and employees meet again to have an interim review. The point of the discussion is to make sure that the personal development plan remains on track and objectives are still relevant. The meeting is a formal stage of the process but there is no rating at this point. Nevertheless, the outcomes of discussions are used to help inform pay rises that take place a few months later, effective from January.

Six months after the interim review, the year ends and managers and staff again meet to review objectives and discuss performance over the previous 12 months. If objectives are not attained, the conversation examines why this was the case, with managers considering their own as well as the individual's role when determining why targets were not achieved. Employees also have the opportunity to explain why they believed targets were not met, outlining any mitigating circumstances. Based on this interaction, the outcomes of discussions lead to a performance rating being awarded and any failed targets usually feed into the following year's objectives. Unlike some other organizations, ratings do not align with a forced distribution and the four potential levels are:

'O':   Failed to meet objectives.

'S':   After assessing performance against objectives has met some of the objectives.

'M':   Meets expectations and has completed all objectives.

'M*':   Achieved significantly more than the agreed objectives so performance was exceptional.

Consistency

A common concern with most, if not all, performance management schemes, is maintaining consistency across the whole organization. To ensure this is achieved, Hitachi Europe's HR staff review objectives at the start of the year to check that they are both 'SMART' and realistic. Further, once the process is completed, results are evaluated to determine whether particular departments or divisions have especially high or low outcomes. In addition, even when there are no discernible differences in departmental rankings as a whole, HR staff still examine any individual outliers to determine whether an unfair rating has occurred.

Where inconsistencies are found, HR staff meet with the line managers concerned and revisit each part of the process to ensure they are taking a consistent and impartial approach. In some cases, rating inconsistency is a symptom of another underlying problem or issue. Some managers, for example, might feel that their staff's salaries are too low, while others may have difficulties managing the expectations of their team.

Line managers and training

Like any initiative originating from human resources that is implemented outside the department, buy-in from the managers at the operational end is crucial. The company says that the attitudes of line managers are generally good, although there are some variations. As a result, a certain amount of chasing is necessary, especially around key dates. Nevertheless, the company's training programme does help in fostering a positive attitude to the process among line managers.

Managers undertake a day's training dedicated to the performance management system that covers the timetable of the process, each component of the appraisal process and how to set objectives. In addition, managers have access to a number of guidance documents available on the intranet, while refresher courses are also available. From a staff perspective, there is no formal training although the performance management system is covered during the induction process.

Link to bonus scheme but not directly to pay

Ratings awarded as a result of the performance management system have no direct link to pay, but there is an indirect link to the January salary review process. Pay awards at the firm are performance related and the outcome of interim review discussions in September and October influence decisions on pay increases in January. There is no formal link or performance rating and managers are given a merit pot to allocate awards among their teams. The pot is allocated to each business or division and managers distribute awards to staff after discussions with HR.

In contrast, the performance ratings allocated at the end of the year do feed into one of Hitachi Europe's bonus schemes. The scheme, known as the performance incentive, is one of the company's five plans. There are multiple schemes due to the fact that many employees are sales professionals, but the performance incentive covers the most employees (around two-thirds of the workforce). Of the other four bonus plans, three are designed for sales people and one is for more senior staff who report directly to the company's managing director.

The four ratings assigned as a result of the performance management system directly affect performance incentive awards.

- Those categorized as 'O', who failed to meet objectives, receive no bonus.

- Those classed 'S', who met some of their targets are awarded a pre-determined bonus that is set by HR and formalized in the plan rules.

- In contrast, the level of bonus awarded to those achieving the top two rating levels is determined by guidance levels along with the relevant manager's discretion.

Royal College of Nursing

The Royal College of Nursing (RCN) represents nurses and nursing, promotes excellence in practice and shapes health policies. In total, the RCN employs around 800 staff, while it also supports a network of activists and shop stewards throughout the country. All employees are covered by performance management arrangements that were recently reviewed following the appointment of a new HR director and ongoing concerns with the way that the organization has managed performance in the past. In particular, there was a view expressed, to varying degrees throughout the RCN, that managers were not managing performance effectively enough and, in turn, a small minority of staff were being allowed to 'coast' unchecked. To remedy the situation, a number of changes to the RCN's performance management arrangements were implemented in order to develop a new, stronger performance culture.

Primarily, the aim is to provide a structure that allows managers to manage and, in this context, ensure that poor levels of performance would become unacceptable. In practice, line managers needed to become clearer about what they could – and could not – do from a management as well as legal perspective, while the type and level of support they could hope to receive from human resources had to become clearer.

Understandably, as a trade union, the RCN has a rather different view of the management–employee relationship compared with most other employers and, in the past, this has been one factor making it difficult to fully embrace the idea of the managers' prerogative to manage. Previously, the college operated a formal performance appraisal system, introduced in 2003, and staff reviews had occurred prior to this, but neither were applied consistently.

Performance management annual cycle

An illustration of the RCN's annual performance management cycle is shown in Chapter 14 (Figure 14.8). Appraisals occur between January and March, after operational and financial planning is completed between September and December. Following this, midway through the year there is a six-month review that provides an opportunity to reassess and document progress against objectives and agreed development aims. It also allows for the changing work context to be incorporated into staff's day-to-day work activities (not a compulsory part of the process but one the RCN recommends as 'best practice').

The RCN appraisal process

As described by the RCN the appraisal process is designed to support the performance and development of staff, by providing individuals with an opportunity to review past and current performance and plan future activity. It is summarized in Table B1.

What it is	What it is not	The benefits of doing it
• A formal meeting which is part of an ongoing discussion between the appraiser and the appraisee • A two-way discussion • A review of activity and performance over the past year • An exploration of any challenges that were faced during the year • An opportunity to explore ways of enhancing motivation and performance • A discussion of future work areas and joint agreement of objectives • An opportunity to discuss and agree development areas for the appraisee	• Simply a one-off, once-a-year exercise • Closed/secret • Disciplinary • A platform for bullying • One-sided • A surprise	If carried out correctly, the RCN appraisal process can benefit the appraisee, appraiser, counter-signer and the organization in a number of ways: • Support the organization in achieving its overall purpose • Link individual activities to departmental operational plans – support the department in better planning workload and deadlines • Create a joint understanding between the appraiser and the appraisee of areas of work • Appraisees can better understand what is required of them and how their areas of work contribute to the departmental operational plan and subsequently the overall purpose of the RCN • Appraiser has clear targets against which to measure performance of the appraisee • Can improve performance of the appraisee • Can improve morale/motivation of the appraisee • Give both the appraiser and the appraisee an understanding of the development needed and plan how best to support this

Table B1   RCN appraisal process

A flow chart of the process is shown in Figure B1. The appraisal form and the preparation for appraisal form are given in Figures B2 and B3 at the end of this appendix.

What appraisals cover

The RCN's appraisals are designed to support the performance and development of staff, by providing individuals with an opportunity to review past and current performance and plan future activity. The appraisal meeting itself is a two-way discussion and, more specifically, the RCN says it should include coverage of:

- exploration of achievements – what contributed to success in the year;

- exploration of challenges – what they were, how they were overcome and learning for the future;

- feedback on performance with reference to relevant competencies if available;

- objective setting, linked to the operational and strategic plans for the year ahead;

- career and succession planning;

- future work areas and any development needs associated with these.

In addition, meetings also cover discussions of how objectives will be met, who will help achieve them and whether any training or other type of course is required.

To ensure that the appraisal meeting does not present any surprises, the RCN also recommends that staff and their line managers engage in one-to-one discussions on a regular basis throughout the year. These are used to discuss all issues that arise, including those related to appraisals, and serve the purpose of a 'catch up'.

Preparing for appraisal

Reinforcing this, the RCN appraisal guidance recommends that both the appraiser and the employee also prepare prior to the appraisal meeting. For this purpose, an 'appraisal preparation form' is provided, as shown in Figure B3. The RCN recommends that both parties complete the form and send it to the other at least two weeks prior to the appraisal meeting. This, it says, will have the advantages of providing a structure to the meeting agenda and also ensures that there are no surprises.

When completing the preparation form, both groups consider the following:

- departmental operational plan;

- job description/person specification;

- RCN management and leadership competencies (for managers in the organization);

- Officer Development Framework (for officers/assistant officers);

- last year's appraisal;

- performance/achievements during the appraisal period;

- priorities for coming year;

- knowledge, skills and experience;

- ways to maintain/improve performance;

- possible training and development needs.

In addition, the appraiser should seek input on the performance and future work areas from the employee's supervisor prior to the appraisal meeting.

The appraisal meeting

There are three key roles in the appraisal process: the appraisee, the appraiser (the line manager) and the counter-signer. The counter-signer is the member of staff who has a three-way discussion with the appraisee and the appraiser to sign-off the appraisal process. This is normally the line manager of the appraisee's line manager.

All members of staff have the right to have an appraisal if they are going to be with the RCN for a year or more; for those that are not, the line manager ensures that objectives are set at the beginning of the period of employment and are reviewed at regular intervals. In such cases, they may use the appraisal form as a template for recording discussions but they do not need to submit the forms to HR.

Objective setting

Key to performance management at the RCN is the setting of objectives for the coming year. Objectives filter down to one degree or other from the organization's overall strategic plan, which sets out the college's aims and aspirations for the coming five years. The intention is that all objectives align with the strategic plan and this is achieved by the overall strategy being translated into more specific operational plans for the RCN's various sections. These in turn determine the objectives of senior managers in each department, which then filter down to determine the individual objectives of more junior staff, as illustrated in the January and February sections of the annual cycle shown in Figure 14.8.

With such a variety of roles, the RCN recognizes that each group will have different priorities, so objective setting also takes account of this, with objectives flowing from the job roles as well as the strategic and operational plans. The finance director's objectives, for instance, are linked closely with the bottom-line elements of the overall strategic plan, while in contrast a union officer's are more weighted towards recruiting, retaining and representing members.

As in many organizations, objectives must be 'SMART', although the RCN adds another condition to the normal five factors – 'reviewability' – giving the acronym 'SMARTR':

Identifying development needs

Appraisals also help to identify development needs to support staff in achieving their objectives via personal development plans that are reviewed every six months. The RCN says that employees should not consider development needs to be a 'wish list' of desired training courses to attend, however; instead they should be aligned to the work objectives identified during the appraisal. Moreover, to ensure that the training budget is managed effectively and does not overrun, the HR department conducts training needs analyses based on the information provided from appraisals.

In addition, RCN guidance says that consideration needs to be given to how learning from any development activity can be applied in practice. Therefore, as well as training courses, there are a variety of other activities that can support staff development, which are outlined on the 'staff development' pages of the RCN's intranet site.

Career planning and succession planning

As well as identifying work and development areas, the appraisal discussion is an opportunity to incorporate future planning for the career of the employee. There may be work areas or development needs linking to the operational plan, for instance, that would support the career of the individual, and this is an opportunity to ensure that these are identified. While letting the employees know that the RCN is interested in their own career aspirations, this aspect of the appraisal process can also assist in succession planning where appropriate.

After the appraisal

Following the discussion, the appraiser completes the appraisal form, setting out a summary of the discussions that took place. This occurs as soon as possible after the meeting so the facts are still fresh in the mind and, once complete, the form is sent to the appraisee for agreement.

Following this, there is a three-way meeting between the employee, the appraiser and the counter-signing manager who review and sign-off the documentation of the appraisal discussion. The meeting is also an opportunity for those overseeing the whole process to ensure that objectives set across the department reflect all areas of the operational plan, and that there are no gaps or duplications. In addition, this allows the person counter-signing to ensure that a consistent approach is being applied by line managers.

If a situation arises where those being appraised disagree with the outcome of their appraisal, they are advised to discuss the situation immediately with their appraiser as it is possible it may be the result of a simple misunderstanding. If disagreement runs deeper, however, then a three-way discussion takes place between the same three people to resolve any issues arising. As a last resort, if there is still no agreement, a meeting with HR and a union representative is arranged to mediate a discussion between the concerned parties with the objective of reaching agreement.

Training

To ensure that the system works effectively, the RCN places great value on its training processes and it uses various ways in which to get its message across to staff and line managers. On appointment, all employees attend a two-day induction workshop, for example, which runs regularly throughout the year. Day two of this workshop provides an introduction to the RCN appraisal process for both appraisers and employees, and it also provides an introduction to key appraisal skills.

For those who are new to conducting appraisals and appraisers who would like to develop their skills in setting objectives, giving feedback and developing basic coaching skills, there are 'Conducting Appraisals' workshops that run every year at the beginning of, and during, the appraisal period. In addition there are:

- 'Investigations' training for managers;
- career development workshops, plus secondment and shadowing policies;
- a two-day performance management programme for those managing others;
- performance management master classes to ensure the message of support for tackling performance is clear.

Performance management master classes

One of the other innovations introduced recently is a series of performance management 'master classes'. These are presented by the HR director and are given to all line managers throughout the organization. The master classes use practical examples to present managers with various scenarios that can arise, illustrating the different ways in which they can be addressed.

In particular, managers are informed of what they can and cannot do in the situations, and helped to consider what is acceptable from a legal perspective. The master classes are also a way for the General Secretary to 'spread the message' about the cultural shift the organization is trying to effect, with a big element focused on trying to change attitudes. In addition, the level of support that can be expected from human resources when such issues arise is also made clear, as one of the aims of HR is to provide a high level and consistent degree of support across the organization.

Management development

Linked to training, and overlapping with the appraisal system, the RCN also has a management development programme in place. This has been running for 18 months and features various modules, including one focused on managing people. Initially, managers undergo a 360-degree appraisal that aims to determine their areas of weakness or those they need to focus on, referring to a number of defined management and leadership competencies. Once the areas of development are determined, individuals are provided with support that enables them to address their development needs. In addition, the managing people module focuses on areas relevant to appraisal such as setting objectives and the need for a clear line of sight, enabling employees to understand how their contribution will benefit performance levels. Following this process, around six months after the end of the management development programme, a further 360-degree appraisal is carried out to monitor progress.

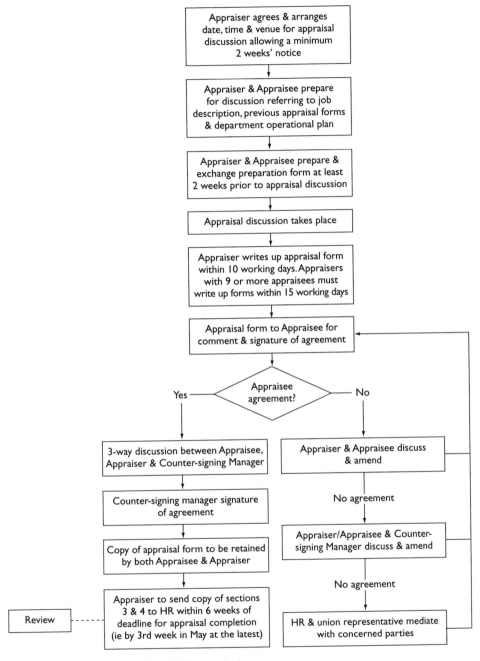

Figure B1   A flow chart of the RCN appraisal process

APPRAISAL FORM
(To be completed by Appraiser in discussion with Appraisee)

Personal Details

Name of Appraisee:

Position held:

Board/Region
Department:

Team:

Date of Meeting:

Appraiser:

Countersigning
Manager:

Appraisal period from   to

Note *This form is to be completed after the discussion and a copy of sections 3 & 4 submitted to the HR Department no later than 6 weeks from the appraisal discussion deadline of end March. Copies of the completed form should be retained by both the Appraiser and the Appraisee.*

Section 1: Performance in the Review Period

1(a) What were the <u>main areas of achievement</u> during the review period?

Achievements

I(b)   What areas are identified as having scope for improvement? How will this be realised?
(Consideration should be given to objectives that were not achieved, problems or obstacles which might have affected Appraisee performance, and possible action to minimise the impact of such factors on future performance)

Objectives not achieved, challenges or areas for improvement	What factors limited success?	How can factors be minimised in future?

Section 2: Identification of Key Areas for the coming year

2   What are the agreed key areas of work for the coming year?

Operational Plan reference number	Key Areas	Personal Objectives (Specific; Measurable; Achievable; Realistic; Timebound; Reviewable)	When?	Review (to be completed after review discussion)

Section 3: Personal Development Plan

3(a)   In order to achieve objectives, are there any areas of work that could be helped by training and development?

This plan should be agreed by both parties. It should include any specific skill requirements for the job (eg. MS Office, Time Management, Organization Skills etc), and any **on-the-job** training requirements. Managers should facilitate protected time out for the Appraisee to undertake the agreed self-development plan.

Consideration should also be given to any professional qualifications / academic qualifications that the Appraisee would be interested in undertaking to further their career opportunities. Such requests will be progressed via the Corporate Development Panel.

Plan

Training/development need	Action	By Whom?	When?	How this learning will be applied in the workplace	Review date

3(b)

Review (to be completed after review discussion)

Development Need	Action taken	Change in performance – how has learning been applied?

Note: Implementation of Personal Development Plan is the responsibility of the Appraiser and the Appraisee. It is recommended that the plan should be reviewed after 6 months.   The plan should not be a wish list of training courses but rather a considered and practical list, realisable within 6 to 12 months

Section 4

4(a) Appraiser comments

We have discussed and agreed the full contents of this document.

Signature: _____   Date: _____

4(b) Appraisee comments and agreement

I have discussed and agreed the full contents of this document with the Appraiser.

Signature: _____   **Date:** _____

4(c) Counter-signing Manager

Signature: _____   **Date:** _____

Figure B2   RCN appraisal form

Royal College of Nursing	**APPRAISAL PREPARATION FORM** *(To be completed by both Appraiser and Appraisee)*

Appraisers and Appraisees are required to exchange information in writing prior to the formal meeting. This will have the advantages of providing a structure to the meeting agenda and ensuring that no surprises arise during the meeting.

Preparation is vital for both parties and listed below you will find areas for you to consider during this preparation. Appraisers and Appraisees should complete this preparation form and copy it to the other party at least 2 weeks prior to the appraisal meeting.

Name of Appraisee

Section 1: Performance in the Review Period

1(a) What were the <u>main areas of achievement</u> during the review period?

Achievements

1(b)   What areas are identified as having scope for improvement? How will this be realised?
(Consideration should be given to objectives that were not achieved, problems or obstacles which might have affected Appraisee performance, and possible action to minimise the impact of such factors on future performance)

Objectives not achieved, challenges or areas for improvement	What factors limited success?	How can factors be minimised in future?

B   **359**

Section 2: Identification of Key Areas for the coming year

2   What are the key areas of work to be addressed in the coming year?

Operational Plan reference number	Key Areas

(Future objectives should be discussed and agreed by both parties during the appraisal meeting)

Section 3: Personal Development

3(a)   What training and development needs does the Appraisee have?

Training/development need

Section 4: Other

What other relevant issues do you wish to raise during the discussion?

Appraiser / Appraisee signature _____ **Date** _____

Figure B3   RCN appraisal preparation form

References

Advisory, Conciliation and Arbitration Service (1988) *Employee Appraisal*, ACAS, London

AMIF (2005) Basic tenets of performance management in financial institutions, *Journal of Performance Management*, **18** (3), pp 17–21

Antonioni, D (1994) Improve the performance management process before discontinuing performance appraisals, *Compensation & Benefits Review*, May–June, pp 29–37

Ariyachandra, T R and Frolick, M (2008) Critical success factors in business performance management: striving for success, *Information Systems Management*, **25** (2), pp 113–20

Arkin, A (2007) Force for good? *People Management*, 8 February, pp 26–29

Armstrong, K and Ward, A (2005) *What Makes for Effective Performance Management?* The Work Foundation, London

Armstrong, M (1976) *A Handbook of Personnel Management Practice*, 1st edn, Kogan Page, London

Armstrong, M and Baron, A (1998) *Performance Management: The New Realities*, CIPD, London

Armstrong, M and Baron, A (2004) *Managing Performance: Performance Management in Action*, CIPD, London

Armstrong, M and Murlis, H (1994) *Reward Management*, Kogan Page, London

Armstrong, M and Murlis, H (1998) *Reward Management*, 4th edn, Kogan Page, London

Atkinson, A A, Waterhouse, J H and Wells, R B (1997) A stakeholder approach to strategic performance measurement, *Sloan Management Review*, **38** (3), pp 25–37

Atwater, L E, Waldman, D A and Brett, J F (2002) Understanding and optimizing multisource feedback, *Human Resource Management*, **41** (2), pp 193–208

Baguley, P (1994) *Improving Organizational Performance*, McGraw Hill, Maidenhead

Bailey, C and Fletcher, C (2002) The impact of multiple source feedback on management development: findings from a longitudinal study, *Journal of Organizational Behaviour*, **23** (7), pp 853–67

Bailey, R T (1983) *Measurement of Performance*, Gower, Aldershot

Bailey, T, Berg, P and Sandy, C (2001) The effect of high performance work practices on employee earnings in the steel, apparel and medical electronics and imaging industries, *Industrial and Labor Relations Review*, **54** (2A), pp 525–43

Bandura, A (1977) *Social Learning Theory*, Prentice-Hall, Englewood Cliffs, NJ

Bandura, A (1982) Self-efficacy mechanism in human agency, *American Psychologist*, **37**, pp 122–47

Bandura, A (1986) *Social Boundaries of Thought and Action*, Prentice-Hall, Englewood Cliffs, NJ

Barlow, G (1989) Deficiencies and the perpetuation of power: latent functions in performance appraisal, *Journal of Management Studies*, September, pp 499–517

Barlow, G (2003) Barriers to appraisals, *Competency & Emotional Intelligence*, **10** (6), pp 29–30

Baron, A and Armstrong, M (1998) Out of the box, *People Management*, 23 July, pp 38–41

Baron, A and Armstrong, M (2004) Get into line, *People Management*, 14 October, pp 44–46

Bates, R A and Holton, E F (1995) Computerized performance monitoring: a review of human resource issues, *Human Resource Management Review*, winter, pp 267–88

Bates, S (2003) Forced ranking, *HR Magazine*, June, pp 65–68

Beaver, G and Harris, L (1995) Performance management and the small firm: dilemmas, tensions and paradoxes, *Journal of Strategic Change*, **4**, pp 109–19

Becker, B E and Huselid, M A (1998) High performance work systems and firm performance: a synthesis of research and managerial implications, *Research on Personnel and Human Resource Management*, **16,** pp 53–101, JAI Press, Stamford, CT

Beer, M (1980) *Organization Change and Development: A systems view*, Goodyear, Santa Monica, CA

Beer, M and Ruh, R A (1976) Employee growth through performance management, *Harvard Business Review*, July–August, pp 59–66

Bernardin, H J and Buckley, M R (1981) Strategies in rater training, *Academy of Management Review*, **6**, pp 205–12

Bernardin, H J, Buckley, M R, Tyler, C L and Wiese, D S (2000) A reconsideration of strategies in rater training, *Research in Personnel and Human Resource Management*, **18**, pp 221–74

Bernardin, H J, Hagan, C and Kane, J (1995) The effects of a 360 degree appraisal system on managerial performance, *Proceedings at the 10th annual conference of the Society for Industrial and Organizational Psychology*, Orlando, FL

Bernardin, H K, Kane, J S, Ross, S, Spina, J D and Johnson, D L (1995) Performance appraisal design, development and implementation, in *Handbook of Human Resource Management*, ed G R Ferris, S D Rosen and D J Barnum, Blackwell, Cambridge, MA

Bevan, S and Thompson, M (1991) Performance management at the crossroads, *Personnel Management*, November, pp 36–39

Bitici, U S, Carrie, A S and McDevitt, L (1997) Integrate performance management systems: audit and development goals, *The TQM Magazine* **9** (1), pp 46–53

Blumberg, M and Pringle, C (1982) The missing opportunity in organizational research: some implications for a theory of work performance, *Academy of Management Review*, **7** (4), pp 560–69

Bones, C (1996) Performance management: the HR contribution, *Address at the Annual Conference of the Institute of Personnel and Development*, Harrogate

Borman, W C and Motowidlo, S J (1993) Expanding the criterion domain to include elements of contextual performance, in *Handbook of Human Resource Management*, ed N Schmitt and W C Borman, Jossey-Bass, San Francisco

Boselie, P, Dietz, G and Boon, C (2005) Commonalities and contradictions in HRM and performance research, *Human Resource Management Journal*, **15** (3), pp 67–94

Bourne, M, Franco, M and Wilkes, J (2003) Corporate performance management, *Measuring Business Excellence*, **7** (3), pp 15–21

Bowles, M L and Coates, G (1993) Image and substance: the management of performance as rhetoric or reality? *Personnel Review*, **22** (2), pp 3–21

Boyett, J H and Conn, H P (1995) *Maximum Performance Management*, Glenbridge Publishing, Oxford

Boxall, P F (1996) The strategic HRM debate and the resource-based view of the firm, *Human Resource Management Journal*, **6** (3), pp 59–75

Boxall, P F and Purcell, J (2003) *Strategy and Human Resource Management*, Palgrave Macmillan, Basingstoke

Brancato, C K (1995) *New Corporate Performance Measures*, The Conference Board, New York

Briscoe, D B and Claus, L M (2008) Employee performance management: policies and practices in multinational enterprises, in *Performance Management Systems: A global perspective*, ed P W Budwah and A DeNisi, Routledge, Abingdon

Brumbach, G B (1988) Some ideas, issues and predictions about performance management, *Public Personnel Management*, winter, pp 387–402

Buchner, T W (2007) Performance management theory: a look from the performer's perspective with implications for HRD, *Human Resource Development International*, **10** (1), pp 59–73

Campbell, J P (1990) Modeling the performance prediction problem in industrial and organizational psychology, in *Handbook of Industrial and Organizational Psychology*, ed M P Dunnette and L M Hugh, Blackwell, Cambridge, MA

Campbell, J P, McCloy, R A, Oppler, S H and Sager, C E (1993) A theory of performance, in *Personnel Selection in Organizations*, ed N Schmitt and W Borman, Jossey-Bass, San Francisco

Cardy, R L and Dobbins, G H (1994) *Performance Appraisal: Alternative perspectives*, South-Western Publishing, Cincinnati, OH

Carlton, I and Sloman, M (1992) Performance appraisal in practice *Human Resource Management Journal*, **2** (3), pp 80–94

Chell, E (1992) *The Psychology of Behaviour in Organisations*, Macmillan, Basingstoke

CIPD (2007) *Coaching Fact Sheet*, CIPD, London

CIPD (2008) *Learning and Development Survey*, CIPD, London

Clayton, H (2004) How to perform under pressure, *People Management*, 29 July, pp 42–43

Clutterbuck, D and Megginson, D (2005) *Making coaching work*, CIPD, London

Coens, T and Jenkins, M (2002) *Abolishing Performance Appraisals: Why they backfire and what to do instead*, Berrett-Koehler, San Francisco

Cone, J W and Robinson, D G (2001) The power of performance, *TD*, August, pp 32–41

Corporate Leadership Council (2002) *Performance Management Survey*, CLC, London

Crosby, P C (1995) *Quality Without Tears*, McGraw-Hill, New York

Cummins, T G and Worley, C G (2005) *Organization Development and Change*, South Western, Mason, OH

Dagan, B (2007) Dashboards and scorecards aid in performance management and monitoring, *Natural Gas & Electricity*, September, pp 23–27

Daniels, A C (1987) What is PM? *Performance Management*, July, pp 8–12

Deloitte & Touche and *Personnel Today* (2002) *Measuring Human Capital Value*, Deloitte & Touche/ *Personnel Today*, London

Deming, W E (1986) *Out of the Crisis*, Massachusetts Institute of Technology Centre for Advanced Engineering Studies, Cambridge, MA

DeNisi, A S (2000) Performance appraisal and performance management: a multilevel analysis, in *Multilevel Theory, Research and Methods in Organizations*, ed K J Klein and S W J Kozlowski, Jossey-Bass, San Francisco

DeNisi, A S and Kluger, A N (2000) Feedback effectiveness: can 360-degree appraisals be improved? *Academy of Management Executive*, **14** (1), pp 129–39

DeNisi, A S and Pritchard, R D (2006) Performance appraisal, performance management and improving individual performance: a motivational framework, *Management and Organization Review*, **2** (2), pp 253–77

Dover, C (2004) Dashboards can change your culture, *Strategic Finance*, October, pp 42–48

Drucker, P (1955) *The Practice of Management*, Heinemann, London

Earley, D C (1986) Computer-generated performance feedback in the magazine industry, *Organisation Behaviour and Human Decision Processes*, **41**, pp 50–64

Edwards, M R and Ewen, A T (1996) *360-degree Feedback*, American Management Association, New York

Edwards, M R, Ewen, A T and O'Neal, S (1994) Using multi-source assessment to pay people not jobs, *ACA Journal*, summer, pp 6–17

Egan, G (1995) A clear path to peak performance, *People Management*, 18 May, pp 34–37

Ellinger, A D (2003) Antecedents and consequences of coaching behavior, *Performance Improvement Quarterly*, **6** (1), pp 5–28

Ellinger, A D, Ellinger, A E and Keller, S B (2003) Supervisory coaching behavior, employee satisfaction, and warehouse employee performance: a dyadic perspective in the distribution industry, *Human Resource Development Quarterly*, **14** (4), pp 435–58

Elliott, S and Coley-Smith, H (2005) Building a new performance management model at BP, *SCM*, August–September, pp 4–8

Engelmann, C H and Roesch, C H (1996) *Managing Individual Performance*, American Compensation Association, Scottsdale, AZ

Epstein, S and O'Brien, E J (1985) The person-situation debate in historical perspective, *Psychological Bulletin*, **83**, pp 956–74

e-reward (2004) *Report on Contingent Pay*, e-reward, Stockport

e-reward (2005) *Survey of Performance Management Practice*, e-reward, Stockport

Evered, R D and Selman, J C (1989) Coaching and the art of management, *Organizational Dynamics*, **18** (2), 16–32

Feedback Project (2001) *360-Degree Feedback: Best practice guidelines*, University of Surrey, Roehampton

Fink, L S and Longenecker, C O (1997) Why managerial performance appraisals are ineffective, *Career Development International*, **2** (5), pp 212–18

Fisher, C M (1994) The difference between appraisal schemes: variation and acceptability – part 1, *Personnel Review*, **23** (8), pp 33–48

Fisher, M (1995) *Performance Appraisals*, Kogan Page, London

Flaherty, J (1999) *Coaching: Evoking Excellence in Others*, Butterworth-Heinemann, Burlington, MA

Flanagan, J C (1954) The critical incident technique, *Psychological Bulletin*, **51**, pp 327–58

Fletcher, C (1993a) Appraisal: an idea whose time has gone? *Personnel Management*, September, pp 34–37

Fletcher, C (1993b) *Appraisal: Routes to improved performance*, Institute of Personnel and Development, London

Fletcher, C (1998) Circular argument, *People Management*, 1 October, pp 46–49

Fletcher, C (2001) Performance appraisal and management: the developing research agenda, *Journal of Occupational and Organizational Psychology*, **74** (4), pp 473–87

Fletcher, C and Williams, R (1992) The route to performance management, *Personnel Management*, **24** (10), pp 42–47

Folger, R and Cropanzano, R (1998) *Organizational Justice and Human Resource Management*, Sage, Thousand Oaks, CA

Folger, R, Konovsky, M A and Cropanzano, R (1992) A due process metaphor for performance appraisal, in *Research in Organizational Behavior*, ed B M Staw and L L Cummings, JAI Press, Greenwich, CT

Fowler, A (1990) Performance management; the MBO of the 90s? *Personnel Management*, July, pp 47–54

Frisch, M H (2001) Going around in circles with '360' tools: have they grown too popular for their own good? *Human Resource Planning*, **24** (2), pp 7–8

Frolick, M and Ariyachandra, T R (2006) Business performance management: one truth, *Information Systems Management*, **23** (1), pp 41–48

Furnham, A (1996) Starved of feedback, *The Independent*, 5 December, p 12

Furnham, A (2004) Performance management systems, *European Business Journal*, **16** (2), pp 83–94

Gannon, M (1995) Personal development planning, in *The Performance Management Handbook*, ed M Walters, Institute of Personnel and Development, London

George, J (1986) Appraisal in the public sector: dispensing with the big stick, *Personnel Management*, May, pp 32–35

Gheorghe, C and Hack, J (2007) Unified performance management: how one company can tame its many processes, *Business Performance Management*, November, pp 17–19

Gjerde, K A and Hughes, S B (2007) Tracking performance: when less is more, *Management Accounting Quarterly*, **9** (1), pp 1–12

Gladwell, M (2008) *Outliers: The story of success*, Allen Lane, London

Goodridge, M (2001) The limits of performance management, *Topics 3*, ER Consultants, pp 23–28

Graham, S, Wedman, J F and Garvin-Kester, B, (1994) Manager coaching skills: what makes a good coach? *Performance Improvement Quarterly*, **7** (2), pp 81–94

Gray, A (2001) Individual differences in 360-degree feedback, in *The Feedback Project*, University of Surrey, Roehampton

Greenberg, R (2004) Beyond performance management: four principles of performance leadership, *Workspan*, September, pp 42–45

Grint, K (1993) What's wrong with performance appraisal? A critique and a suggestion, *Human Resource Management Journal*, spring, pp 61–77

Gross, S E (1995) *Compensation for Teams*, Hay, New York

Grote, D (1996) *The Complete Guide to Performance Appraisal*, Amacom, New York

Guest, D E (1996) The management of performance, *Address to the annual conference of the Institute of Personnel and Development*, October, Harrogate

Guest, D E and Conway, N (1998) An analysis of the results of the IPD performance management survey, in *Performance Management: The new realities*, ed M Armstrong and A Baron, IPD, London

Guin, K A (1992) *Successfully Integrating Total Quality and Performance Appraisal*, spring, Faulkner and Gray, New York

Hallbom, T and Warrenton-Smith, A (2005) *Journal of Innovative Management*, summer, pp 39–48

Hamlin, R G, Ellinger, A D and Beattie, R S (2006) Coaching at the heart of managerial effectiveness: a cross-cultural study of managerial behaviours, *Human Resource Development International*, **9** (3), pp 305–31

Hampson, S E (1982) *The Construction of Personality*, Routledge and Kegan Paul, London

Handley, C (2001) Feedback skills, in *The Feedback Project*, University of Surrey, Roehampton

Handy, C (1989) *The Age of Unreason*, Business Books, London

Handy, L, Devine, M and Heath, L (1996) *360-degree Feedback: Unguided missile or powerful weapon?* Ashridge Management Group, Berkhamstead,

Harrington-Mackin, D (1994) *The Team Building Tool Kit*, AMACOM, New York

Harrison, R (1997) *Employee Development*, IPM, London

Hartle, F (1995) *Transforming the Performance Management Process*, Kogan Page, London

Hedge, L M, Borman, W C and Birkeland, S A (2001) History and development of multisource feedback as a methodology, in *Handbook of Multisource Feedback*, ed D W Bracken, C W Timmwreck and A H Church, Jossey-Bass, San Franciso

Hendry, C, Bradley, P and Perkins, S (1997) Missed, *People Management*, 15 May, pp 20–25

Herzberg, F (1968) One more time: how do you motivate your employees? *Harvard Business Review*, Jan–Feb, pp 109–120

Hobbs, N (2004) How to appraise board members, *People Management*, 20 May, pp 42–43

Hoehn, W K (2003) Managing organizational performance: linking the balanced scorecard to a process improvement technique, *Proceedings of the 4th Annual Symposium in Engineering Management*, Tucson, AZ

Houldsworth, E and Jirasinghe, D (2006) *Managing and Measuring Employee Performance*, Kogan Page, London

Hull, C (1951) *Essentials of Behaviour*, Yale University Press, New Haven, CT

Humble, J (1972) *Management by Objectives*, Management Publications, London

Hutchinson, S and Purcell, J (2003) *Bringing Policies to Life: The vital role of front line managers in people management*, CIPD, London

IDS Study No 626 (1997) *Performance Management*, Incomes Data Services, London

Industrial Society (1996) *Managing Best Practice: Rewarding performance*, Industrial Society, London

Institute of Personnel Management (1992) *Performance Management in the UK: An analysis of the issues*, IPM, London

International Society for Performance Improvement (2004) Will employees perform better if you reward them? *HR Focus*, December, pp 10–13

IRS Employment Review (2003) Performance management: policy and practice, *IRS Employment Review*, August, pp 12–19

Jarvis, J (2004) *Coaching and Buying Coaching Services: A guide*, CIPD, London

Jawahar, I M and Williams, C R (1997) Where all children are above average: the performance appraisal purpose effect, *Personnel Psychology*, **50**, pp 905–25

Joelle, D, Elicker, J F, Levy, P E and Hall, R J (2006) The role of leader-member exchange in the performance appraisal process, *Journal of Management*, **32** (4), pp 531–51

Jones, P, Palmer, J, Whitehead, D and Needham, P (1995) Prisms of performance, *The Ashridge Journal*, April, pp 10–14

Jones, T W (1995) Performance management in a changing context, *Human Resource Management*, **34** (3), pp 425–42

Kane, J S (1996) The conceptualization and representation of total performance effectiveness, *Human Resource Management Review*, summer, pp 123–45

Kane, J S and Bernardin, H J (1982) Behavioral observation scales and the evaluation of performance appraisal effectiveness, *Personnel Psychology*, **35** (3), pp 635–41

Kaplan, R S and Norton, D P (1992) The balanced scorecard: measures that drive performance, *Harvard Business Review*, January–February, pp 71–79

Kaplan, R S and Norton, D P (1996) Using the balanced scorecard as a strategic management system, *Harvard Business Review*, January–February, pp 75–85

Kaplan, R S and Norton, D P (2000) Having trouble with your strategy? Then map it, *Harvard Business Review*, September–October, pp 167–76

Katz, D and Kahn, R (1966) *The Social Psychology of Organizations*, John Wiley, New York

Katzenbach, J and Smith, D (1993) *The Magic of Teams*, Harvard Business School Press, Boston, MA

Kearns, P (2000) How do you measure up? *Personnel Today*, 21 March, pp 21–22

Kermally S (1997) *Managing Performance*, Butterworth-Heinemann, Oxford

Kessler, I and Purcell, J (1992) Performance-related pay: objectives and application, *Human Resource Management*, spring, pp 16–33

Kessler, I and Purcell, J (1993) *The Templeton Performance-Related Pay Project: Summary of key findings*, Templeton College, Oxford

Kluger, A N and DeNisi, A (1996) The effects of feedback interventions on performance: A historical review, a meta-analysis, and a preliminary feedback theory, *Psychological Bulletin*, **119**, pp 254–84

Kochanski, J (2007) Sibson reveals secrets of successful performance management, *Employee Benefit News*, September, pp 22–23

Koontz, H (1971) *Appraising Managers as Managers*, McGraw-Hill, New York

Krames, J A (2004) *The Welch Way*, McGraw-Hill, New York

Lampron, F and Koski, L (2004) Implementing web-enabled performance management, *Workspan*, January, 35–38

Latham, G P and Locke, E A (1979) Goal setting: a motivational technique that works, *Organizational Dynamics*, autumn, pp 442–47

Latham, G P and Locke, E A (2006) Enhancing the benefits and avoiding the pitfalls of goal setting, *Organizational Dynamics*, **35** (4), pp 332–40

Latham, G P and Wexley, K N (1977) Behavioural observation scales, *Personnel Psychology*, **30,** pp 255–68

Latham, G, Sulsky, L M and Macdonald, H (2007) Performance management, in *Oxford Handbook of Human Resource Management*, ed Peter Boxall, John Purcell and Patrick Wright, Oxford University Press, Oxford

Latham, G P, Almost, J, Mann, S and Moore, C (2005) New developments in performance management, *Organizational Dynamics*, **34** (1), pp 77–87

Lawler, E E (1994) Performance management: the next generation, *Compensation & Benefits Review*, **26** (3), pp 16–19

Lawler, E E (2003) Reward practices and reward system effectiveness, *Organizational Dynamics*, November, pp 396–404

Lawler, E E and McDermott, M (2003) Current performance management practices, *WordatWork Journal*, second quarter, pp 49–60

Lawler, E E, Mohrman, A M and Resnick, S M (1984) Performance appraisal revisited, *Organizational Dynamics*, **13** (1), pp 20–35

Lawson, P (1995) Performance management: an overview, in *The Performance Handbook*, ed M Walters, Institute of Personnel and Development, London

Lazer, R I and Wikstrom, W S (1977) *Appraising Managerial Performance: Current practices and new directions*, The Conference Board, New York

Lee, C D (2005) Rethinking the goals of your performance management system, *Employment Relations Today*, **32** (3), pp 53–60

Lespinger, R and Lucia, A D (1997) 360-degree feedback and performance appraisal, *Training*, **34** (9), pp 62–70

Leventhal, G S (1980) What should be done with equity theory? New approaches to the study of fairness in social relationships, in *Social Exchange: Advances in Theory and Research*, ed K Gerken, M Greenberg and R Willis, Plenum Press, New York

Levinson, H (1970) Management by whose objectives? *Harvard Business Review*, July–August, pp 125–134

Levinson, H (1976) Appraisal of *what* performance? *Harvard Business Review*, July–August, pp 30–46

Lindbom, D (2007) A culture of coaching: the challenge of managing performance for long-term results, *Organization Development Journal*, **25** (1), pp 101–06

Local Government Management Board (1995) *Guide to 360-degree feedback*, Local Government Management Board, London

Locke, E A and Latham, G P (1990) Work motivation and satisfaction: light at the end of the tunnel, *Psychological Science*, **1** (4), pp 240–46

Locke, E A and Latham, G P (2002) Building a practically useful theory of goal setting and task motivation, *American Psychologist*, **57** (9), pp 705–17

Lockett, J (1992) *Effective Performance Management*, Kogan Page, London

London, M and Beatty, R W (1993) 360-degree feedback as competitive advantage, *Human Resource Management*, **32** (2/3), pp 353–72

London, M, Mone, E M, and Scott, J C (2004) Performance management and assessment: methods for improved rater accuracy and employee goal setting, *Human Resource Management*, **43** (4), pp 319–36

Long, P (1986) *Performance Appraisal Revisited*, Institute of Personnel Management, London

Longenecker, C and Ludwig, D (1995) Ethical dilemmas in performance appraisal revisited, in *Performance Measurement and Evaluation*, ed J Holloway, J Lewis and J Mallory, Sage, London

Machine Design (2007) Forced ranking of employees bad for business (editorial), September, pp 2–3

Maier, N (1958) *The Appraisal Interview*, Wiley, New York

Martone, D (2003) A guide to developing a competency-based performance management system, *Employment Relations Today*, **30** (3), pp 23–32

Maurer, T, Mitchell, D and Barbiette, F (2002) Predictors of attitudes towards a 360-degree feedback system and involvement in post-feedback management development activity, *Journal of Occupational and Organizational Psychology*, **75**, pp 87–107

McAdam, R, Hazlett, S-A and Casey, C (2005) Performance management in the UK public sector: addressing multiple stakeholder complexity, *International Journal of Public Sector Management*, **18** (3), pp 256–73

McDonald, D and Smith, A (1991) A proven connection: performance management and business results, *Compensation & Benefits Review*, January–February, pp 59–64

McGregor, D (1957) An uneasy look at performance appraisal, *Harvard Business Review*, May–June, pp 89–94

McGregor, D (1960) *The Human Side of Enterprise*, McGraw-Hill, New York

Meisler, A (2003) Dead man's curve, *Workforce Management*, June, pp 44–49

Michaels, E G, Handfield-Jones, H and Axelrod, B (2001) *The War for Talent*, Harvard Business School Press, Boston, MA

Milkovich, G and Wigdor, A C (1991) *Pay for Performance: Evaluating performance appraisal and merit pay*, National Academy Press, Washington DC

Miller, E and Rice, A (1967) *Systems of Organization*, Tavistock, London

Mohrman, A M and Mohrman, S A (1995) Performance management is 'running the business', *Compensation & Benefits Review*, July–August, pp 69–75

Mone, E M and London, M (2002) Fundamentals of performance management, *Spiro*, London

Morgan, A, Cannan, K and Culinane, K (2005) 360-degree feedback: a critical enquiry, *Personnel Review*, **34** (6), pp 663–80

Moretti, L (2007) The performance connection, *Organization Development Journal*, **25** (2), pp 213–17

Moullin, M (2002) *Delivering Excellence in Health and Social Care*, Open University Press, Buckingham

Murphy, K R and Balzer, W K (1989) Rater errors and rating accuracy, *Journal of Applied Psychology*, **74** (4), pp 619–24

Murphy, K R and Cleveland, J (1995) *Understanding Performance Appraisal*, Sage, London

Nadler, D A and Tushman, M (1980) A congruence model for diagnosing organizational behaviour, in *Resource Book in Macro-Organizational Behaviour*, ed R H Miles, Goodyear Publishing, Santa Monica, CA

Neary, D B (2002) Creating a company-wide, on-line, performance management system: a case study at TRW INC, *Human Resource Management*, **41** (4), pp 491–98

Neely, A, Adams, C and Kennerley, M (2002) *The Performance Prism: The scorecard for measuring and managing business success*, Pearson Education, Harlow

Newton, T and Findlay, P (1996) Playing god? The performance of appraisal, *Human Resource Management Journal*, **6** (3), pp 42–56

Novations (2006) *Uncovering the Growing Disenchantment with Forced Ranking Performance Management Systems*, wwwnovationscom

O'Malley, M (2003) Forced ranking, *WorldatWork Journal*, first quarter, pp 31–39

Pedler, M, Burgoyne, J and Boydell, T (1986) *Manager's Guide to Self Development*, 2nd edn, McGraw-Hill, Maidenhead

Pfeffer, J and Sutton, R I (2006) *Hard facts, Dangerous Half-Truths and Total Nonsense*, Harvard Business School Press, Cambridge, MA

Philpott, L and Sheppard, L (1992) Managing for improved performance, in *Strategies for Human Resource Management*, ed Michael Armstrong, Kogan Page, London

Plachy, R J and Plachy, S J (1988) *Getting Results From Your Performance Management and Appraisal System*, AMACOM, New York

Pollack, D and Pollack, L (1996) Using 360-degree feedback in performance appraisal, *Public Personnel Management*, **25** (4), pp 507–28

Porter, L W and Lawler, E E (1968) *Managerial Attitudes and Performance*, Irwin Dorsey, Homewood, IL

Posthumus, R A and Campion, M A (2008) 20 best practices for just performance reviews, *Compensation & Benefits Review*, January–February, pp 47–55

Pritchard, A (2008) The new BPM: enterprise performance management, *Business Performance Management*, March, pp 28–30

Pulakos, E D (2004) *A Roadmap for Developing, Implementing and Evaluating Performance Management*, SHRM Foundation, Alexandria, VA

Pulakos, E D, Mueller-Hanson, R A and O'Leary, R S (2008) Performance management in the US, in *Performance Management Systems: A global perspective*, ed A Varma, P S Budhwar and A DeNisi, Routledge, Abingdon

Purcell, J, Hutchinson, S and Kinnie, N (1998) *The Lean Organisation*, IPD, London

Purcell, J, Kinnie, N, Hutchinson, S, Rayton, B and Swart, J (2003) *People and Performance: How people management impacts on organizational performance*, CIPD, London

Quinn, F J (2003) Measurement – the right way, *Logistics Management*, **42** (3), p 9

Randell, G H (1973) Performance appraisal: purpose, practices and conflicts, *Occupational Psychology*, **47**, pp 221–24

Renwick, D and MacNeil, C M (2002) Line manager involvement in careers, *Career Development International*, **7** (7), pp 407–14

Reynolds, J (2004) *Helping People Learn*, CIPD, London

Risher, H (2003) Re-focusing performance management for high performance, *Compensation & Benefits Review*, October, pp 20–30

Risher, H (2005) Getting serious about performance management, *Compensation & Benefits Review*, November–December, pp 18–26

Roberts, E R (1994) Maximizing performance appraisal system acceptance: perspectives from municipal government personnel administrators, *Public Personnel Management*, **23** (4), pp 525–48

Robertson, I T, Smith, M and Cooper, C L (1992) *Motivation*, Institute of Personnel and Development, London

Rodgers, R and Hunter, J E (1991) Impact of management by objectives on organizational performance, *Journal of Applied Psychology*, **76** (2), pp 322–36

Rogers, R (2004) *Realizing the Promise of Performance Management*, DDI Press, Bridgevile, PA

Rothwell, W (2002) *Models for Human Resource Improvement*, 2nd edn, American Society for Training and Development, Alexandria, VA

Rousseau, D M (2006) Is there such a thing as evidence-based management? *Academy of Management Review*, **31** (2), pp 256–69

Rowe, K (1964) An appraisal of appraisals, *Journal of Management Studies*, **1** (1), pp 1–25

Rucci, A J, Kirn, S P and Quinn, R T (1998) The employee–customer–profit chain at Sears, *Harvard Business Review*, January–February, pp 82–97

Schaffer, R H (1991) Demand better results and get them, *Harvard Business Review*, March–April, pp 142–49

Schiff, C (2008) Three things you should know about dashboards, *DM Review*, June, p 29

Schneiderman, A M (1999) Why balanced score cards fail, *Journal of Strategic Performance Measurement*, January, pp 6–10

Shih, H-A, Chiang, Y-H and Hsu, C-C (2005) Can high performance work systems really lead to better performance? *Academy of Management Conference Paper*, pp 1–6

Silverman, M, Kerrin, M and Carter, A (2005) *360-degree Feedback: Beyond the spin*, Institute of Employment Studies, Brighton

Sink, D S and Tuttle, T C, (1990) The performance management question in the organization of the future, *Industrial Management*, **32** (1), pp 4–12

Smith, P C and Kendall, L M (1963) Retranslation of expectations: an approach to the construction of unambiguous answers for rating scales, *Journal of Applied Psychology*, **47**, pp 853–85

Sparrow, P (1996) Too good to be true, *People Management*, 5 December 1996, pp 22–27

Sparrow, P (2008) Performance management in the UK, in *Performance Management Systems: A global perspective*, ed A Varma, P S Budhwar and A DeNisi, Routledge, Abingdon

Stewart, V and Stewart, A (1982) *Managing the Poor Performer*, Gower, Aldershot

Stiles, P, Gratton, L, Truss, C, Hope-Hailey, J and McGovern, P (1997) Performance management and the psychological contract, *Human Resource Management Journal*, **2** (1), pp 57–66

Storey, J (1985) The means of management control, *Sociology*, **19** (2), pp 193–212

Strebler, M T, Bevan, S and Robertson, D (2001) *Performance Review: Balancing objectives and content*, Institute of Employment Studies, Brighton

Sulsky, L M and Balzer, W K (1988) The meaning and measurement of performance rating accuracy: Some methodological and theoretical concerns, *Journal of Applied Psychology*, **73**, pp 497–506

Summers, L (2005) Integrated pay for performance: the high-tech marriage of compensation management and performance management, *Compensation & Benefits Review*, January–February, pp 18–25

Swanson, R A (1994) *Analysing for Improved Performance*, Berrett-Koelher, New York

Tamkin, P, Barber, L and Hirsh, W (1995) *Personal Development Plans: Case studies of practice*, The Institute for Employment Studies, Brighton

Taylor, F W (1911) *Principles of Scientific Management*, Harper, New York

Taylor, M S, Masterson, S S, Renard, M K and Tracy, K B (1998) Managers' reactions to procedurally just performance management systems, *Academy of Management Journal*, **41** (5), pp 568–79

Taylor, M S, Tracy, K B, Renard, M K, Harrison, J K and Carroll, S J (1995) Due process in performance appraisal: a quasi-experiment in procedural justice, *Administrative Science Quarterly*, **40**, pp 495–523

Thomas, C (1995) Performance management, *Croner Pay and Benefits Bulletin*, August, pp 4–5

Thompson, T, Purdy, J and Summers, D B (2008) A five factor framework for coaching middle managers, *Organization Development Journal*, **26** (3), pp 63–71

Thor, G G (1995) Using measurement to reinforce strategy, in *The Performance Imperative*, ed H Rishner and C Fay, Jossey Bass, San Francisco

Townley, B (1990) A discriminating approach to appraisal, *Personnel Management*, December, pp 34–37

Townley, B (1990/1991) Appraisal into UK universities, *Human Resource Management Journal*, **1** (2), pp 27–44

Townley, B (1993) Performance appraisal and the emergence of management, *Journal of Management Studies*, **30** (2), pp 221–38

Turnow, W W (1993) Introduction to special issue on 360-degree feedback, *Human Resource Management*, **32** (2/3), pp 211–19

van de Vliet, A (1997) The new balancing card, *Management Today*, July, pp 78–79

Van Fleet, D D, Peterson, T O and Van Fleet, E W (2005) Closing the performance feedback gap with expert systems, *Academy of Management Executive*, **19** (2), pp 38–53

Vaughan, S (2003) Performance: self as the principal evaluator, *Human Resource Development International*, September, pp 371–85

Vroom, V (1964) *Work and Motivation*, Wiley, New York

Walters, M (1995a) Developing organizational measures, in *The Performance Management Handbook*, ed M Walters, Institute of Personnel and Development, London

Walters, M (1995b) *The Performance Management Handbook*, Institute of Personnel and Development, London

Ward, P (1997) *360-Degree Feedback*, Institute of Personnel and Development, London

Warr, P and Ainsworth, E (1999) 360-degree feedback: some recent research, *Selection and Development Review*, **15** (3), pp 302–16

Warren, M (1972) Performance management: a substitute for supervision, *Management Review*, October, pp 28–42

Welfare, S (2006) A whole world out there: managing global HR, *IRS Employment Review*, 862, 29 December, pp 8–12

Wheatley, M (1996) How to score performance management, *Human Resources*, May–June, pp 24–26

Wherry, R J and Bartlett, C J (1982) The control of bias in ratings: a theory of rating, *Personnel Psychology*, **35** (3), pp 521–51

Williams, R (1998) *Performance Management*, Thompson Business Press, London

Williams, S (1991) Strategy and objectives, in *The Handbook of Performance Management*, ed F Neale, Institute of Personnel and Development, London

Willmore, J (2004) The future of performance, *Training and Development (USA)*, August, pp 26–31

Wingrove, C (2003) Developing an effective blend of process and technology in the new era of performance management, *Compensation & Benefits Review*, January–February, pp 25–31

Winstanley, D and Stuart-Smith, K (1996) Policing performance: the ethics of performance management, *Personnel Review*, **25** (6), pp 66–84

Wolff, C (2008) Managing employee performance, *IRS Employment Review*, 890, 4 February, pp 1–12

Woodruffe, C (2008) Could do better? *Must* do better! *British Journal of Administrative Management*, January, pp 14–16

Wortzel-Hoffman, N and Boltizar, S (2007) Performance and development planning: a culture shift perspective, *Organization Development Journal*, **25** (2), pp 195–200

Ziegler, R (2002) The business ROI of e-learning, *e-learning*, April, pp 85–86

Zigon, J (1994) Measuring the performance of work teams, *ACA Journal*, autumn, pp 18–32

Subject Index